TEPS 달인이 되는 법 Final 문법

저자 | 남윤이
초판 1쇄 발행 | 2008년 3월 3일
초판 5쇄 발행 | 2010년 1월 10일

발행인 | 박효상
편집책임 | 김상호
편집 | 조승주
영업책임 | 이종선
영업 | 이태호
출판등록 | 제 10-1835호
발행처 | 사람in
주소 | 121-839 서울시 마포구 서교동 378-16 4F
전화 | 02) 338-3555(代)
팩스 | 02) 338-3545
e-mail | esaramin@nate.com
Homepage | www.saramin.com

만든 사람들
표지 디자인 | 장선숙
내지 디자인 | 한현식
Native Consultant | Joel Park, Anton Brinza

● 책값은 표지 뒷면에 있습니다.
● 파본은 바꾸어 드립니다.

ISBN 978-89-6049-071-0 13740
ISBN 978-89-6049-041-3 (세트)

사람 in
saramin.com

머리말

〈TEPS 달인이 되는 법-기본 종합〉을 낸지 엊그제 같은데 벌써 Final 문제의 출간을 앞두게 되었습니다. 〈TEPS 달인이 되는 법-기본 종합〉은 TEPS를 처음 접하시는 분들에게 전체적인 유형과 함께 기본기를 다질 수 있는 책이었던 반면 〈TEPS 달인이 되는 법-Final〉은 더 많은 기출 변형 문제를 접하시고 싶은 분들을 위해 집필하였습니다. 〈TEPS 달인이 되는 법-기본 종합〉을 통해 기본은 다졌지만 막상 문제에 적용을 못하시는 분들을 위해 약 8세트 문제의 양을 4주간 계획적으로 풀어봄으로써 고득점을 얻을 수 있도록 구성된 교재입니다. 모든 파트가 골고루 섞인 실전 시험의 난이도로 구성된 문제를 풀어 볼 수 있기 때문에 이 교재를 통해서 고득점을 향한 실력을 쌓는 발판을 마련하실 수 있을 것입니다.

실전에서 TEPS를 공부하는 많은 학생들을 보면서 그들이 어려워하고 필요로 하는 것을 몸소 체험하게 되었고, 그것을 바탕으로 이러한 교재들을 집필할 수 있게 되었습니다. 좋은 교사는 정답을 가르쳐 주는 것이 아니라 정답의 방향과 길을 제시하는 것이라 생각합니다. 아무쪼록 이 교재가 TEPS를 준비하는 모든 학생들에게 등대와 같이 방향을 제시하는 책이 되길 기대합니다.

남윤이

First of all, all the glory to God.
This book could never have been completed without the support and help from my family and friends. They are the people whom I can always rely on, and they are always there for me in times of need. My parents influenced me to become who I am and what I am today. Without their love and trust I would have never been able to take my first steps in each area. They have never questioned my decisions, and have always showed love and support.

To my colleagues, I thank you for always offering a lending hand and making the work environment so pleasant. Also, I'd like to extend my thanks to Miss Hwang, Joel, Anton, Mr. Yoon, and Mr. Jeon. It is a blessing to have the trust and support of so many special people throughout my life.

Contents

청해 Listening Comprehension

Contents

어휘 Vocabulary

1st Week

2nd Week

3rd Week

4th Week

이 책의 특징

이 책은 TEPS 문법의 완벽한 마무리를 위한 최종 실전서이다. 문법 출제 유형을 20개로 정리해서 출제 포인트를 확인할 수 있으며, 실전에 가장 가까운 기출 문제와 예상 문제로 충분히 연습한 다음 1회분 모의고사로 최종 점검을 할 수 있도록 구성했다.

1. 20일로 TEPS를 마무리할 수 있다

20개의 유형 정리로 TEPS 문법을 유형별로 완벽하게 정리했다. 실전 시험을 앞두고 모든 파트를 매일 골고루 풀어 봄으로써 실전에 대한 감을 키우도록 한다. 마지막에 실전 모의고사 1회분을 풀어봄으로써 실전을 단기간에 대비한다. 이론적 기반은 있으나 TEPS 유형에 아직 익숙하지 않아 실전 시험에서 실력발휘를 제대로 못하는 학습자는 문법 유형을 빠르게 파악할 수 있고 문제를 풀면서 충분하게 유형 연습을 할 수 있다.

2. 실전에 가장 가까운 문제를 풀 수 있다

최근 3년간의 기출 문제를 완벽하게 분석해서 각 파트별 비율에 맞게 문제를 구성했다. 8회분 400문제는 TEPS 고득점을 위해 엄선된 문제이다. 학습자는 기출 변형 Catch Up, 예상 문제 Build Up, 1회분 모의고사 Final Check 문제를 풀면서 정기시험과 유사한 문제 유형을 익힐 수 있다.

3. 전문 TEPS 강사의 노하우를 배울 수 있다

매월 TEPS 정기시험을 보는 전문 강사가 TEPS의 특징과 텝스에서 요구하는 공부 방식을 담았다. 학습자는 TEPS의 특징과 TEPS에서 요구하는 공부방식을 배울 수 있다.

4. Handy Book을 통해 부족한 부분을 보완할 수 있다

문법 문제는 나오는 문제의 유형들이 어느 정도 정해져 있으므로 Handy Book으로 틀린 문제를 적어 두고 다시는 그 문법 요소와 관련된 문제를 틀리지 않도록 예방하는 훈련을 할 수 있다. 또한 문법 핵심 포인트 20개를 실어 어디에서든지 중요 포인트를 가지고 다니면서 정리할 수 있도록 했다.

이 책의 구성 및 활용

TEPS 어휘를 20일에 끝낼 수 있게 다음 구성에 따라 학습한다.

1. 핵심 정리 20

가장 중요한 TEPS 문법 포인트를 20개로 정리했다. 20개의 핵심 정리를 Catch Up과 Build Up 문제를 통해 확인한다면 시험 전에 핵심 문법을 빠르게 정리할 수 있을 것이다.

2. 기출로 감을 익히는 Catch Up

기출변형 문제로 실제 시험문제와 가장 가까운 지문들을 다뤄볼 수 있다. TEPS 문법 영역의 각 파트별로 정리하여 실전감각을 더욱 익히도록 하였다.

3. 예상 문제로 실전 감각을 익히는 Build Up

TEPS 문법 영역 4개 파트의 다양한 유형의 문제를 다뤘다. 실전에 대비할 수 있는 연습이 충분히 되도록 하였다.

4. 최종 실전 점검 Final Check

문법 1회분 모의고사를 실었다. 난이도는 정기시험과 동일하다. 실전 난이도와 유형의 문제를 통하여 실전에 대비할 수 있고, 정확한 자기 실력을 파악할 수 있다.

5. 한 눈에 보는 정답 및 해설

본문의 내용과 함께 지문과 해석, 해설을 〈정답 및 해설〉에 모두 실어 문제 풀이와 보충 학습을 〈정답 및 해설〉 한 권만으로도 가능하게 했다.

TEPS 문법 유형 및 형식

문법(Grammar) 50문항

밑줄 친 부분 중 오류를 식별하는 유형 등의 단편적이며 기계적인 문법 지식 학습을 조장할 우려가 있는 분리식 시험 유형을 배제하고, 의미 있는 문맥을 근거로 오류를 식별하는 유형을 통하여 진정한 의사소통 능력의 바탕이 되는 살아있는 문법, 어법 능력을 문어체와 구어체를 통하여 측정한다.

PART 1	20문항

Choose the best answer for the blank.

A: How come you came home so early today?
B: Our boss ___________ us go home early today, which surprised everyone.

(a) was made
(b) allowed
(c) got
(d) let

Part 1은 A, B 두 사람의 짧은 대화를 통해 전치사 표현력, 구문 이해력, 품사 이해도, 시제, 접속사 등 문법에 대한 이해력을 묻는 형태로 되어 있다. 주로 후자(B)의 대화 중에 빈칸이 있고, 그 곳에 들어갈 적절한 표현을 고르는 형식이다.

PART 2	20문항

Choose the best answer for the blank.

John _________ a lot. He always has a cigarette in his mouth.

(a) smoked
(b) is smoking
(c) smokes
(d) used to smoke

Part 2는 문어체 질문을 다룬다. 서술문 속의 빈칸을 채우는 문제로 총 20문항으로 되어 있다. 이 파트에서는 문법 자체에 대한 이해도는 물론 구문에 대한 이해력이 중요하다.

<table>
<tr><td>PART 3</td><td>5문항</td></tr>
</table>

Identify the option that contains an awkward expression or an error in grammar.

(a) A: Are you up already?
(b) B: Yes, it is my turn to prepare breakfast.
(c) A: Oh, don't worry about it. Susan makes some
  pancakes for everyone.
(d) B: Hmm. Yes, I can smell that. OK, wake me up
  again when the breakfast is ready.

Part 3는 대화문에서 어법상 틀리거나 어색한 부분이 있는 문장을 고르는 다섯 문항으로 구성되어 있다. 이 영역 역시 문법뿐만 아니라 정확한 구문 파악, 회화 내용의 식별 능력이 대단히 중요하다.

<table>
<tr><td>PART 4</td><td>5문항</td></tr>
</table>

Identify the option that contains an awkward expression or an error in grammar.

(a) Helen Keller was born in a small rural town in the US. (b) She was born with full sight and hearing. (c) In February 1882, when Helen was nineteen months old, she fell ill. To this day the nature of her ailment remains a mystery. (d) The doctors of the time calls it "brain fever."

Part 4는 한 문단을 주고 그 가운데 문법적으로 틀리거나 어색한 문장을 고르는 다섯 문항으로 되어 있다. 틀린 부분을 신속하게 골라야 하므로 속독 능력도 중요한 작용을 한다.

GRAMMAR

Week 1

Day 1 ▶▶ 시제

1. 현재와 현재진행의 차이점을 알아둔다.
2. 과거와 현재완료의 차이점을 구분하도록 한다.
3. 시간·조건 부사절에서는 현재나 현재완료가 미래를 대신한다.

Day 2 ▶▶ 조동사

1. 조동사 본연의 의미를 파악한다. 이는 LC스크립트를 잘 활용하면 도움이 된다.
2. 〈조동사 과거형 ＋have p.p.〉의 형태를 알아둔다.
3. 조동사의 관용적 표현의 쓰임을 알아둔다.

Day 3 ▶▶ 수동태

1. Part III와 Part IV에서 자동사가 수동태로 쓰이지 않았는지 확인한다.
2. 자동사와 타동사가 둘 다 가능한 동사를 알아둔다.
3. 감정 동사는 수동태로도 많이 쓰이지만 능동태로도 가능함을 알아둔다.

Day 4 ▶▶ 가정법

1. 가정법의 쓰임을 파악해 둔다.
2. 주장·요구·제안 등의 동사, 형용사, 명사 등이 조동사 should가 생략되어 함께 쓰이는 용법을 파악해 둔다.
3. if 가정법에서 if가 생략되면 도치가 이루어진다.

Day 5 ▶▶ to부정사

1. to부정사를 목적어로 취하는 동사를 파악한다. 특히 to부정사를 목적격 보어로 취하는 5형식 동사들을 파악한다.
2. to부정사의 형용사적 용법을 이해하고 파악해 둔다.
3. 대부정사의 쓰임을 알아둔다.

TEPS **Day 1**

시제

영어의 시제는 매우 세분화되어 있다. 다행히 TEPS에서는 세밀한 시제 차이를 묻는 질문은 잘 나오지 않고 시제의 큰 그림을 묻는 편이다. 그러므로 시험에 빈출되는 시제 유형을 중심으로 시험에 대비하도록 한다.

1. 현재시제: 현재 상태나 습관, 일반적 사실, 자연 법칙처럼 확실성이 큰 상황에 사용한다. 또한 빈도부사와 함께 자주 사용된다.

I usually get up early. (반복적 동작) 나는 주로 일찍 일어난다.
Steve drives a bus. (사실) 스티브는 버스를 운전한다. (운전기사라는 의미)
cf. **Steve is driving a bus.** (현재 진행: 현재의 일시적 시점을 나타냄) 스티브는 (지금) 버스를 운전한다.

2. 과거 표시 단어나 부사구가 있으면 반드시 과거시제를 사용한다.

last~, yesterday, at that time, ago, the other day 일전에 **just now** 방금
I saw her last week. 지난주에 그녀를 보았다.

3. 현재완료: 과거에서 현재까지 이어지는 기간의 개념이다.

I think I have met her once before. (과거부터 지금까지)
그녀를 전에 한 번 봤던 것 같다.

4. 과거완료: 기준 시점이 과거이고 그보다 이전의 일에 대해 언급할 때 〈had+p.p.(대과거)〉를 사용한다. 주로 두 가지의 과거 일이 언급될 때 그 중 하나가 이전의 일임을 강조할 때 쓰인다.

They had already left when I arrived at the office.
내가 사무실에 도착했을 때 그들은 이미 떠나고 없었다.

5. 미래완료: 기준 시점이 미래이고 그 미래 시점 이전에 완결된 미래의 행동을 의미할 때 사용한다. 〈by+시간 부사구〉나 by the time과 함께 자주 쓰인다.

I will have studied for 3 hours by the time my mom comes home.
엄마가 집에 오실 때가 되면 나는 3시간을 공부한 것이 된다.

6. 시간 · 조건 접속사(if, when, as, after, before, until, as soon as, etc.)가 나오는 절에서는 현재나 현재완료가 미래를 대신한다. 그러나 이러한 부사절이 나온다고 해서 무조건 시제를 현재나 현재완료로 하는 것이 아니라 주절이 미래형이나 명령문일 때 이러한 문법이 형성됨을 잊지 말자.

When you arrive tonight, we will go out for dinner.
오늘 밤 당신이 돌아오면 우리는 외식하러 나갈 거예요.

# Catch Up 

시제 관련 TEPS 주요 문제들을 풀어보도록 한다.

Part I Fill in the blank with the most appropriate word or phrase.

1. A: Erica, you look so tired! Have you been busy all day?
B: What a day! I've been working since 8 a.m. and ___________ a chance to eat!

(a) didn't even have
(b) haven't even had
(c) hadn't even had
(d) wouldn't have even had

2. A: Are you going to the festival?
B: Sure. I am excited to go to the festival because I expect ___________ fun.

(a) it was
(b) it's
(c) it'll be
(d) it's being

Part II Fill in the blank with the most appropriate word or phrase.

3. What a good deal! If you _________ a pair of pants at full price, you get another one for 50% off!

(a) purchase
(b) purchased
(c) will purchase
(d) will have purchased

4. Mom _________ furious when she found out that Bobby broke her crystal vase.

(a) was
(b) had been
(c) has been
(d) have been

Part III Identify the grammatical error in the dialogue.

5. (a) A: Joel! Long time no see! I thought you were in Paris!
(b) B: I was, but I've moved back in February.
(c) A: How come? Weren't you attending design school?
(d) B: I was, but I graduated and decided to move back.

Answers

Catch Up에서 푼 문제의 해석과 해설을 점검한다.

1

A: Erica, you look so tired! Have you been busy all day?
B: What a day! I've been working since 8 a.m. and ________________ a chance to eat!

(a) didn't even have
(b) haven't even had
(c) hadn't even had
(d) wouldn't have even had

A: 에리카, 너 피곤해 보인다. 하루 종일 바빴니?
B: 세상에! 아침 8시부터 일해서 밥 먹을 틈조차 없었어.

해설 시제에 관한 문제이다. 아침 8시부터 일을 시작해서 말하는 시점까지 밥 먹을 틈이 없었다는 내용이므로 과거 시점(8 a.m.)부터 현재까지 아우르는 기간의 개념인 '현재완료'가 가장 적절하다. (c)와 같은 과거완료는 과거의 한 시점을 기준으로 그 이전의 일을 나타내므로 여기서는 적절하지 않다.

2

A: Are you going to the festival?
B: Sure. I am excited to go to the festival because I expect ________________ fun.

(a) it was
(b) it's
(c) it'll be
(d) it's being

A: 너 그 축제에 갈 거니?
B: 물론이지. 그 축제가 재미있을 것 같아서 기대돼.

해설 축제에 가는 것은 미래의 상황이므로 '그것이 재미있을 것 같다'는 의미가 되도록 미래 조동사 will이 쓰이는 것이 가장 적절하다.

3

What a good deal! If you ______________ a pair of pants at full price, you get another one for 50% off!

(a) purchase
(b) purchased
(c) will purchase
(d) will have purchased

너무나 좋은 기회입니다! 바지 한 벌을 정가에 구입하시면 또 다른 한 벌을 50% 할인된 가격으로 사실 수 있습니다.

해설   if가 조건인지 가정인지는 주절을 보고 판단한다. 여기서는 if가 가정법이 아닌 '조건'의 의미로 쓰였기 때문에 현재시제로 쓰는 것이 맞다. 조건 부사절에서는 현재시제가 미래의 의미를 대신한다. 그러므로 (a)가 정답이 된다.

4

Mom ______________ furious when she found out that Bobby broke her crystal vase.

(a) was
(b) had been
(c) has been
(d) have been

엄마는 바비가 그녀의 크리스털 꽃병을 깬 것을 알았을 때 화내셨다.

해설   시간 부사절(when절)의 시제가 과거(found out)이므로 주절의 본동사가 와야 하는 빈칸에는 '과거형'이 적절하다. 또한 엄마가 발견을 한 후 엄마가 화가 난 것이므로 (b)와 같은 과거완료는 적절치 않다.

5

(a) A: Joel! Long time no see! I thought you were in Paris!
(b) B: I was, but (I've moved → I moved) back in February.
(c) A: How come? Weren't you attending design school?
(d) B: I was, but I graduated and decided to move back.

(a) A: 조엘! 오랜만이다! 난 네가 파리에 있는 줄 알았어.
(b) B: 있었지. 근데 2월에 돌아 왔어.
(c) A: 왜? 디자인 학교에 다니지 않았니?
(d) B: 다녔었지. 근데 졸업하고 돌아오기로 결심했어.

해설   현재완료는 현재를 기점으로 과거의 한 시점부터 현재까지의 기간을 아우르는 개념의 시제이다. 그러나 여기서는 과거의 한 시점(in February)에 일어난 일을 말하고 있으므로 단순 과거시제가 적절하다. 그러므로 현재완료(I've moved)를 과거형(I moved)로 바꾸는 것이 적절하다.

Answers

1. (b) 2. (c) 3. (a) 4. (a) 5. (b) I've moved → I moved

Build Up

TEPS 전 문법 요소가 모의고사 형식으로 골고루 섞인 4파트의 문제를 골고루 풀어 본다.

▶▶ **Part I**   Fill in the blank with the most appropriate word or phrase.

1. A: What did the witness say?
   B: The witness testified that she ______________ the convicted murderer in the alleyway behind the diner at 9:13 p.m.

   (a) saw
   (b) see
   (c) have seen
   (d) had seen

2. A: Hurry! I need to stop by the gas station before I go ______________ the airport.
   B: OK. I will be ready in a minute.

   (a) at
   (b) to
   (c) for
   (d) from

3. A: The waitress asked us what we _________ like to drink.
   B: I want a Coke. What about you?

   (a) should
   (b) would
   (c) could
   (d) can

4. A: ____________ the basketball team wins this game, will they compete in the playoffs?
   B: Yes, they will.

   (a) To assume
   (b) Assumed
   (c) Assuming
   (d) Assume

▶▶ **Part II**   Fill in the blank with the most appropriate word or phrase.

5. Alcohol _________ people's cognitive processes; therefore, they make bad decisions.

   (a) influenced
   (b) influences
   (c) is influenced
   (d) is influencing

6. Joshua ordered the laptop two weeks ago, but he hasn't received it __________.

  (a) still
  (b) yet
  (c) already
  (d) then

7. College applicants are expected __________ four years of high school English courses.

  (a) to have completed
  (b) to completing
  (c) to have completion
  (d) to be completing

8. Very __________ people lack credit cards because they are easier to carry.

  (a) little
  (b) a little
  (c) a few
  (d) few

▶▶ **Part III** Identify the grammatical error in the dialogue.

9. (a) A: How did you do on your exam?
  (b) B: Horribly, but let's not talk about it.
  (c) A: I thought you did well since you studied a week in advance!
  (d) B: I think so, too! I don't understand it.

10. (a) A: What's wrong, Tina?
  (b) B: It's my daughter. She wants to move out and live on her own.
  (c) A: That's great! She's growing up.
  (d) B: Yes, she is, but I am hard to accept that she's growing up.

▶▶ **Part IV** Identify the ungrammatical sentence in the passage.

11. (a) There are several different theories regarding losing weight. (b) Some people believe that there are supplements that can help increase their metabolism to lose weight. (c) Today, many believe that the best way to lose weight is to exercise and eat in small portions. (d) Although there is no solid evidence support the supplement theory, it seems that it is becoming more and more popular these days.

12. (a) There are over 100 children at the new pre-school. (b) Because there are so many children, it is difficult to give each child the proper attention that they need. (c) In order to accommodate this problem, they must divide into smaller groups. (d) By doing this, the teacher-to-student ratio is much better.

정답: 186p

<table><tr><td>**Day 1**</td><td>▶▶ 시제</td></tr></table>

1. 현재와 현재진행의 차이점을 알아둔다.
2. 과거와 현재완료의 차이점을 구분하도록 한다.
3. 시간·조건 부사절에서는 현재나 현재완료가 미래를 대신한다.

<table><tr><td>**Day 2**</td><td>▶▶ 조동사</td></tr></table>

1. 조동사 본연의 의미를 파악한다. 이는 LC 스크립트를 잘 활용하면 도움이 된다.
2. 〈조동사 과거형 +have p.p.〉의 형태를 알아둔다.
3. 조동사의 관용적 표현의 쓰임을 알아둔다.

<table><tr><td>**Day 3**</td><td>▶▶ 수동태</td></tr></table>

1. Part III와 Part IV에서 자동사가 수동태로 쓰이지 않았는지 확인한다.
2. 자동사와 타동사가 둘 다 가능한 동사를 알아둔다.
3. 감정 동사는 수동태로도 많이 쓰이지만 능동태로도 가능함을 알아둔다.

<table><tr><td>**Day 4**</td><td>▶▶ 가정법</td></tr></table>

1. 가정법의 쓰임을 파악해 둔다.
2. 주장·요구·제안 등의 동사, 형용사, 명사 등이 조동사 should가 생략되어 함께 쓰이는 용법을 파악해 둔다.
3. if 가정법에서 if가 생략되면 도치가 이루어진다.

<table><tr><td>**Day 5**</td><td>▶▶ to부정사</td></tr></table>

1. to부정사를 목적어로 취하는 동사를 파악한다. 특히 to부정사를 목적격 보어로 취하는 5형식 동사들을 파악한다.
2. to부정사의 형용사적 용법을 이해하고 파악해 둔다.
3. 대부정사의 쓰임을 알아둔다.

조동사

> TEPS에서 조동사 관련 문제가 나오면 대부분 해석을 통해 풀어야 하는, 조동사의 본래 의미를 물어보는 문제이다. 또한 〈조동사 과거형＋have p.p.〉의 쓰임이 가장 많이 나온다.

1. would, could, might, should는 과거형 이외에 조동사 본연의 뜻을 가지고 있다.

That could be true. 그것이 진실일 수도 있다.
You might meet Eric after the concert. 너는 그 콘서트 후에 에릭을 만날 수도 있다.
He would be in time. 그는 제시간에 올 것이다.
He should study harder. 그는 더 열심히 공부해야 한다.

2. 주어의 강한 의지, 고집, 습성을 나타내는 will(～할 것이다, ～하려고 하다, ～하기 마련이다)

This window won't open. 이 창문은 열리지 않는다. (고집)

3. 과거의 습관을 나타내는 would와 used to (～하곤 했다)

I would take a nap after lunch. 점심을 먹고 낮잠을 자곤 했다.
그러나 과거의 상태를 말할 때는 used to를 써야 함을 기억하자.
He used to be a singer. 그는 가수였다.
He would be a singer. (X)

4. 조동사 과거형＋have p.p.

I shouldn't have done it. 그것을 하지 말았어야 했다.
I could have arrived earlier. 좀 더 일찍 도착할 수 있었다.

5. must (～임에 틀림없다) ↔ cannot (～일 리 없다)

must not (～해서는 안 된다)
must have p.p. (～였음에 틀림없다), **should have p.p.** (～했어야 했다)

You must have been very tired by the time you finished the exams.
시험을 끝냈을 때 매우 피곤했었겠다.

6. 관용적 표현

1) **may well V** V 하는 것은 당연하다

She may well be proud of her daughter. 그녀가 딸을 자랑스러워하는 것은 당연하다.

2) **would rather A than B** B하느니 A하는 것이 더 낫다

I would rather stay at home than go with him. 그 남자와 함께 가느니 차라리 집에 있겠다.

3) **cannot ~ too+(형용사/부사)** 아무리 ～해도 지나치지 않다

You cannot be too careful when you drive a car. 차를 운전할 때는 아무리 조심해도 지나치지 않다.

Catch Up 

조동사 관련 TEPS 주요 문제들을 풀어보도록 한다.

Part I Fill in the blank with the most appropriate word or phrase.

1. A: Thomas, let's go! We _________________ home an hour ago.
B: Okay, Mom. I'm coming.

(a) should have left
(b) should be leaving
(c) must have left
(d) could be leaving

2. A: I don't like my history class.
B: The semester just started. You __________ probably go to the office and change the class.

(a) must
(b) will
(c) would
(d) could

Part II Fill in the blank with the most appropriate word or phrase.

3. If you want a seat at the symphony, tickets __________ be purchased in advance.

(a) will
(b) must
(c) would
(d) shall

4. The diet __________ be maintained, without change, for at least six months if you want it to work.

(a) should not
(b) may not
(c) should
(d) may

Part IV Identify the ungrammatical sentence in the passage.

5. (a) Jogging, bicycling, swimming, and other popular exercise activities rarely produce serious injuries. (b) However, people who are just beginning a regular exercise program often feel stiff and sore after the first few days. (c) More physical types of exercise, such as weightlifting and football, can cause long lasting muscle and joint problems. (d) To avoid these risks, it is recommended that you would find an appropriate stretching routine and get in the habit of completing it before exercising.

 # Answers 

Catch Up에서 푼 문제의 해석과 해설을 점검한다.

1

A: Thomas, let's go! We ______________ home an hour ago.
B: Okay, Mom. I'm coming.

(a) should have left
(b) should be leaving
(c) must have left
(d) could be leaving

A: 토마스, 가자. 우리 한 시간 전에 떠났어야 해.	
B: 네, 엄마. 가요.	

해설 should have p.p.는 과거에 하지 못한 일에 대한 '후회, 유감' 등을 나타낼 때 쓰인다. 여기서는 an hour ago가 적절한 조동사 표현을 고르는 데 중요한 포인트가 된다. 즉, 한 시간 전에 떠났어야 했는데 그렇지 못했다고 말하는 것이므로 (a)가 정답이 된다. (c)에서 must have p.p.는 '~했음에 틀림 없다'는 의미로 과거에 대한 확실한 추측을 나타내기 때문에 정답이 될 수 없다.

2

A: I don't like my history class.
B: The semester just started. You ______ probably go to the office and change the class.

(a) must
(b) will
(c) would
(d) could

A: 역사 수업이 맘에 들지 않아.
B: 학기 초잖아. 그러니까 사무실 가서 바꿀 수 있어.

해설 조동사 본연의 의미를 고르는 문제일 경우 해석을 통해 빈칸에 들어갈 가장 적절한 조동사를 선택지에서 골라야 한다. 여기서는 (d)의 could가 가능성을 나타내는 조동사로서 빈칸에 가장 적절한 의미가 되므로 정답이 된다. probably라는 부사 때문에 의무를 나타내는 must는 적절치 않고, would는 (불확실한) 추측을 나타내므로 적절치 않다.

3

> **If you want a seat at the symphony, tickets _________ be purchased in advance.**
>
> (a) will   (b) must
> (c) would   (d) shall

연주회에서 좌석을 원한다면 미리 표를 구매하셔야 합니다.

해설 여기서는 must가 '필요, 의무'의 뜻으로 쓰여 빈칸에 가장 적절한 조동사가 된다. should가 선택지에 있었다면 정답이 될 수도 있다. (d)의 shall은 오늘날 일상 영어 회화에서 1인칭(I, we)에 한정되어 쓰이는 경향이 있으며 상대방의 의지를 묻거나 단순 미래를 나타낼 때 쓰인다.

4

> **The diet _________ be maintained, without change, for at least six months if you want it to work.**
>
> (a) should not
> (b) may not
> (c) should
> (d) may

그 다이어트가 효과가 있으려면 적어도 6개월간 지속해서 해야 한다.

해설 must, ought to보다 뜻이 약한 should는 '제안, 권고'의 의미를 가지고 있다. 빈칸에는 막연한 추측을 나타내는 may보다 권고의 의미를 가지고 있는 should가 들어가야 문장의 해석이 자연스러우므로 (c)가 정답이 된다.

5

> **(a) Jogging, bicycling, swimming, and other popular exercise activities rarely produce serious injuries. (b) However, people who are just beginning a regular exercise program often feel stiff and sore after the first few days. (c) More physical types of exercise, such as weightlifting and football, can cause long lasting muscle and joint problems. (d) To avoid these risks, it is recommended that you (would find → (should) find) an appropriate stretching routine and get in the habit of completing it before exercising.**

(a) 달리기, 자전거 타기, 수영 그리고 다른 인기 있는 운동들은 심한 부상을 거의 만들지 않는다. (b) 그러나 규칙적인 운동을 시작하는 사람들은 운동 시작 며칠 후에 뻣뻣하고 쑤시는 느낌을 받곤 한다. (c) 역도와 축구 같이 몸을 더 쓰는 운동의 경우 근육과 관절에 문제가 생길 수 있다. (d) 이러한 위험을 피하기 위해서는 적절한 스트레칭 절차를 찾아 운동 전에 스트레칭을 완벽하게 하는 습관을 들여야 한다.

해설 주장, 명령, 제안, 권고를 나타내는 recommend, insist, suggest 뒤에 이어지는 명사절의 동사는 〈should +동사원형〉의 형태가 된다. 그러나 should는 종종 생략되고 동사원형만 쓰이기도 한다.

Answers

1. (a)   2. (d)   3. (b)   4. (c)   5. (d) would find → (should) find

Build Up

TEPS 전 문법 요소가 모의고사 형식으로 골고루 섞인 4파트의 문제
를 골고루 풀어 본다.

▶▶ **Part I** Fill in the blank with the most appropriate word or phrase.

1. A: How does Sarah like her new job?
B: She hasn't decided yet, __________ there for three days.

(a) she'll only work
(b) she's only worked
(c) she only worked
(d) she'd only worked

2. A: Roger ruined the party yesterday.
B: You're right, he __________ have ever come.

(a) wouldn't
(b) can't
(c) shouldn't
(d) won't

3. A: Are you going to perform at the concert tomorrow?
B: No, I __________ able to practice at all.

(a) weren't
(b) hadn't been
(c) don't
(d) wasn't

4. A: I love watching the firework show __________ the city puts on every Independence Day.
B: Me, too. They are very pretty.

(a) that
(b) when
(c) whichever
(d) how

▶▶ **Part II** Fill in the blank with the most appropriate word or phrase.

5. Certain species of parrots are known for their extremely long lifespans, though there are
__________ very short lifespans.

(a) some have
(b) those have
(c) some having
(d) none having

6. This is a difficult experiment because you have no ___________ for error.

    (a) the room
    (b) room
    (c) rooms
    (d) a room

7. We can throw everything in the trash, except for those photo albums ___________ are piled in the corner.

    (a) who
    (b) for whom
    (c) which
    (d) where

8. A dental analysis proved that the skeleton found in the tomb ___________ a female pharaoh between the years B.C. 300 and B.C. 100.

    (a) should be
    (b) should not have been
    (c) would not be
    (d) must have been

▶▶ **Part III**   Identify the grammatical error in the dialogue.

9. (a) A: How did the dinner with your parents go?
    (b) B: Awful! It was nice to see my parents, but we ate at such horrible a restaurant.
    (c) A: I'm glad you told me that because I have a reservation there for tonight.
    (d) B: I would cancel it if I were you. I am never going back there again.

10. (a) A: How did you do on your calculus exam?
    (b) B: I don't have the exam until next period. How did you do?
    (c) A: I think I did really well. I should have since I and Wendy studied all weekend.
    (d) B: Well, I didn't have much time to study, so I hope it's not too difficult.

▶▶ **Part IV**   Identify the ungrammatical sentence in the passage.

11. (a) Many people read literature for leisure. (b) Of these people, a great number prefer to purchase their books, as opposing to borrowing them. (c) They enjoy the close proximity of a useful book. (d) Once they have read a book, it can be quite a pleasure to glance back at the pages or to reference the book freely at a later time.

12. (a) In modern times technology has taken incredible strides. (b) For thousands of years science and technology evolved very slowly, taking hundreds of years at a time for any major changes to occur. (c) However, as human knowledge of the physical world continues to grow, we gained the ability to push our technology even further. (d) Advances in communication, for instance, have allowed this rapid growth to continue its acceleration.

정답:188p

<table>
<tr><td>Day 1</td><td>

▶▶ 시제

1. 현재와 현재진행의 차이점을 알아둔다.
2. 과거와 현재완료의 차이점을 구분하도록 한다.
3. 시간·조건 부사절에서는 현재나 현재완료가 미래를 대신한다.

</td></tr>
<tr><td>Day 2</td><td>

▶▶ 조동사

1. 조동사 본연의 의미를 파악한다. 이는 LC스크립트를 잘 활용하면 도움이 된다.
2. 〈조동사 과거형 + have p.p.〉의 형태를 알아둔다.
3. 조동사의 관용적 표현의 쓰임을 알아둔다.

</td></tr>
<tr><td>Day 3</td><td>

▶▶ 수동태

1. Part III와 Part IV에서 자동사가 수동태로 쓰이지 않았는지 확인한다.
2. 자동사와 타동사가 둘 다 가능한 동사를 알아둔다.
3. 감정 동사는 수동태로도 많이 쓰이지만 능동태로도 가능함을 알아둔다.

</td></tr>
<tr><td>Day 4</td><td>

▶▶ 가정법

1. 가정법의 쓰임을 파악해 둔다.
2. 주장·요구·제안 등의 동사, 형용사, 명사 등이 조동사 should가 생략되어 함께 쓰이는 용법을 파악해 둔다.
3. if 가정법에서 if가 생략되면 도치가 이루어진다.

</td></tr>
<tr><td>Day 5</td><td>

▶▶ to부정사

1. to부정사를 목적어로 취하는 동사를 파악한다. 특히 to부정사를 목적격 보어로 취하는 5형식 동사들을 파악한다.
2. to부정사의 형용사적 용법을 이해하고 파악해 둔다.
3. 대부정사의 쓰임을 알아둔다.

</td></tr>
</table>

Day 3
수동태

자동사가 수동태로 쓰이지 않았는지 Part III와 Part IV에서 확인해야 한다.

1. 전형적인 자동사는 수동태가 불가능하다.

happen, occur, arrive, become, remain, appear, disappear, fall, come

The house has been remained empty for a long time. (X)
The house has remained empty for a long time. (O) 그 집은 오랫동안 비어져 있다.

2. It ~ that 구문으로 수동태로 쓰이는 동사

believe, consider, find, report, think, say, expect, suppose, know

It is said that he was once famous. 그는 한때 유명했다고 한다.

3. 수동태 뒤에 명사(구)가 올 수 있는 4형식·5형식 동사

give, offer, consider, call, elect

They gave her the money. 그들은 그녀에게 돈을 주었다.
→ **She was given the money (by them).**
We elected her mayor. 우리는 그녀를 시장으로 선출했다.
→ **She was elected mayor (by us).**

4. 지각동사, 사역동사의 목적격 보어인 원형부정사는 수동태에서는 to부정사로 바뀐다.

She saw him break the window. 그녀는 그가 창문을 깨는 것을 보았다.
→ **He was seen to break the window.** 그가 창문 깨는 것이 목격되었다.

5. 감정 동사(scare, frighten, interest, disappoint, surprise, satisfy)가 수동태로만 쓰인다는 생각을 버려야 한다.

The result satisfied me. 그 결과는 나를 만족시켰다. (능동태)
I was satisfied with the result. 나는 그 결과에 만족했다. (수동태)

6. 자동사와 타동사 둘 다 가능한 동사

write 쓰다/ 써지다   **cut** 자르다/(날이) 들다
sell 팔다 /팔리다   **read** 읽다/~라고 쓰여 있다
clean 청소하다/깨끗해지다   **hurt** 다치게 하다/아프다
grow 기르다/자라다   **peel** 벗기다/벗겨지다

The house has been sold. 그 집은 팔렸다. (타동사)
The books sell well. 그 책들은 잘 팔린다. (자동사, 수동 불가능)

Catch Up 

수동태 관련 TEPS 주요 문제들을 풀어보도록 한다.

Part I Fill in the blank with the most appropriate word or phrase.

1. A: Some people believe in the existence of UFOs.
B: Yes, but they remain to ____________.

(a) see
(b) be seen
(c) have seen
(d) have been seen

2. A: For my history assignment, I'm writing a paper about notorious rulers. Will you give me
some suggestions on who to write about?
B: There are many, but Adolf Hitler ___________ one of the most infamous rulers of the
twentieth century.

(a) considers
(b) considered
(c) is considered
(d) will be considered

Part II Fill in the blank with the most appropriate word or phrase.

3. I needed some eggs to bake a cake, but the store was ___________.

(a) closing
(b) closed
(c) to close
(d) close

4. New Nobel laureates ___________ to the list of Nobel Prize winners every year.

(a) add
(b) are added
(c) are adding
(d) adding

Part IV Identify the ungrammatical sentence in the passage.

5. (a) I'm going to call Tim to be told him that Dad's in the hospital. (b) I'm not sure how he
will react because they are so close. (c) However, I think it would be wrong for me to wait
for things to settle down. (d) The situation might get worse.

Answers

Catch Up에서 푼 문제의 해석과 해설을 점검한다.

1

A: Some people believe in the existence of UFOs.
B: Yes, but they remain to ____________.

(a) see
(b) be seen
(c) have seen
(d) have been seen

A: 어떤 사람들은 UFO가 있다고 믿어.
B: 응. 근데 목격되지 않은 채로 남아 있어.

해설 remain to V는 '~하지 않고 남아 있다' 라는 의미가 있다. see는 '~을 보다' 라는 타동사이므로 '목격되다' 라는 수동의 의미가 되려면 수동태인 (b)가 정답이 된다.

2

A: For my history assignment, I'm writing a paper about notorious rulers. Will you give me some suggestions on who to write about?
B: There are many, but Adolf Hitler ____________ one of the most infamous rulers of the twentieth century.

(a) considers
(b) considered
(c) is considered
(d) will be considered

A: 역사 숙제로 악명 높은 통치자에 대해서 쓰고 있어. 누구에 대해 쓸지 제안 좀 해줄래?
B: 많지. 그런데 아돌프 히틀러가 20세기의 가장 악명 높은 통치자 중에 한 명으로 간주되잖아.

해설 consider는 〈consider + 목적어 + 목적격 보어〉의 구문을 취하는 5형식 동사로 '~을 …으로 간주하다' 라는 의미가 있다. 여기서는 히틀러가 20세기의 가장 악명 높은 통치자 중에 하나로 '간주되어지는' 것이므로 '수동' 의 형태가 되어야 한다. 그러므로 정답은 (c) 이다.

3

I needed some eggs to bake a cake, but the store was __________.

(a) closing
(b) closed
(c) to close
(d) close

케이크를 굽기 위해서 달걀이 필요했는데 가게가 닫혀 있었다.

해설 close는 '~을 닫다, 차단하다' 라는 의미의 타동사이다. 여기서는 가게가 '닫힌' 상태였으므로 '수동' 의 형태가 가장 적절하다. 그러므로 정답은 (b)가 된다.

4

New Nobel laureates __________ to the list of Nobel Prize winners every year.

(a) add
(b) are added
(c) are adding
(d) adding

새로운 노벨상 수상자들이 매년 노벨상 수상자 명단에 추가된다.

해설 add는 '더하다, 가산하다' 라는 의미의 타동사이다. 여기서는 '추가된다' 는 '수동' 의 의미가 되어야 하므로 (b)가 정답이 된다.

5

(a) I'm going to call Tim to (be told → tell) him that dad's in the hospital. (b) I'm not sure how he will react because they are so close. (c) However, I think it would be wrong for me to wait for things to settle down. (d) The situation might get worse.

(a) 나는 팀에게 아빠가 병원에 있다고 말하기 위해 전화하려고 한다. (b) 그들이 너무 친하기 때문에 그가 어떻게 반응할지 모르겠다. (c) 그러나 문제가 해결될 때까지 기다리는 것은 잘못된 것 같다. (d) 상황이 심각해질 수도 있기 때문이다.

해설 tell은 '~을 말하다' 라는 의미의 타동사이다. be told는 말을 하는 것이 아니라 듣는 것이므로 여기서는 의미상 적절치 않다. 또한 tell 뒤에 간접목적어 him이 있으므로 능동의 형태로 쓰는 것이 적절하다.

Answers

1. (b) 2. (c) 3. (b) 4. (b) 5. (a) be told → tell

Build Up

TEPS 전 문법 요소가 모의고사 형식으로 골고루 섞인 4파트의 문제
를 골고루 풀어 본다.

▶▶ **Part I**   Fill in the blank with the most appropriate word or phrase.

1.   A: I can't believe smoking is still allowed in restaurants!
   B: Why don't we petition ________________________?

   (a) the government to do something about it
   (b) to the government to do something about it
   (c) for the government to stop
   (d) for a stop to the government

2.   A: Why do you watch so many cooking shows?
   B: I enjoy learning the art of making __________.

   (a) the meal
   (b) meal
   (c) the meals
   (d) meals

3.   A: Do you recognize anyone in this picture?
   B: I think I remember __________ the woman in the purple shirt.

   (a) saw
   (b) to see
   (c) seeing
   (d) seen

4.   A: Slow down! There's an injured dog over there!
   B: Oh, no! I __________ that!

   (a) don't see
   (b) didn't see
   (c) hadn't seen
   (d) have seen

▶▶ **Part II**   Fill in the blank with the most appropriate word or phrase.

5.   ________________ Richard was in an accident was given to his wife.

   (a) A message is that
   (b) The message that
   (c) The message which
   (d) From the message

6. As the war continued and the number of injured soldiers grew, _________________ for medical supplies and bigger facilities.

(a) so the need did
(b) so did the need
(c) such was the need
(d) as such was the need

7. Contrary to popular belief, _________________ most crimes occur.

(a) at dawn is when
(b) dawn is at when
(c) when is at dawn
(d) when at is dawn

8. Dr. James came _________________ as the leading authority on the subject because he conducted studies on it for 33 years.

(a) to be recognized
(b) to recognize
(c) recognized to be
(d) to recognized be

▶▶ **Part III**   Identify the grammatical error in the dialogue.

9. (a) A: Do you have any pets?
(b) B: I have a cat, but most of time it wanders outside of my home.
(c) A: Is your cat hard to take care of?
(d) B: Not really. It seems that my cat is very well trained.

10. (a) A: What do you plan on doing after graduating?
(b) B: I plan on opening a business, but I need a partner.
(c) A: Are you talking about the bakery you talked about?
(d) B: That's which I want to discuss with you.

▶▶ **Part IV**   Identify the ungrammatical sentence in the passage.

11. (a) Many supporters of the Chicago Cubs tend to be fair-weather fans. (b) More fans are eager to switch sides when the Chicago White Sox are doing well. (c) However, when both teams are doing well, they try to prevent from cheering for the wrong team by staying with the Chicago Cubs. (d) That is what happened during the 2002-2003 regular baseball season.

12. (a) Many kinds of dinosaurs roamed the earth thousands of years ago. (b) There is fossils that prove that they existed. (c) Many of these fossils have been excavated and placed as display in museums. (d) People can go to museums and see what dinosaurs looked like.

정답: 190p

GRAMMAR
Week 1

Day 1 ▶▶ 시제

1. 현재와 현재진행의 차이점을 알아둔다.
2. 과거와 현재완료의 차이점을 구분하도록 한다.
3. 시간 · 조건 부사절에서는 현재나 현재완료가 미래를 대신한다.

Day 2 ▶▶ 조동사

1. 조동사 본연의 의미를 파악한다. 이는 LC스크립트를 잘 활용하면 도움이 된다.
2. 〈조동사 과거형 ＋have p.p.〉의 형태를 알아둔다.
3. 조동사의 관용적 표현의 쓰임을 알아둔다.

Day 3 ▶▶ 수동태

1. Part III와 Part IV에서 자동사가 수동태로 쓰이지 않았는지 확인한다.
2. 자동사와 타동사가 둘 다 가능한 동사를 알아둔다.
3. 감정 동사는 수동태로도 많이 쓰이지만 능동태로도 가능함을 알아둔다.

Day 4 ▶▶ 가정법

1. 가정법의 쓰임을 파악해 둔다.
2. 주장 · 요구 · 제안 등의 동사, 형용사, 명사 등이 조동사 should가 생략되어 함께 쓰이는 용법을 파악해 둔다.
3. if 가정법에서 if가 생략되면 도치가 이루어진다.

Day 5 ▶▶ to부정사

1. to부정사를 목적어로 취하는 동사를 파악한다. 특히 to부정사를 목적격 보어로 취하는 5형식 동사들을 파악한다.
2. to부정사의 형용사적 용법을 이해하고 파악해 둔다.
3. 대부정사의 쓰임을 알아둔다.

1. 가정법 과거: 현재와 반대되는 상황을 가정한다.

If+S+과거형 동사(be동사 → were), S+would/could/should/might+동사원형:
~한다면 ~할 텐데 (현재로 해석함)

If I knew his number, I would invite him to the party. 그의 전화번호를 안다면 그를 파티에 초대할 텐데.

2. 가정법 과거완료: 과거와 반대되는 상황을 가정한다.

If+S+had p.p., S+would/could/should/might+have p.p. : ~했다면 ~했을 텐데 (과거로 해석함)

If I had known his number, I would have invited him to the party.
그의 전화번호를 알았다면 그를 파티에 초대했을 텐데.

3. 도치: if절에서 if를 생략하면 도치가 이루어진다.

If it had not been for your help, I wouldn't have finished this project in time.
= Had it not been for your help, I wouldn't have finished this project in time.
당신의 도움이 아니었더라면 나는 이 프로젝트를 제시간에 끝낼 수 없었을 것이다.

4. 제안, 요구, 주장, 소망 표현

행동의 중요성을 표현하는 명사, 형용사, 동사 뒤에 that절이 오는 경우 that절의 동사는 〈(should+) 동사원형〉을 쓴다.
동사: **suggest, recommend, insist, demand, propose, advise, decide, claim, require**
형용사: **essential, important, advisable, required, urgent, necessary, imperative**
명사: **suggestion, wish, advice, decision, request, command, requirement**

He suggested that the government (should) pay more attention to the handicapped.
그는 정부가 장애자들에게 더 많은 관심을 가져야 한다고 제안했다.

that절 이하가 아직 일어나지 않은 내용 즉, '~해야 한다', '~하겠다' 등의 제안의 의미가 없을 때는 should가 생략됐다고 볼 수 없으므로 무조건 동사원형을 넣어서는 안 된다.

She insisted that she wasn't at home at that time.
그 여자는 그 당시 집에 없었다고 주장했다. → (사실을) 주장하다

7. 가정법 특수 구문

1) **It is (high/about) time (that)+S+과거동사:** ~할 때이다

It is about time you studied harder. 이제 더 열심히 공부해야 할 때다.

2) **주어+wish+(that) 주어+과거 동사:** 현재 사실 반대 소망
　　　　　　　had p.p.: 과거 사실 반대 소망

3) **as if/as though 주어+과거 동사:** 마치 ~인 것처럼
　　　　　　had p.p.: 마치 ~였던 것처럼

She talks as if she ran the company. 그녀는 마치 그녀가 그 회사를 운영하는 것처럼 말한다.

# Catch Up 

가정법 관련 TEPS 주요 문제들을 풀어보도록 한다.

Part I Fill in the blank with the most appropriate word or phrase.

1. A: The boss told us we will now be starting work two hours earlier.
B: Good, __________ that way. I don't like getting finished so late.

(a) it will be
(b) should it be
(c) it should be
(d) will it should

2. A: That was a great game, but we almost lost.
B: Yeah, we __________ if it hadn't been for your great play at the end.

(a) would have lost
(b) would lose
(c) did lose
(d) could lose

Part II Fill in the blank with the most appropriate word or phrase.

3. The team claimed they ______________ the project without working through the weekend.

(a) didn't finish
(b) couldn't finish
(c) couldn't have finished
(d) will not finish

4. You're having car problems again? I think it's about time you __________ a new car.

(a) had gotten
(b) should get
(c) get
(d) got

5. The police officer suggested we ____________ driving because of the parade today.

(a) avoid
(b) had avoided
(c) avoided
(d) didn't avoid

Answers 

Catch Up에서 푼 문제의 해석과 해설을 점검한다.

1

A: The boss told us we will now be starting work two hours earlier.
B: Good, __________ that way. I don't like getting finished so late.

(a) it will be
(b) should it be
(c) it should be
(d) will it should

A: 사장님이 이제 2시간 일찍 일을 시작할 거라고 말씀하셨어.
B: 잘됐다. 그래야 돼. 난 늦게 끝나는 게 싫거든.

해설 조동사 본연의 뜻을 묻는 질문은 해석을 해야 하므로 여기서도 앞뒤 문장의 해석을 통해서 적절한 조동사를 골라야 한다. A의 말에 Good이라고 반응하고, 빈칸 뒤에 오는 문장을 보면 늦게 끝나는 것을 싫어한다고 말하고 있으므로 '그렇게 되어야 한다' 는 의미가 되어야 함을 알 수 있다. should가 여기서는 '마땅히 ~하다' 라는 의미로 쓰이고 있고 도치될 이유가 없으므로 (c)가 정답이 된다.

2

A: That was a great game, but we almost lost.
B: Yeah, we __________ if it hadn't been for your great play at the end.

(a) would have lost
(b) would lose
(c) did lose
(d) could lose

A: 정말 멋진 경기였어. 하지만 우리가 거의 질 뻔 했지.
B: 맞아. 마지막에 네가 경기를 잘하지 않았더라면 우리는 졌을지도 몰라.

해설 가정법 과거완료의 문제이다. 가정법 과거완료는 과거 상황과 반대되는 상황을 가정하는 것으로 〈if+S+had p.p.~, S+would/could/should/might+have p.p.~〉의 형태로 표현한다. 여기서도 가정을 하는 시점이 과거이므로 주절도 가정법 과거완료로 표현한 (a)가 정답이 된다.

3

<table>
<tr><td>

The team claimed they _____________ the project without working through the weekend.

(a) didn't finish
(b) couldn't finish
(c) couldn't have finished
(d) will not finish

</td><td>

그 팀은 그들이 주말 내내 일하지 않았다면 그 프로젝트를 끝낼 수 없었을 것이라고 말했다.

</td></tr>
</table>

해설 〈조동사(would/could/should/might)+have p.p.〉는 과거 상황에 대한 추측이나 후회, 유감, 가능성 등을 표현할 때 사용된다. 여기서는 주절의 시제가 과거이고 과거의 반대 상황을 가정하는 것이므로 (c)가 가장 적절하다.

4

<table>
<tr><td>

You're having car problems again? I think it's about time you __________ a new car.

(a) had gotten
(b) should get
(c) get
(d) got

</td><td>

차가 또 고장났습니까? 제 생각엔 새 차를 사실 때가 된 것 같네요.

</td></tr>
</table>

해설 〈It is (about/high) time+S+과거 동사〉는 가정법의 관용 표현으로 아직 하지 않은 일에 대해서 '이제는 ~할 시간이다'라는 의미가 된다. 그러므로 빈칸에는 과거 동사인 got이 가장 적절하다.

5

<table>
<tr><td>

The police officer suggested we _____________ driving because of the parade today.

(a) avoid
(b) had avoided
(c) avoided
(d) didn't avoid

</td><td>

경찰관은 오늘 행진 때문에 운전을 피하라고 말했다.

</td></tr>
</table>

해설 주장, 요구, 제안 등의 동사(suggest, insist, demand, require)의 목적절이 아직 일어나지 않은 일에 대한 제안의 의미가 있을 때 should가 생략됐다고 보고 동사원형이 오게 된다. 여기서도 원래는 should avoid였으나 should가 생략되고 avoid가 남게 되었다.

Answers

1. (c) 2. (a) 3. (c) 4. (d) 5. (a)

Build Up 

TEPS 전 문법 요소가 모의고사 형식으로 골고루 섞인 4파트의 문제
를 골고루 풀어 본다.

▶▶ **Part I** Fill in the blank with the most appropriate word or phrase.

1. A: You should really take your dog to the veterinarian.
B: I know, I ___________, but I don't have enough money to pay the bill.

(a) want it to do
(b) want to do it
(c) want
(d) want to

2. A: Tom and I are getting married next month, and you are invited.
B: Wow, congratulations! I ___________ there.

(a) was
(b) must have been
(c) will be
(d) could be

3. A: I thought you were planning to move away from Chicago.
B: I was, but over the last year I've grown ___________ the city.

(a) with love
(b) loving for
(c) to love
(d) loving

4. A: Have you ever seen ___________ of the seven natural wonders of the world?
B: I've only seen the Grand Canyon.

(a) any
(b) those
(c) some
(d) every

▶▶ **Part II** Fill in the blank with the most appropriate word or phrase.

5. Passing the bar exam ___________ than I had expected.

(a) was difficult
(b) was more difficult
(c) were difficult
(d) were more difficult

6. Five miles _________ the longest I had ever run before I ran in the marathon this afternoon.

    (a) has been
    (b) was
    (c) were
    (d) have been

7. When we were children, we learned _________ to protect ourselves in the case of fire.

    (a) how
    (b) when
    (c) what
    (d) why

8. _________ all their money at the casino, the Smiths had to end their vacation early and head home.

    (a) Wasting
    (b) Having wasted
    (c) To have wasted
    (d) Wasted

▶▶ **Part III**   Identify the grammatical error in the dialogue.

9. (a) A: Tonight is the final night that the Munich Symphony will be in town.
    (b) B: I know. I'm very excited for the performance.
    (c) A: You're going, too? After the show we are all going out to dinner. Can you come?
    (d) B: I wish I could, but I must go for home afterwards so I can finish some paperwork.

10. (a) A: Hello, can we check in for flight 402 here?
    (b) B: You sure can, sir. Can I see your your boarding passes and photo IDs'?
    (c) A: Sure. Also, I want to make sure that my wife and I are seating next to each other.
    (d) B: I'll see what I can do, Mr. Park, but it might be difficult. This flight is filled to capacity.

▶▶ **Part IV**   Identify the ungrammatical sentence in the passage.

11. (a) No one had ever taught Jeff how to swim, but he very much wanted to learn. (b) He had nothing to do this weekend, so he decided to drive to nearby Lake Wikoma. (c) Entering the water, the wind grew strong and the waves became too large for a novice swimmer. (d) Jeff was disappointed that he would have to wait for another day, but he knew it was dangerous for him to be in the lake in those conditions.

12. (a) The following is a reminder to all returning students. (b) There has been a great increase in the number of new students who have joined our institution this coming semester. (c) Many of them will be confused and will require your patient assistance in order to help get their bearings here. (d) Please be willing to offer directions, advice, and any other sort of aid, should you come across any students appeared lost or disoriented.

정답: 192p

| **Day 1** |  시제 |

1. 현재와 현재진행의 차이점을 알아둔다.
2. 과거와 현재완료의 차이점을 구분하도록 한다.
3. 시간·조건 부사절에서는 현재나 현재완료가 미래를 대신한다.

| **Day 2** |  조동사 |

1. 조동사 본연의 의미를 파악한다. 이는 LC스크립트를 잘 활용하면 도움이 된다.
2. 〈조동사 과거형 ＋have p.p.〉의 형태를 알아둔다.
3. 조동사의 관용적 표현의 쓰임을 알아둔다.

| **Day 3** |  수동태 |

1. Part III와 Part IV에서 자동사가 수동태로 쓰이지 않았는지 확인한다.
2. 자동사와 타동사가 둘 다 가능한 동사를 알아둔다.
3. 감정 동사는 수동태로도 많이 쓰이지만 능동태로도 가능함을 알아둔다.

| **Day 4** |  가정법 |

1. 가정법의 쓰임을 파악해 둔다.
2. 주장·요구·제안 등의 동사, 형용사, 명사 등이 조동사 should가 생략되어 함께 쓰이는 용법을 파악해 둔다.
3. if 가정법에서 if가 생략되면 도치가 이루어진다.

| **Day 5** |  to부정사 |

1. to부정사를 목적어로 취하는 동사를 파악한다. 특히 to부정사를 목적격 보어로 취하는 5형식 동사들을 파악한다.
2. to부정사의 형용사적 용법을 이해하고 파악해 둔다.
3. 대부정사의 쓰임을 알아둔다.

Day 5
to부정사

1. 의문사 + to V: 명사구로서 주어, 목적어, 보어로 쓰인다.

〈의문사 + to부정사〉를 목적어로 취하는 동사
know, wonder, discover, find out, show, see, explain, understand, tell, learn
I don't know what to say. 나는 무슨 말을 해야 할지 모르겠다.

2. to부정사가 목적격 보어가 되는 경우: V + O + to V (5형식 문장)

force, ask, enable, cause, want, allow, encourage, expect, persuade, require, urge, compel
He forced me to sign the paper. 그는 나에게 서류에 사인하도록 강요했다.

3. N + to V: 명사를 후치 수식하여 '~할', '~하기 위한'의 의미가 있다. (한정 용법)

the only, the first, ~thing + to V
She does not have friends to play with. 그녀는 함께 놀 친구가 없다.
I have nothing to be afraid of. 나는 두려워 할 게 없다.

4. 자동사 + to V

never fail to V 반드시 ~하다　**manage to V** 간신히(용케) ~해내다　**come to V** 서서히 ~하다
get to V ~하게 되다　**deserve to V** ~할 만하다　**prove to V** ~으로 판명되다　**afford to V** ~할 여유가 있다
seem/appear to V ~처럼 생각나다(보이다)　**grow to V** 서서히 ~하게 되다

5. to부정사를 목적어로 취하는 동사

care, decide, determine, choose, expect, fail, hope, manage, mean, plan, pretend, promise, refuse, want, wish, hesitate, seek, offer, afford

6. to부정사의 관용표현: be + 형용사 + to부정사

be ready to V ~할 준비가 되어 있다　　　　**be able to V** ~할 능력이 있다
be available to V ~할 수 있는 상황이다　　　**be eager to V** 열망하다
be hesitant to V ~하기를 주저하다　　　　　**be sure/certain to V** 반드시 ~하다
be reluctant to V ~하기를 꺼려하다　　　　　**be likely to V** ~할 가능성이 있다
be supposed to V ~하기로 예상되다　　　　　**be apt to V** ~하기 쉽다
feel free to V 마음껏 ~하다　　　　　　　　**be bound to V** 틀림없이 ~하다
be enough N to V / be 형용사 enough to V 충분하다　**be willing to V** 기꺼이 ~하다

7. 대부정사: 같은 동사구의 반복을 피하기 위해 동사를 생략하고 to만 쓰는 부정사를 말한다.

You don't have to go if you don't want to. 네가 가기 싫다면 가지 않아도 된다.

8. 완료시제: to have p.p. (본동사보다 한 시제 앞선 시제)

She seems to have been ill. 그녀는 아팠던 것 같다.

Catch Up 

to부정사 관련 TEPS 주요 문제들을 풀어보도록 한다.

Part I   Fill in the blank with the most appropriate word or phrase.

1. A: What's wrong, Julie? You seem very upset.
B: My little brother collapsed, so I _______________ right now.

(a) need you to take me home
(b) need to take home
(c) need you to take home
(d) need to take you home

2. A: New York City is a rich, diverse city and there are many places _______________.
B: Do you think you can give me a tour?

(a) here to visit around
(b) here around to visit
(c) to visit here around
(d) to visit around here

3. A: You can't force me to stay here!
B: Okay, you can go if ___________.

(a) you want it
(b) you want to
(c) you want go
(d) you want going

Part II   Fill in the blank with the most appropriate word or phrase.

4. The new movie is supposed ___________ at the local theatre starting this Friday.

(a) to playing
(b) playing
(c) to play
(d) to have played

5. My youngest daughter loves to be noticed and always tries _________ attention to herself.

(a) draw
(b) drawn
(c) to draw
(d) drawing

Answers 

Catch Up에서 푼 문제의 해석과 해설을 점검한다.

1

A: What's wrong, Julie? You seem very upset.
B: My little brother collapsed, so I _______________ right now.

(a) need you to take me home
(b) need to take home
(c) need you to take home
(d) need to take you home

A: 무슨 일이야, 쥴리? 너 걱정스러워 보인다.
B: 내 동생이 쓰러졌어. 그러니 네가 나를 집에 데려다 줘야겠어.

해설 〈take＋목적어＋home〉은 '~를 집에 바래다주다'라는 의미이다. 여기서는 의미상 you가 I를 집에 데려다 줘야 한다는 말이 의미상 맞으므로 '내가 너를 집에 데려다 줘야 한다'는 (d)는 논리상 맞지 않다.

2

A: New York City is a rich, diverse city and there are many places _______________.
B: Do you think you can give me a tour?

(a) here to visit around
(b) here around to visit
(c) to visit here around
(d) to visit around here

A: 뉴욕은 풍요롭고 다양성이 있는 도시야. 이 근처에는 방문할 장소가 많아.
B: 네가 안내 좀 해 줄 수 있니?

해설 to부정사구의 어순을 묻는 문제이다. 여기서 to visit은 명사(many places)를 수식하는 형용사 역할을 한다. 장소를 나타내는 표현인 전치사구 around here는 to부정사 뒤에 오게 된다.

3

A: You can't force me to stay here!
B: Okay, you can go if __________.

(a) you want it
(b) you want to
(c) you want go
(d) you want going

A: 넌 나를 여기 억지로 머물게 할 수 없어!
B: 알았어. 네가 원하면 가도 돼.

해설   대부정사와 관련된 문제이다. 명사의 반복을 피하기 위해 대명사를 쓰고, 동사의 반복을 피하기 위해서 대동사를 쓰듯이 to부정사의 동일한 동사구의 반복을 피하기 위해서 동사구를 생략하고 to까지만 쓰는 것을 대부정사라고 한다. 그러므로 (b)가 정답이 된다. TEPS에서 자주 출제되는 문제 유형이므로 반드시 알아두도록 한다.

4

The new movie is supposed __________ at the local theatre starting this Friday.

(a) to playing
(b) playing
(c) to play
(d) to have played

새 영화가 이번 금요일부터 극장에서 상영될 예정이야.

해설   be supposed to V는 '~하기로 되어 있다' 라는 의미이다. 여기서 to는 to부정사로 뒤에 동사원형이 와야 한다. 또한 이번 금요일에 상영된다는 의미의 미래 용법으로 to부정사가 쓰여야 하기 때문에 to부정사의 완료형인 (d)는 적절치 않다. 그러므로 정답은 (c)이다.

5

My youngest daughter loves to be noticed and always tries __________ attention to herself.

(a) draw
(b) to be drawn
(c) to draw
(d) drawing

내 막내 딸은 주목 받기를 좋아해서 항상 자신에게로 주의를 끌려고 노력한다.

해설   try는 to부정사와 동명사를 둘 다 취할 수 있는 동사이다. 그러나 의미는 각각 다르다. try to V는 '~하려고 애쓰다(노력하다)' 라는 의미이고, try -ing는 '~을 시도하다' 라는 의미가 있다. 여기서는 문맥상 전자의 의미로 쓰였으므로 (c)가 정답이 된다. draw attention to~는 '~에 이목(주의)를 끌다' 라는 의미이다.

Answers

1. (a) 2. (d) 3. (b) 4. (c) 5. (c)

Build Up

TEPS 전 문법 요소가 모의고사 형식으로 골고루 섞인 4파트의 문제를 골고루 풀어 본다.

▶▶ Part I Fill in the blank with the most appropriate word or phrase.

1. A: Who's the fastest runner on the track team?
B: Jordan is definitely the fastest. He runs __________ the second fastest runner.

(a) faster than three times as
(b) as three times fast as
(c) three times as fast as
(d) as three times faster than

2. A: Which candidate did you vote for?
B: I voted for George Bush, __________ my wife did.

(a) although
(b) as
(c) as if
(d) when

3. A: Everyone failed the chemistry midterm!
B: I know. __________ how difficult it would be, I would've studied more!

(a) I could've known
(b) Had I known
(c) Have I known
(d) If I knew

4. A: John is __________ in the attic.
B: Oh! I thought he was studying downstairs in the basement!

(a) up
(b) down
(c) back
(d) around

▶▶ Part II Fill in the blank with the most appropriate word or phrase.

5. Being able __________ music takes a lot of dedication and understanding of music.

(a) to composing
(b) to be composed of
(c) to compose
(d) to have composed

6. It is _______________ decent housing in the south side of Chicago.

   (a) likely to find
   (b) to find it likely
   (c) to find likely
   (d) likely to find it

7. Although Ms. Franzen has a strict restroom policy, she __________ let you go to the restroom during class if it is an emergency.

   (a) might have
   (b) used to
   (c) may
   (d) did

8. Nobody really knows ______________________________.

   (a) for sure where the movie theater is
   (b) for sure the movie theater is there
   (c) how for sure the movie theater is
   (d) how for sure the movie theater was

▶▶ **Part III**   Identify the grammatical error in the dialogue.

9. (a) A: Are you nervous when you took the exam?
   (b) B: Not at all! I was as cool as a cucumber.
   (c) A: Wow! Most people were panicking right before the exam!
   (d) B: Yeah, but I felt very prepared since I attended every lecture and studied a lot.

10. (a) A: How are your golf lessons?
   (b) B: The lessons helped me improve my backswing.
   (c) A: How long have you been taking lessons?
   (d) B: Since over two months.

▶▶ **Part IV**   Identify the ungrammatical sentence in the passage.

11. (a) In the United States, a bill must be approved with Congress before it becomes a law. (b) The bill is read and reviewed at a legislative meeting. (c) Members of Congress may debate the bill and offer amendments. (d) Members then vote on the bill and the bill becomes a law if the majority of Congress approves it.

12. (a) All college students participating in any athletics will be tested for drugs. (b) From next year, each athlete will need to go through proper testing including a personal interview. (c) The fine for a first positive test will result in a suggestion to be treated. (d) After their second positive test, players will receive a full season suspension.

정답: 195p

GRAMMAR
Week 2

Day 6   ▶▶ 동명사

1. 동명사를 목적어로 취하는 동사를 파악한다.
2. 동명사의 의미상의 주어는 소유격이나 목적격으로 표현한다.
3. to부정사와 동명사를 둘 다 목적어로 취할 수 있으나 의미가 다른 동사들의 쓰임을 알아둔다.

Day 7   ▶▶ 분사

1. 명사를 수식하는 분사가 현재분사인지 과거분사인지 확인하는 절차를 알아둔다.
2. 감정 동사의 분사 용법을 알아둔다.
3. 분사구문을 만드는 절차를 알아둔다.

Day 8   ▶▶ 명사와 관사

1. 가산명사일 경우 단수나 복수 표시를 해야 한다.
2. 양 표시어와 수 표시어를 확인하고 Part Ⅲ나 Part Ⅳ에서 이들이 바르게 표기되었는지 확인한다.
3. 관사의 위치를 파악하여 순서를 외워두도록 한다.

Day 9   ▶▶ 대명사

1. 대명사와 그것을 받고 있는 명사와의 수, 성, 격이 일치하는지 확인한다.
2. one과 it의 차이점을 알아둔다.
3. 부정대명사의 종류와 쓰임을 알아둔다.

Day 10   ▶▶ 형용사

1. 서술적 용법으로만 쓰이는 형용사를 알아둔다.
2. 복합 형용사로 쓰이는 것은 복수로 표시하지 않는다.
3. 수량 형용사를 파악하고 수의 일치가 되는지 확인한다.

Day 6
동명사

1. 동명사의 의미상 주어는 소유격으로 표시한다.

I don't mind your smoking here. 여기서 담배 피우셔도 됩니다.
= I don't mind you smoking here. (구어체에서는 목적격도 가능)

2. need, want, require + -ing: 수동 의미

본래 to부정사 수동형을 취하나 그 의미가 수동일 때 동명사를 취할 수 있는 동사

My car needs washing. 내 차는 세차되어야 한다.
= My car needs to be washed.

3. 동명사를 목적어로 취하는 동사

finish, consider, enjoy, suggest, quit, abandon, avoid, mind, delay, permit, admit, resist, deny, prohibit, anticipate

He suggested going on a picnic. 그가 피크닉 가는 것을 제안했다.

4. 동명사를 취하는 관용어구

look forward to -ing ~을 기대하다
fall to -ing ~에 빠져들기 시작하다
be used to -ing ~하는 데 익숙하다
object/oppose to -ing ~을 반대하다
be devoted to -ing ~에 몰두하다
be committed to -ing 전념하다
be equal to -ing ~과 동등하다
be busy (in) -ing ~하느라 바쁘다
be worth -ing ~할 만한 가치가 있다
come close to -ing ~에 근접하다
there is no use/good -ing ~해도 소용없다
have difficulty/trouble/a hard time (in) -ing ~하는 데 어려움을 겪다
when it comes to -ing ~의 점에서는
What do you say to -ing? ~하는 것이 어떻습니까?

5. to부정사와 동명사를 취할 때 의미가 다른 경우

remember/forget + to V (앞으로 할 것)
                       -ing (이미 완료된 것)
regret + to V 유감스럽다
        -ing 후회하다
try+ to V ~하려고 노력하다
      -ing 시험 삼아 ~해보다

Sam often forgets to lock the door. 샘은 종종 문 잠그는 것을 잊곤 한다.
I will never forget seeing the Alps for the first time. 처음 알프스를 봤을 때를 잊지 못할 것이다.

# Catch Up 

동명사 관련 TEPS 주요 문제들을 풀어보도록 한다.

Part I Fill in the blank with the most appropriate word or phrase.

1. A: What do you do when you want to relax?
B: I enjoy ___________ baseball games.

(a) watching
(b) to watch
(c) watched
(d) the watching

2. A: What did you and your wife do on vacation?
B: We spent most of our time ___________ on the beach.

(a) in relaxing
(b) having relaxed
(c) relaxing
(d) to relax

3. A: Why does your dad seem so angry today?
B: His new computer doesn't work, but the salesman objected ___________ his money.

(a) to reimburse
(b) to reimbursing
(c) reimbursing
(d) the reimbursement of

Part II Fill in the blank with the most appropriate word or phrase.

4. Harry always has a difficult time ___________ his appointments.

(a) to remember
(b) remember
(c) of remembering
(d) remembering

5. Even though we live far apart, my sister always suggests ___________ during the holidays.

(a) getting together
(b) to get together
(c) having gotten together
(d) of getting together

Answers

Catch Up에서 푼 문제의 해석과 해설을 점검한다.

1

A: **What do you do when you want to relax?**
B: **I enjoy __________ baseball games.**
(a) **watching**
(b) **to watch**
(c) **watched**
(d) **the watching**

A: 쉬고 싶을 때 무엇을 하니?
B: 야구 경기 보는 것을 즐겨.

해설 enjoy는 동명사를 목적어로 취하는 동사이다. 그러므로 동명사 watching이 정답이 된다.

2

A: **What did you and your wife do on vacation?**
B: **We spent most of our time __________ on the beach.**
(a) **in relaxing**
(b) **having relaxed**
(c) **relaxing**
(d) **to relax**

A: 아내하고 휴가 때 무엇을 했니?
B: 해변에서 쉬면서 대부분의 시간을 보냈어.

해설 〈spend+목적어+-ing〉는 '(때를) 보내다, 지내다' 라는 의미가 있다. 빈칸에는 동명사의 형태가 와야 하므로 (c)가 정답이다.

3

A: Why does your dad seem so angry today?
B: His new computer doesn't work, but the
   salesman objected __________ his money.

(a) to reimburse
(b) to reimbursing
(c) reimbursing
(d) the reimbursement of

A: 오늘 너희 아빠가 왜 그리 화난 것 같니?
B: 컴퓨터가 고장났는데 판매원이 돈을 상환해
   주지 않았어.

해설 reimburse는 '변상하다, 상환하다' 라는 의미이다. object to -ing는 '～하는 것을 반대하다' 는 의미로 여기서의 to는 전치사 to로
뒤에 동명사를 취한다.

4

Harry always has a difficult time __________ his
appointments.

(a) to remember
(b) remember
(c) of remembering
(d) remembering

해리는 약속을 기억하는 데 항상 어려움을 겪는
다.

해설 have a difficult time -ing는 '～하는 데 어려움을 겪다' 라는 의미이다. 빈칸에는 동명사가 와야 하므로 (d)가 정답이다.

5

Even though we live far apart, my sister always
suggests __________ during the holidays.

(a) getting together
(b) to get together
(c) having gotten together
(d) of getting together

우리는 서로 떨어져 살지만 내 여동생은 휴일 때
에는 같이 모이자고 항상 제안한다.

해설 suggest는 목적어로 that절을 취하기도 하지만 동명사(-ing)를 목적어로 취하기도 한다. 그러므로 (a)가 정답이 된다.

Answers

1. (a) 2. (c) 3. (b) 4. (d) 5. (a)

Build Up

TEPS 전 문법 요소가 모의고사 형식으로 골고루 섞인 4파트의 문제
를 골고루 풀어 본다.

▶▶ **Part I** Fill in the blank with the most appropriate word or phrase.

1. A: I won the tennis match.
   B: Good for __________!

   (a) them
   (b) him
   (c) you
   (d) her

2. A: Do you have any __________ classes this semester?
   B: Yes, I'm taking a really great history class.

   (a) to interest
   (b) interesting
   (c) interested
   (d) interest

3. A: How long until you have to pay the bill?
   B: It __________ by July 19th.

   (a) paid
   (b) must pay
   (c) has to be paid
   (d) is paid

4. A: Is there anything wrong with your dog?
   B: Not at all. __________ is to be petted.

   (a) All she wants
   (b) She all wants
   (c) she needs all
   (d) All wants it

▶▶ **Part II** Fill in the blank with the most appropriate word or phrase.

5. __________ made a more important contribution to psychiatry than Sigmund Freud.

   (a) All psychiatrists
   (b) No other psychiatrist has
   (c) Any psychiatrist has
   (d) Any other psychiatrists have

6. After _________ hard for months, Alex was able to buy a brand-new car.

    (a) worked
    (b) he working
    (c) his work
    (d) working

7. The organization receives many donations _________ local citizens.

    (a) by
    (b) with
    (c) to
    (d) from

8. We can perform this entire experiment without _________ materials at all.

    (a) any
    (b) the
    (c) some
    (d) no

▶▶ **Part III** Identify the grammatical error in the dialogue.

9. (a) A: You seem really sick! You should just stay in bed today.
    (b) B: I think I will. Could you get me a glass of water?
    (c) A: Of course. Do you need anything else?
    (d) B: Maybe some chicken soup either, if you don't mind.

10. (a) A: It's so nice to see you, Kelly! I thought you couldn't come to the party.
    (b) B: I wouldn't miss your birthday party for the world.
    (c) A: Well, I'm glad you're here, but how was the work you have to do?
    (d) B: I've worked very hard for the past week, so I was able to finish it all in time.

▶▶ **Part IV** Identify the ungrammatical sentence in the passage.

11. (a) Wendy, congratulations on your promotion at work. (b) I just stopped by to be given to you these flowers, but you weren't here. (c) It's been a long time since we've been able to spend any quality time together, but I understand how busy you must be with all your new responsibilities. (d) Good luck with everything and call me soon, so we can have lunch.

12. (a) Rock climbing ranks high among outdoor enthusiasts as one of the most rewarding outdoor activities. (b) However, it is also one of the most physically demanding and dangerous activities. (c) Without proper training and steady understanding of safety procedures, you risk serious injury, or even death. (d) Rock climbing without proper certification is prohibited in all national parks, so you might complete a training course before you begin.

정답: 197p

GRAMMAR
Week 2

Day 6 ▶▶ 동명사

1. 동명사를 목적어로 취하는 동사를 파악한다.
2. 동명사의 의미상의 주어는 소유격이나 목적격으로 표현한다.
3. to부정사와 동명사를 둘 다 목적어로 취할 수 있으나 의미가 다른 동사들의 쓰임을 알아둔다.

Day 7 ▶▶ 분사

1. 명사를 수식하는 분사가 현재분사인지 과거분사인지 확인하는 절차를 알아둔다.
2. 감정 동사의 분사 용법을 알아둔다.
3. 분사구문을 만드는 절차를 알아둔다.

Day 8 ▶▶ 명사와 관사

1. 가산명사일 경우 단수나 복수 표시를 해야 한다.
2. 양 표시어와 수 표시어를 확인하고 Part III나 Part IV에서 이들이 바르게 표기되었는지 확인한다.
3. 관사의 위치를 파악하여 순서를 외워두도록 한다.

Day 9 ▶▶ 대명사

1. 대명사와 그것을 받고 있는 명사와의 수, 성, 격이 일치하는지 확인한다.
2. one과 it의 차이점을 알아둔다.
3. 부정대명사의 종류와 쓰임을 알아둔다.

Day 10 ▶▶ 형용사

1. 서술적 용법으로만 쓰이는 형용사를 알아둔다.
2. 복합 형용사로 쓰이는 것은 복수로 표시하지 않는다.
3. 수량 형용사를 파악하고 수의 일치가 되는지 확인한다.

1. 명사를 수식하는 분사가 현재분사인지 과거분사인지를 확인하는 절차

① 동사가 타동사인지 자동사인지 확인한다.
② 타동사일 땐 명사(의미상 주어)와 분사(의미상 동사)의 관계가 능동인지 수동인지를 파악하여 결정한다.
③ 자동사일 땐 명사(의미상 주어)와 분사(의미상 동사)의 관계가 진행인지 완료인지를 파악하여 결정한다.

2. 분사 + 명사

a sleeping baby 자는 아기 (sleep은 자동사 – 진행의 의미)
a returned solider 돌아온 군인 (return은 자동사 – 완료의 의미)
an exciting show 흥미진진한 쇼 (excite는 타동사 – 능동의 의미)
disappointed people 실망한 사람들 (disappoint는 타동사 – 수동의 의미)

3. 명사 + 분사: 〈주격 관계대명사+be동사〉가 생략된 경우가 많다.

The man (who is) talking over the phone is the manager of the restaurant.
전화 통화중인 저 남자가 그 레스토랑 매니저다.
Those (who are) invited to the party are not allowed to bring any electronics inside.
파티에 초대된 사람들은 어떤 전자제품도 안에 가져갈 수 없다.

4. 감정 동사의 분사 용법

감정의 원인은 현재분사(능동)를 쓰고, 감정을 느끼는 주체(주로 사람)에게는 과거분사(수동)를 사용한다.

bore 지루하게 하다　**interest** 흥미를 일으키다　**excite** 흥분시키다　**surprise** 놀라게 하다　**scare** 겁나게 하다
frighten 놀라게 하다　**satisfy** 만족시키다　**please** 즐겁게 하다　**amuse** 즐겁게 하다　**disappoint** 실망시키다
confuse 당황하게 하다　**satisfy** 만족시키다　**annoy** 성가시게 굴다　**bewilder** 당황하게 하다
irritate 짜증나게 하다　**exhaust** 지치게 하다　**astonish** 놀라게 하다　**embarrass** 당황하게 하다

5. 분사구문 만드는 법: 종속절의 주어와 주절의 주어가 일치할 때 접속사와 종속절의 주어를 생략한다.

접속사 + S1 + V~(종속절), S + V~(주절). (S1 = S)
　없앰　　없앰　　V+-ing ~, S + V~.

Since she was eliminated, she had to go back to the hotel immediately and pack her belongings. 여자는 탈락되었기 때문에 즉시 호텔로 돌아가 짐을 꾸려야 했다.
→ **Being eliminated, she had to go back to the hotel immediately and pack her belongings.** (분사구문에서 Being/Having been은 생략 가능하다.)
→ **Eliminated, she had to go back to the hotel immediately and pack her belongings.**

Catch Up

분사 관련 TEPS 주요 문제들을 풀어보도록 한다.

Part I   Fill in the blank with the most appropriate word or phrase.

1.   A: I start my new job next week.
B: You must _______________.

(a) excite
(b) be excited
(c) be exciting
(d) excited

2.   A: I can't decide which university to go to.
B: _______________________, you must take your time and make an informed decision.

(a) When chose a university
(b) Choose a university
(c) When choosing a university
(d) University chosen

Part II   Fill in the blank with the most appropriate word or phrase.

3.   Since there weren't any more concerns __________ from the team members, the meeting was brought to an end.

(a) arises
(b) arisen
(c) arising
(d) arose

4.   Five members split the cost of the remaining 50%, each now __________ a 10% share of the new company.

(a) own
(b) owns
(c) owned
(d) owning

Part III   Identify the grammatical error in the dialogue.

5.   (a) A: Hey! Long time no see! How are you?
(b) B: I'm okay. I'm just tired from work.
(c) A: Are you sure? Your face says otherwise. You seem distracting.
(d) B: I guess I am, but I don't want to talk about it.

Answers

Catch Up에서 푼 문제의 해석과 해설을 점검한다.

1

A: I start my new job next week.
B: You must __________.
(a) excite
(b) be excited
(c) be exciting
(d) excited

A: 다음주에 새로운 일을 시작해.
B: 기쁘겠구나.

해설 excite는 '흥분 시키다' 라는 의미의 타동사이다. 여기서 주어 you가 흥분을 느끼는 대상이 되므로 수동으로 표현한 과거분사의 형태가 되어야 하고 과거분사는 형용사이므로 be동사가 필요하다. 그러므로 (b)가 정답이 된다.

2

A: I can't decide which university to go to.
B: __________________, you must take your time and make an informed decision.
(a) When chose a university
(b) Choose a university
(c) When choosing a university
(d) University chosen

A: 어느 대학을 가야 할지 정할 수가 없어.
B: 대학을 정할 땐 시간을 가지고 정보에 근거한 결정을 해야 돼.

해설 분사구문을 고르는 문제이다. choose는 목적어를 취하는 타동사이고 목적어 a university가 있으므로 능동의 분사구문인 (c)가 정답이 된다. 원래 문장은 when you choose a university가 된다.

3

Since there weren't any more concerns __________ from the team members, the meeting was brought to an end.

(a) arises
(b) arisen
(c) arising
(d) arose

팀원들로부터 더 이상의 사안이 나오지 않았기 때문에 그 회의는 끝났다.

해설 arise는 자동사로 '(문제 등이) 생기다, 발생하다' 라는 의미이다. 이것의 수식을 받는 명사 concerns와의 관계가 능동의 완료로 보기 힘들기 때문에 과거분사 arisen이 아닌 현재분사 arising이 되어야 한다. 그러므로 (c)가 정답이다.

4

Five members split the cost of the remaining 50%, each now __________ a 10% share of the new company.

(a) own
(b) owns
(c) owned
(d) owning

새 회사의 10% 지분을 각각 소유하면서 5명의 회원이 남아 있는 50%의 비용을 분담한다.

해설 own은 '~을 소유하다' 라는 타동사이고 뒤에 목적어가 있으므로 능동 형태의 분사구문이 되어야 한다. 그러므로 (d)가 정답이 된다.

5

(a) A: Hey! Long time no see! How are you?
(b) B: I'm okay. I'm just tired from work.
(c) A: Are you sure? Your face says otherwise. You seem (distracting → distracted).
(d) B: I guess I am, but I don't want to talk about it.

(a) A: 안녕. 오랜만이다. 어떻게 지내?
(b) B: 난 괜찮아. 그냥 일 때문에 피곤해.
(c) A: 정말이야? 아닌 것 같은데. 심란해 보여.
(d) B: 그런 것 같아. 근데 그것에 대해 얘기하고 싶지 않아.

해설 distract는 '혼란시키다' 라는 타동사이다. 여기서는 주어 you가 혼란을 느끼는 상태이므로 수동의 과거분사형으로 고쳐야 한다. 또한 (c)에서 otherwise는 부사로 '다르게, 달리' 라는 의미로 사용되었다.

Answers

1. (b) 2. (c) 3. (c) 4. (d) 5. (c) distracting → distracted

Build Up

TEPS 전 문법 요소가 모의고사 형식으로 골고루 섞인 4파트의 문제를 골고루 풀어 본다.

▶▶ **Part I**   Fill in the blank with the most appropriate word or phrase.

1. A: Is Mary not feeling well?
B: No. She __________ when I got home.

(a) slept
(b) is sleeping
(c) has slept
(d) was sleeping

2. A: Thank you for the dinner, William.
B: It was my pleasure. I would like __________ again.

(a) to seeing you
(b) to see you
(c) of you seeing
(d) you to see

3. A: Dinosaurs __________ once the largest creatures to roam the earth.
B: Neat! What happened to them?

(a) was
(b) were
(c) have been
(d) had been

4. A: Why were you late to the board meeting?
B: __________ to drop off my sister at the airport, but then I got stuck in traffic.

(a) I had
(b) I had had
(c) I have had
(d) I have

▶▶ **Part II**   Fill in the blank with the most appropriate word or phrase.

5. The computer manufacturer recommends __________ the battery every 2 years.

(a) for changing
(b) for change
(c) changing
(d) to change

6. I will go to the barbeque ___________ it doesn't rain.

(a) if
(b) although
(c) unless
(d) while

7. The company ___________ once the leading producer of soy products.

(a) is
(b) was
(c) have
(d) has

8. Many great writers emerged from the Harlem Renaissance ___________ Langston Hughes was one of the most talented and well-known.

(a) that
(b) what
(c) whose
(d) of which

▶▶ **Part III**   Identify the grammatical error in the dialogue.

9. (a) A: I went to Olive Garden with Jim.
(b) B: Wow! They serve big portions. Did you have any leftovers?
(c) A: Yes, I brought some back with me. I probably eat them later. Do you want some?
(d) B: Sure! I'll be happy to share them with you!

10. (a) A: Did you hear that someone left a newborn baby outside of Dr. Thornton's clinic?
(b) B: Really? What did he do?
(c) A: He tried finding the parents of the baby who couldn't find.
(d) B: Wow, that is very sad to hear.

▶▶ **Part IV**   Identify the ungrammatical sentence in the passage.

11. (a) I need to speak to John about his failing grade. (b) He was doing well in class for a while, especially in the beginning of the year. (c) However, he stopped doing his homework and his attendance was far from being acceptable. (d) His test scores also dropped drastically, which affected his grade a lot.

12. (a) Relationships, whether they are business, romantic, or platonic, are important in life. (b) It is difficult, however, to maintain of them. (c) Many people do not understand that relationships take commitment and compromise. (d) Both parties must be willing to commit and sacrifice in order to make things work.

정답: 199p

GRAMMAR
Week2

Day 6 ▶▶ 동명사

1. 동명사를 목적어로 취하는 동사를 파악한다.
2. 동명사의 의미상의 주어는 소유격이나 목적격으로 표현한다.
3. to부정사와 동명사를 둘 다 목적어로 취할 수 있으나 의미가 다른 동사들의 쓰임을 알아둔다.

Day 7 ▶▶ 분사

1. 명사를 수식하는 분사가 현재분사인지 과거분사인지 확인하는 절차를 알아둔다.
2. 감정 동사의 분사 용법을 알아둔다.
3. 분사구문을 만드는 절차를 알아둔다.

Day 8 ▶▶ 명사와 관사

1. 가산명사일 경우 단수나 복수 표시를 해야 한다.
2. 양 표시어와 수 표시어를 확인하고 Part III나 Part IV에서 이들이 바르게 표기되었는지 확인한다.
3. 관사의 위치를 파악하여 순서를 외워두도록 한다.

Day 9 ▶▶ 대명사

1. 대명사와 그것을 받고 있는 명사와의 수, 성, 격이 일치하는지 확인한다.
2. one과 it의 차이점을 알아둔다.
3. 부정대명사의 종류와 쓰임을 알아둔다.

Day 10 ▶▶ 형용사

1. 서술적 용법으로만 쓰이는 형용사를 알아둔다.
2. 복합 형용사로 쓰이는 것은 복수로 표시하지 않는다.
3. 수량 형용사를 파악하고 수의 일치가 되는지 확인한다.

Day 8
명사와 관사

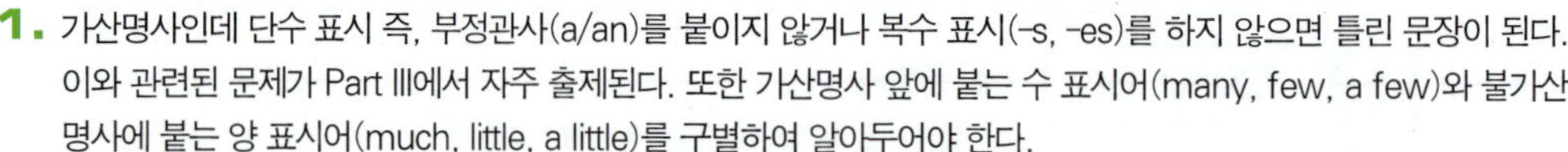

1. 가산명사인데 단수 표시 즉, 부정관사(a/an)를 붙이지 않거나 복수 표시(-s, -es)를 하지 않으면 틀린 문장이 된다. 이와 관련된 문제가 Part III에서 자주 출제된다. 또한 가산명사 앞에 붙는 수 표시어(many, few, a few)와 불가산 명사에 붙는 양 표시어(much, little, a little)를 구별하여 알아두어야 한다.

2. 부정관사: (a/an) '하나, ~에, ~당, 어떤' 이라는 의미를 갖는다.

He didn't say a word about it. 그는 그것에 대해 한 마디도 하지 않았다
She visits her parents once a week. 그녀는 일주일에 한 번 부모님을 방문한다.

3. 부정관사의 쓰임: 같은 명사라 하더라도 그 의미에 따라 가산명사 혹은 불가산명사 취급을 받을 때가 있다. 대체적으로 그 단어가 일반적인 의미로 쓰일 때는 불가산명사로 보고, 구체적인 하나의 개별체로 볼 때는 가산명사로 본다. 이와 관련된 문제가 출제되니 그 의미 파악을 먼저 하도록 한다.

hair 머리 숱	**a hair** 머리카락
noise 소음	**a noise** 소리
room 공간	**a room** 방
paper 종이	**a paper** 신문; 논문
work 일	**a work** 작품
light 빛	**a light** 조명

4. 정관사: 부정관사가 '막연한 것' 을 가리키는 반면 정관사는 '특정한 것' 을 지칭한다.

형용사구(절)나 전치사구에 의해 수식을 받을 때, last, only, next, same, 형용사의 최상급, 서수사 등이 명사를 수식하여 그 명사가 특정한 사람이나 사물을 가리키게 될 때, 〈by the+단위 명사〉 등의 경우에 정관사 the가 그 명사 앞에 붙는다.

All the candidates in B group are safe. B그룹에 있는 모든 후보는 통과했다.
He is paid by the week. 그는 주급을 받는다.

5. 관사의 위치

1) **such, many, quite, what+ (a/an)+형용사+명사**
   It's quite an easy question. 그건 꽤 쉬운 질문이다.
2) **so, how, too +형용사+(a/an)+명사**
   This is too good an opportunity. 너무 좋은 기회이다.

Catch Up 

명사와 관사 관련 TEPS 주요 문제들을 풀어보도록 한다.

Part I Fill in the blank with the most appropriate word or phrase.

1. A: Your meal comes to $22.00.
B: Here's $25.00. You can keep __________.

(a) changing
(b) the changes
(c) the change
(d) a change

Part II Fill in the blank with the most appropriate word or phrase.

2. __________ is the largest rainforest in the world.

(a) Amazons
(b) The Amazon
(c) An Amazon
(d) The Amazons

3. Not much is understood about __________________.

(a) the ecosystem of the oceans
(b) ecosystem of the oceans
(c) the ecosystem of oceans
(d) ecosystem of oceans

4. Most of the locals earn a living by catering to the __________.

(a) tourist's trade
(b) tourist trades
(c) tourist trade
(d) tourists trades

Part III Identify the grammatical error in the dialogue.

5. (a) A: What is tomorrow's meeting going to be about?
(b) B: I'm going to talk about organization in the work place.
(c) A: Good idea. Don't forget to mention something about the time management.
(d) B: Yes, many of our employees do need a lesson in that.

 # Answers 

Catch Up에서 푼 문제의 해석과 해설을 점검한다.

1

A: Your meal comes to $22.00.
B: Here's $25.00. You can keep __________.
(a) changing
(b) the changes
(c) the change
(d) a change

A: 식사값은 22달러입니다.
B: 여기 25달러 있습니다. 잔돈은 됐습니다.

해설 change는 '잔돈, 거스름돈'의 의미로 정관사 the와 함께 keep the change는 '잔돈을 가져가다'라는 의미가 된다. 하나의 관용적 표현으로 알아두도록 한다.

2

__________ is the largest rainforest in the world.
(a) Amazons
(b) The Amazon
(c) An Amazon
(d) The Amazons

아마존은 세계에서 가장 큰 열대우림이다.

해설 the의 쓰임에 대한 문제이다. 강 이름 앞에는 the를 붙이기 때문에 '아마존 강'을 지칭하는 Amazon 앞에도 the를 붙여야 한다. 그러므로 (b)가 정답이다.

3

Not much is understood about ______________.

(a) the ecosystem of the oceans
(b) ecosystem of the oceans
(c) the ecosystem of oceans
(d) ecosystem of oceans

해양 생태계에 대한 이해가 부족하다.

해설 'of 명사구'의 수식을 받고 있는 명사가 한정된 생태계를 의미하므로 ecosystem 앞에 정관사 the가 와야 한다. 또한 세계에 존재하는 대양들을 의미하므로 'ocean' 앞에도 정관사가 오게 된다.

4

Most of the locals earn a living by catering to the ______________.

(a) tourist's trade
(b) tourist trades
(c) tourist trade
(d) tourists trades

그 지역민들 대부분이 관광업 서비스로 생계를 유지한다.

해설 tourist trade는 '관광업'이라는 뜻이지만 tourist's trade는 '관광객의 산업'이라는 의미가 되므로 (a)는 적절치 않다. 그러므로 (c)가 정답이 된다.

5

(a) A: What is tomorrow's meeting going to be about?
(b) B: I'm going to talk about organization in the workplace.
(c) A: Good idea. Don't forget to mention something about (the time management → time management).
(d) B: Yes, many of our employees do need a lesson in that.

(a) A: 내일 회의는 무엇에 관한 것이지?
(b) B: 직장 조직에 대해서 말할 거야.
(c) A: 좋은 생각이다. 시간 관리에 대해서 언급하는 거 잊지 마.
(d) B: 응. 많은 직원이 그것에 대한 교훈이 필요해.

해설 일반적인 시간 관리(time management)에 대해서 말하고 있으므로 the는 필요치 않다. 그러므로 the를 빼야 한다.

Answers

1. (c) 2. (b) 3. (a) 4. (c) 5. (c) the time management → time management

Build Up 

TEPS 전 문법 요소가 모의고사 형식으로 골고루 섞인 4파트의 문제
를 골고루 풀어 본다.

▶▶ **Part I** Fill in the blank with the most appropriate word or phrase.

1. A: My parents have invited you over for dinner. Can you come?
B: Enough __________. You know I could never turn down their invitation.

(a) to say
(b) said
(c) says
(d) saying

2. A: How long has the search for the missing girl been going on?
B: I think they've been ______________ for a few weeks.

(a) searched
(b) searching
(c) being searched
(d) search

3. A: What do you plan to do on vacation?
B: I am going to hike the mountain __________ camp near the peak.

(a) but
(b) so
(c) also
(d) and

4. A: Have you and Tom ever done this _________?
B: No, we have never been scuba diving.

(a) long
(b) ago
(c) before
(d) since

▶▶ **Part II** Fill in the blank with the most appropriate word or phrase.

5. Jason said he had never seen ___________________ at the symphony before.
(a) such a small attendance
(b) such small an attendance
(c) such small attendance
(d) such attendance small

6. Small fish are easy to catch, __________ larger fish aren't.

(a) besides
(b) rather than
(c) otherwise
(d) whereas

7. The Industrial Revolution _______________, starting in the England in the late 1700s.

(a) lasted over 150 years
(b) has lasted over 150 years
(c) over 150 years lasted
(d) did 150 years last over

8. Some people claim that a cellphone __________ radiation that affects the user's brain.

(a) producing
(b) has produced
(c) is producing
(d) produces

▶▶ **Part III** Identify the grammatical error in the dialogue.

9. (a) A: Your cat's still ill? Didn't you take her to the veterinarian?
(b) B: I did, last week. And I took care of her just like the vet told me.
(c) A: Well, it will take a little time for her to be cured.
(d) B: I know, but I am starting to get a little worried.

10. (a) A: I missed Anna's wedding. How was it?
(b) B: It was very nice and something hilarious happened while they said their vows.
(c) A: Weddings aren't supposed to be funny. What happened?
(d) B: A little girl ran up to Anna, then she hugged Anna's leg and mustn't let go.

▶▶ **Part IV** Identify the ungrammatical sentence in the passage.

11. (a) One of my favorite vacation destinations is Thailand. (b) Thailand has everything you could want, from tropical beaches to beautiful mountains and forests. (c) And of course there is the modern metropolis and capital city, Bangkok, a place to which I always return to. (d) I love the city because it has a certain energy flowing through it that I've never felt anywhere else.

12. (a) Construction workers have been brought in to make the school look more sleek and modern. (b) However, their work has done nothing but cause a disturbance for the students and faculty. (c) Not only do they make loud, disruptive noises all day long, but also the dust from the construction gets everywhere making it hard to breathe. (d) Also, it covers all the desks and chairs so that each class period the students must wipe their desks and chairs a layer of dust off.

정답:201p

GRAMMAR
Week2

Day 6	▶▶ 동명사

1. 동명사를 목적어로 취하는 동사를 파악한다.
2. 동명사의 의미상의 주어는 소유격이나 목적격으로 표현한다.
3. to부정사와 동명사를 둘 다 목적어로 취할 수 있으나 의미가 다른 동사들의 쓰임을 알아둔다.

Day 7	▶▶ 분사

1. 명사를 수식하는 분사가 현재분사인지 과거분사인지 확인하는 절차를 알아둔다.
2. 감정 동사의 분사 용법을 알아둔다.
3. 분사구문을 만드는 절차를 알아둔다.

Day 8	▶▶ 명사와 관사

1. 가산명사일 경우 단수나 복수 표시를 해야 한다.
2. 양 표시어와 수 표시어를 확인하고 Part III나 Part IV에서 이들이 바르게 표기되었는지 확인한다.
3. 관사의 위치를 파악하여 순서를 외워두도록 한다.

Day 9	▶▶ 대명사

1. 대명사와 그것을 받고 있는 명사와의 수, 성, 격이 일치하는지 확인한다.
2. one과 it의 차이점을 알아둔다.
3. 부정대명사의 종류와 쓰임을 알아둔다.

Day 10	▶▶ 형용사

1. 서술적 용법으로만 쓰이는 형용사를 알아둔다.
2. 복합 형용사로 쓰이는 것은 복수로 표시하지 않는다.
3. 수량 형용사를 파악하고 수의 일치가 되는지 확인한다.

TEPS Day 9
대명사

1. 대명사가 나오면 그것이 가리키는 명사와 수, 성, 격이 일치하는지를 반드시 확인한다.

They are taking preliminary steps to protect themselves.
그들 자신을 보호하기 위해 조기 조치를 취하고 있다.

2. **one**: 〈a +명사〉 대신 쓰이며 동일한 종류의 것을 받는다.

it: 〈the/소유격+명사〉 대신으로 쓰이며 동일한 바로 '그것' 을 받는다.

A: I bought this dress in Zara yesterday. 나 어제 이 드레스 자라에서 샀어.
B: ① **It's beautiful. I want to buy one.** (동일한 종류의 드레스를 사고 싶다는 의미)
  ② **It's beautiful. I want to buy it.** (A가 산 옷을 B가 사고 싶다는 의미)

3. 부정대명사

부정대명사란 정해지지 않은 막연한 사람이나 사물, 수량을 나타내는 대명사로 some, any, one, another, other, each, every 등이
있다.
1) **any, no, some, the + other +단수 명사**
  There is no other way. 다른 방법이 없다.
2) **another + 숫자+ 복수 명사**: another 가 '더 많은' 이라는 의미를 지칭할 때
  Could you wait for another ten minutes for me? 10분만 더 기다려 주시겠어요?
3) **every+ 숫자 + 복수 명사**
  She works at the store every two weeks. (= every second week, every other week)
  그녀는 이 주일에 한 번씩 그 가게에서 일한다.

4. 〈so+주어+동사〉의 어순: so는 yes의 뜻이 되어 '정말 그래' 의 뜻.

〈so+동사+주어〉의 어순: so는 also의 뜻이 되어 '~도 역시 그래' 의 뜻.

You said the concert would be awesome and so it was. 그 콘서트가 멋질 거라더니 정말 그렇더라.
His father was a singer and so is he. 그의 아버지는 가수셨는데 그도 가수이다.

5. 관용적 용법

1) **(A is) one thing, (B is) another** A와 B는 별개다
2) **one ~, the other ...** (둘 중에서) 하나는 ~, 다른 하나는 …
  one ~, another ... the other/third - (셋 중에서) 하나는 ~, 둘째는 …, 셋째는 -
3) **one ~, the others ...** (셋 이상 중에서) 하나는 ~, 나머지 전부는 …
4) **some ~, others ...** 어떤 것(사람)들은 ~, 다른 일부(사람)는 … (전체 수가 정해지지 않았을 때)
5) **each other**는 '(둘 사이에) 서로 서로,' **one another**는 '(셋 이상의 사이에) 서로 서로'

Catch Up

대명사 관련 TEPS 주요 문제들을 풀어보도록 한다.

Part I Fill in the blank with the most appropriate word or phrase.

1. A: Why is your stomach upset? Did you eat or drink anything bad today?
B: Not really. I had a sandwich and __________.

(a) teas
(b) no tea
(c) the teas
(d) some tea

2. A: I have to choose between the boring history class and the difficult economics class.
B: Wow, you have no __________ choice?

(a) some
(b) other
(c) another
(d) the other

Part II Fill in the blank with the most appropriate word or phrase.

3. The objective of the game is to get all the balls onto __________ side of the court.

(a) others
(b) another
(c) the other
(d) the others

4. Do you want me to get you __________ from the grocery store while I'm there?

(a) anything
(b) something
(c) nothing
(d) everything

Part III Identify the grammatical error in the dialogue.

5. (a) A: What is Ms. Robinson's number one classroom rule?
(b) B: I think it is to treat another with respect.
(c) A: Do you think it improves the classroom environment?
(d) B: Yeah, because everyone wants to be treated well.

Answers

Catch Up에서 푼 문제의 해석과 해설을 점검한다.

1

A: Why is your stomach upset? Did you eat or drink anything bad today?
B: Not really. I had a sandwich and ___________.

(a) teas
(b) no tea
(c) the teas
(d) some tea

A: 왜 배가 아프니? 오늘 뭐 잘못 먹거나 마셨니?
B: 아니. 샌드위치하고 차를 마셨어.

해설 some은 '얼마간, 다소의'란 의미로 뒤에 가산명사가 오면 '복수형'의 명사가, 불가산명사가 오면 '단수형'이 오게 된다. 여기서는 tea가 불가산 명사이므로 단수형이 오게 됐다.

2

A: I have to choose between the boring history class and the difficult economics class.
B: Wow, you have no ___________ choice?

(a) some
(b) other
(c) another
(d) the other

A: 난 지루한 역사 수업과 어려운 경제 수업 중에 골라야 돼.
B: 어머, 다른 선택은 없니?

해설 other는 보통 뒤에 복수 명사를 취하여 '다른, 그 밖의~'의 의미를 가지게 된다. some은 주로 긍정문에서 쓰이며, 의문문에서 쓰일 경우에는 권유를 나타내거나 yes의 답을 기대하는 경우에 쓰이므로 여기서는 적절치 않다. 그러므로 other가 가장 적절한 답이 된다.

3

The objective of the game is to get all the balls onto __________ side of the court.

(a) others
(b) another
(c) the other
(d) the others

그 게임의 목적은 모든 공을 그 코트의 다른 쪽 위로 가게 하는 것이다.

해설　⟨the other ＋단수 명사⟩는 '(둘 중에) 다른 하나, 다른 쪽, 반대(의 것)'을 의미한다. another은 an＋other로 ⟨another＋단수 명사⟩는 '또 다른 하나'를 의미한다. 그러므로 여기서는 (c)가 가장 적절하다.

4

Do you want me to get you __________ from the grocery store while I'm there?

(a) anything
(b) something
(c) nothing
(d) everything

내가 식료품점에서 뭐 좀 사다 줄까?

해설　anything은 의문문과 조건절에서 '무엇인가'라는 의미로 쓰이는 부정대명사이다. 여기서도 문장이 의문문이므로 의미상 anything이 가장 적절하다. something은 보통 긍정문에 쓰이며 의문문에서 쓰일 때에는 권유나 yes를 기대하는 경우에만 쓰이므로(e.g. Would you like some tea?) 여기서는 적절치 않다.

5

(a) A: What is Ms. Robinson's number one classroom rule?
(b) B: I think it is to treat (another → others) with respect.
(c) A: Do you think it improves the classroom environment?
(d) B: Yeah, because everyone wants to be treated well.

(a) A: 로빈슨 선생님이 교실에서 제일 우선순위로 치는 규칙이 무엇이니?
(b) B: 다른 사람들을 존중하는 것 같은데.
(c) A: 그것이 교실 환경을 향상시키는 것 같니?
(d) B: 응. 왜냐면 누구나 대우받기를 원하잖아.

해설　another는 부정대명사로 '또 다른 하나, 또 한 사람'이란 의미가 있다. 그러나 여기서는 의미상 '다른 사람들'이라는 의미가 적절하므로 others(＝other people)로 고쳐야 한다.

Answers

1. (d) 2. (b) 3. (c) 4. (a) 5. (b) another → others

Build Up

Part I Fill in the blank with the most appropriate word or phrase.

1. A: Hey, the bus is here! I have to go.
B: Okay. Remember! Dinner at six. __________

(a) See there you!
(b) There you see
(c) You see there!
(d) See you there!

2. A: Benjamin placed first in the track tournament.
B: I'm not so surprised considering ______________ training for it a year in advance.

(a) for him to begin
(b) of him to begin
(c) at him began
(d) that he began

3. A: Thank you so much for your help today.
B: No problem. Let me know if you have ____________________________.

(a) something of you to do
(b) something I want to do
(c) anything you want me to do
(d) anything do you want me to do

4. A: Were you in the middle of something when the fire alarm went off?
B: Yes, I was working on my essay, __________ my own business.

(a) mind
(b) to mind
(c) minding
(d) minded

Part II Fill in the blank with the most appropriate word or phrase.

5. Because of the stock market crash, Mickey lost more than ______________ and stocks.

(a) halving his earnings
(b) half of his earnings
(c) his half of earnings
(d) earnings in half

6. What gift should we get for John __________ his birthday?

    (a) at
    (b) on
    (c) of
    (d) upon

7. James was in __________ to learn more about the student organization.

    (a) hurry
    (b) a hurry
    (c) hurries
    (d) the hurry

8. The firefighters worked for seventeen hours to extinguish __________ spreading in different areas of the forest.

    (a) blazes
    (b) a blaze
    (c) all blaze
    (d) the blazes

▶▶ **Part III**   Identify the grammatical error in the dialogue.

9. (a) A: Are you okay? You seem unfocusing and worried.
    (b) B: I guess. I received a phone call from my mom about my cousin.
    (c) A: Was it bad news?
    (d) B: I'm not sure yet, but she told me that my cousin found a lump on her chest.

10. (a) A: Why are you so happy?
    (b) B: Our boss just promoted several people included me and others!
    (c) A: That's fantastic! You definitely deserve it.
    (d) B: Thank you! I worked hard for this promotion.

▶▶ **Part IV**   Identify the ungrammatical sentence in the passage.

11. (a) There are many reasons why the ecosystem is deteriorating. (b) One of the reasons are because of pollution. (c) Another reason is because people don't put in the effort to recycle or clean up the environment. (d) Also, humans destroy natural resources every year by demolishing and building over forests.

12. (a) Women should be careful at night-time and for the good reason too. (b) They are very vulnerable to sexual harassment and assault. (c) Women should carry around a whistle or other noise device for emergency situations. (d) They should also try not to walk alone because they are more susceptible to being attacked.

정답 : 203p

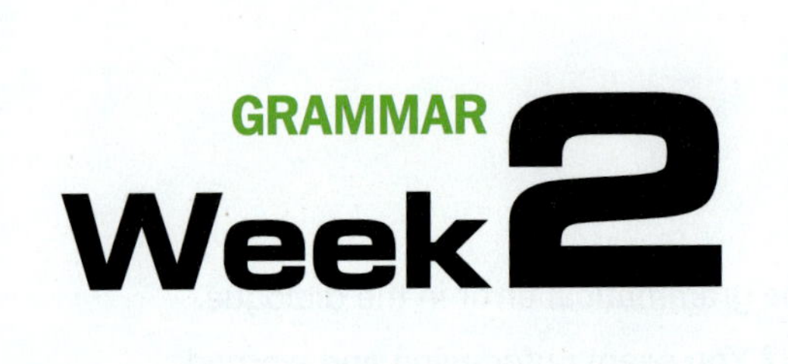
GRAMMAR
Week 2

Day 6 ▶▶ 동명사

1. 동명사를 목적어로 취하는 동사를 파악한다.
2. 동명사의 의미상의 주어는 소유격이나 목적격으로 표현한다.
3. to부정사와 동명사를 둘 다 목적어로 취할 수 있으나 의미가 다른 동사들의 쓰임을 알아둔다.

Day 7 ▶▶ 분사

1. 명사를 수식하는 분사가 현재분사인지 과거분사인지 확인하는 절차를 알아둔다.
2. 감정 동사의 분사 용법을 알아둔다.
3. 분사구문을 만드는 절차를 알아둔다.

Day 8 ▶▶ 명사와 관사

1. 가산명사일 경우 단수나 복수 표시를 해야 한다.
2. 양 표시어와 수 표시어를 확인하고 Part III나 Part IV에서 이들이 바르게 표기되었는지 확인한다.
3. 관사의 위치를 파악하여 순서를 외워두도록 한다.

Day 9 ▶▶ 대명사

1. 대명사와 그것을 받고 있는 명사와의 수, 성, 격이 일치하는지 확인한다.
2. one과 it의 차이점을 알아둔다.
3. 부정대명사의 종류와 쓰임을 알아둔다.

Day 10 ▶▶ 형용사

1. 서술적 용법으로만 쓰이는 형용사를 알아둔다.
2. 복합 형용사로 쓰이는 것은 복수로 표시하지 않는다.
3. 수량 형용사를 파악하고 수의 일치가 되는지 확인한다.

Day 10
형용사

형용사는 명사를 수식하며 보어로 쓰인다.

1. 서술적 용법으로만 쓰이는 형용사

afraid 두려운 **alike** 같은 **alive** 살아 있는 **alone** 혼자인 **ashamed** 부끄러운 **asleep** 잠든
awake 깨어 있는 **aware** 알고 있는

When you enter the building, you need to be aware that you shouldn't forget to bring your ID card. 그 건물에 들어갈 때 ID 카드를 가지고 가는 것을 잊으면 안 된다.

2. 복합 형용사

명사 앞에 하이픈(-)으로 연결된 어군이 명사를 수식하는 경우가 있는데 이를 하나의 복합 형용사로 본다. 이때 수식하는 명사는 반드시 단수형으로 쓴다.

It's a two-days trip. (X)
It's a two-day trip. (O) 이틀간의 여행이다.

3. 수량 형용사

1) many +명사의 복수형
〈many a/an+단수 명사〉는 단수로 취급한다.
Many a student likes the band. 많은 학생이 그 밴드를 좋아한다.

2) much+ 명사의 단수형
I have too much homework to do. 해야 할 숙제가 너무 많다.

3) a few와 a little
a few + 가산명사의 복수형: 소수의
a little + 불가산명사의 단수형: 소량의
some은 수와 양을 모두 나타낼 수 있다.

4) few 와 little: '별로 없는, 거의 없는' 이라는 부정의 의미를 나타내는 표현이 된다.
There is little hope. 희망이 별로 없다.
cf. **There is a little hope.** 약간의 희망이 있다.

5) 수의 단위인 hundred, thousand, million, billion, trillion 등은 그 앞에 복수의 수가 붙어도 복수형으로 쓰지 않는다.
two hundreds (X)   two hundred (O)

6) hundred, thousand, million이 복수형으로 뒤에 위치한 명사와 of로 연결되면 '수백, 수천, 수백만' 의 뜻을 갖는다.
Hundreds of fans are waiting for him in front of his house.
수백 명의 팬들이 그의 집 앞에서 그를 기다리고 있다.

# Catch Up 

형용사 관련 TEPS 주요 문제들을 풀어보도록 한다.

Part I Fill in the blank with the most appropriate word or phrase.

1. A: Why are you going to the grocery store?
B: I want to get ____________ grapes.

(a) white fresh some
(b) some fresh white
(c) fresh white some
(d) fresh some white

2. A: Which of the houses you've been looking at are you going to buy?
B: Well, I think ____________________ is the condominium closest to my work.

(a) the possible smartest option
(b) the smartest option possible
(c) the option smartest possible
(d) the option possible smartest

3. A: You don't look pleased. Is there something the matter?
B: I can't live this lifestyle anymore, I ________________.

(a) go to bankruptcy
(b) am to go bankrupt
(c) went bankruptcy
(d) am going bankrupt

Part II Fill in the blank with the most appropriate word or phrase.

4. White blood cells ____________ for a body to fight off infectious diseases.
(a) make possible
(b) make it possible
(c) makes it possible
(d) makes possible one

5. In many career fields, __________ experience you've gained the better.
(a) the bigger
(b) the large
(c) the more
(d) the better

Catch Up에서 푼 문제의 해석과 해설을 점검한다.

1

A: Why are you going to the grocery store?
B: I want to get _______________ grapes.

(a) white fresh some
(b) some fresh white
(c) fresh white some
(d) fresh some white

A: 식료품 가게는 왜 가니?
B: 신선한 백포도를 사고 싶어서.

해설 형용사의 순서를 묻는 문제이다. 형용사가 여러 개 나올 경우는 〈한정사 – 수량(서수 – 기수) – 성질(대소 – 형상 · 성질 – 신구 – 색채 – 재료 · 소속＋명사)〉의 순서로 나열한다. 여기서도 부정대명사 즉, 한정사 some이 가장 먼저, 다음에 성질을 나타내는 fresh, 그 다음에 색채를 나타내는 white 순으로 나열해야 한다. 보통은 가장 중요한 내용의 형용사가 명사 전에 오므로 그것을 먼저 판단하여 순서를 정리하도록 한다.

2

A: Which of the houses you've been looking at are you going to buy?
B: Well, I think _____________________ is the condominium closest to my work.

(a) the possible smartest option
(b) the smartest option possible
(c) the option smartest possible
(d) the option possible smartest

A: 네가 봤던 집들 중에 어떤 집을 살 거니?
B: 직장에서 가장 가까운 분양 아파트가 제일 현명한 선택일 것 같아.

해설 최상급과 함께 온 명사를 –able, –ible로 끝나는 형용사가 수식할 경우 명사 뒤에서 후치 수식한다. 즉, 〈최상급＋명사＋–able/ –ible〉의 어순이 된다. 그러므로 (b)가 정답이다.

3

A: You don't look pleased. Is there something the matter?

B: I can't live this lifestyle anymore, I ___________.

(a) go to bankruptcy
(b) am to go bankrupt
(c) went bankruptcy
(d) am going bankrupt

A: 기분이 안 좋아 보이는데. 무슨 일 있니?
B: 더이상 이런 식으로는 살 수 없어. 파산하겠어.

해설 go bankrupt는 '파산하다' 라는 의미로 go는 형용사 bankrupt와 결합하여 become의 의미로 쓰였다.

4

White blood cells ________________ for a body to fight off infectious diseases.

(a) make possible
(b) make it possible
(c) makes it possible
(d) makes possible one

백혈구는 몸이 전염병을 퇴치하는 것을 가능하게 한다.

해설 make는 3형식(make+목적어)혹은 5형식 문장(make+목적어+목적격 보어)을 취하는 동사이다. 여기서는 후자로 쓰였으며 it은 가목적어, 진목적어는 to부정사 이하가 된다. 〈make, find, think, believe+it(가목적어)+형용사+for 명사(의미상의 주어)+to부정사(진목적어)〉

5

In many career fields, ____________ experience you've gained the better.

(a) the bigger
(b) the large
(c) the more
(d) the better

많은 직업 분야에서는 경험이 많으면 많을수록 더 좋다.

해설 〈the 비교급+주어+동사, the 비교급+주어+동사〉는 '더 ~하면 할수록 더욱 더 ~하다' 라는 의미이다. the better 뒤에는 you become이 생략되었다.

Answers

1. (b) 2. (b) 3. (d) 4. (b) 5. (c)

 **Build Up** 

TEPS 전 문법 요소가 모의고사 형식으로 골고루 섞인 4파트의 문제
를 골고루 풀어 본다.

▶▶ **Part I** Fill in the blank with the most appropriate word or phrase.

1. A: Did you have fun playing tennis yesterday?
B: Yes! But I wish you __________ with me.

(a) played
(b) had play
(c) have played
(d) had played

2. A: Do you know why there's going to be a parade next week?
B: It's because on August 12th the island __________ established for 200 years.

(a) was
(b) will have been
(c) must have been
(d) will be

3. A: Hi, Lloyd! ______________ play on the school soccer team?
B: I'm not sure yet, they haven't announced the lineup.
(a) Would you
(b) Did you
(c) Were you chosen to
(d) Were you choosing to

4. A: I'm confused, ______________________? I thought it was further up the street.
B: No. It's always been right here, but many of these buildings have been renovated.

(a) where did we eat dinner last year
(b) where we ate dinner last year
(c) is this where did we eat last year
(d) is this where we ate dinner last year

▶▶ **Part II** Fill in the blank with the most appropriate word or phrase.

5. We must teach young athletes __________ losing, but rather to learn from it.

(a) never hate
(b) no hate
(c) not to hate
(d) to hate not

6. __________ of the thieve's guilt was found in his basement, where he stored the things he stole.

(a) Proofs
(b) A proof
(c) Proof
(d) The proofs

7. Young kids do not realize that cellphones were rare _____________________.

(a) too not in the distant past
(b) in the not too distant past
(c) past in the not too distant
(d) in not too the distant past

8. __________ I am not fond of New York City, I think the rest of the States is beautiful.

(a) Since
(b) But
(c) While
(d) When

▶▶ **Part III** Identify the grammatical error in the dialogue.

9. (a) A: The Smiths and the Walters are planning to vacation Florida this summer.
(b) B: Must we go to Florida again? We've been there the last three summers.
(c) A: But wouldn't you rather go where our friends are going?
(d) B: Not if it means seeing and doing the same things we do every year.

10. (a) A: What is the best way to gain advancement in your career?
(b) B: I've always been told that making a five-year plan is effective.
(c) A: That's right. And do you know why those methods are effective?
(d) B: Because it helps keep your progress on the course for meeting your goals.

▶▶ **Part IV** Identify the ungrammatical sentence in the passage.

11. (a) When learning to drive a car, the most important lesson is to learn to be comfortable while behind the wheel. (b) Too many drivers focus too closely on the physical act of driving. (c) A good driver is always aware of the road, the cars, and the conditions, at the same time perfectly comfortable and relaxed. (d) Also, in order to be both aware and comfortable, the driver should not be concentrating on what could happen, but rather on how to react to his or her surroundings.

12. (a) Native Americans were not always native in the Western Hemisphere. (b) We call them native because they were there long before the Europeans ever realized those continents existed. (c) When did the Native Americans arrive they came across the Bering Strait, which separates Russia from Alaska. (d) During very cold winters the Strait froze over, creating a safe, solid route from Asia to the Americas.

정답:205p

GRAMMAR
Week 3

Day 11 ▶▶ 부사

1. 부사는 보어로 쓰일 수 없음을 알아두고 Part III나 Part IV에서 부사가 보어로 쓰이지 않았는지 확인한다.
2. 형용사와 부사의 형태가 같은 것을 알아둔다.
3. 뜻이 다른 두 가지 형태의 부사를 알아둔다.

Day 12 ▶▶ 관계사

1. 선행사와 관계대명사의 수가 일치하는지 확인한다.
2. 관계대명사의 격이 제대로 쓰였는지 확인한다.
3. 관계대명사 뒤에는 불완전한 절이 와야 한다.

Day 13 ▶▶ 접속사

1. 접속사 뒤에는 절이 오고, 전치사 뒤에는 구가 온다.
2. 대등 접속사와 등위접속사에서 문법 단위가 동일한 품사끼리 병렬 구조가 되었는지 확인한다.
3. 상관접속사의 연결어구가 알맞게 연결되었는지 확인한다.

Day 14 ▶▶ 전치사

1. 기본적인 시간, 장소의 전치사를 확인해 둔다.
2. 많은 전치사의 쓰임을 알기 위해서 평소에 LC에 나오는 쓰임을 확인해 둔다.
3. 관용적인 전치사구의 쓰임을 알아둔다.

Day 15 ▶▶ 시험에 잘 나오는 문장 어순

1. 보어 자리엔 부사가 올 수 없다.
2. 목적보어를 취하는 타동사들을 알아둔다.
3. 목적보어로 to부정사를 취하는 동사들을 확인한다.

Day 11
부사

> 부사는 동사, 형용사 또는 다른 부사를 수식하거나 문장 전체를 수식할 때 쓰이고 보어가 될 수 없다.
>
> **What he did for me makes me specially. (X)**
>
> **→ What he did for me makes me special. (O)** 그가 나를 위해 한 것이 날 특별하게 만든다.

1. 주의해야 할 부사

1) very는 형용사나 부사의 원급, 현재분사, 형용사화된 과거분사를 수식한다.
   I am much tired. (X) → I am very tired. (O)

2) much는 동사, 형용사나 부사의 비교급 · 최상급, 서술적 형용사를 수식한다.
   You should be much more careful. 좀 더 조심해야 한다.

2. 형용사와 부사의 형태가 같은 것

1) **hard** → 형용사: 어려운
   → 부사: 열심히

2) **fast** → 형용사: 빠른
   → 부사: 빠르게

3) **long** → 형용사: 긴
   → 부사: 오래

4) **late** → 형용사: 늦은
   → 부사: 늦게

3. 뜻이 다른 두 가지 부사의 형태

free 무료로 — **freely** 자유롭게	**hard** 열심히 — **hardly** 거의 ~않는
wide 넓게/완전히 — **widely** 널리(범위)	**late** 늦게 — **lately** 최근에
near 가까이 — **nearly** 거의	**right** 정확히 — **rightly** 올바르게
direct 똑바로 — **directly** 곧바로	**sharp** 정각에 — **sharply** 심하게
deep 깊게 — **deeply** 매우, 철저히	**high** 높게 — **highly** 매우, 대단히

I got up very late today. 오늘 늦게 일어났다.
Have you seen Tom lately? 최근에 탐 본 적 있니?

Catch Up 

부사 관련 TEPS 주요 문제들을 풀어보도록 한다.

Part I Fill in the blank with the most appropriate word or phrase.

1. A: This chocolate cake __________ delicious!
B: I told you that it's tasty.

(a) sure
(b) sure is
(c) surely does
(d) does surely

Part II Fill in the blank with the most appropriate word or phrase.

2. Charles Darwin's theory of evolution states that __________________________.

(a) the only fittest may remain
(b) only the fittest may remain
(c) may the fittest only remain
(d) may only the fittest remain

3. After he was rebuked for his insensitivity, Andy treated people very __________ and with respect.

(a) difference
(b) differed
(c) differently
(d) different

Part III Identify the grammatical error in the dialogue.

4. (a) A: I want to go on a road trip with my friends.
(b) B: Where would you guys go?
(c) A: I'm not sure. Maybe California?
(d) B: That would be fun. I would like to do that with my friends either.

5. (a) A: Amos, I heard you were sick!
(b) B: Yeah, my stomach's upset and I've been vomiting all day.
(c) A: Oh, no! Do you know why?
(d) B: Yeah, I think I had undercooked meat and ate it too fastly.

Answers

Catch Up에서 푼 문제의 해석과 해설을 점검한다.

1

A: This chocolate cake __________ delicious!
B: I told you that it's tasty.

(a) sure
(b) sure is
(c) surely does
(d) does surely

A: 이 초콜릿 케이크는 진짜 맛있어!
B: 내가 맛있다고 했잖아.

해설 빈칸에는 '확실히'라는 의미의 부사와 be동사가 들어가야 한다. 보통 부사는 be동사 뒤에 위치하지만 부사 sure은 be동사 앞에 위치하게 된다.

2

Charles Darwin's theory of evolution states that
__________________________.

(a) the only fittest may remain
(b) only the fittest may remain
(c) may the fittest only remain
(d) may only the fittest remain

찰스 다윈의 진화론은 가장 적응을 잘 하는 것만이 살아남는다고 말한다.

해설 부사 only의 위치를 고르는 문제이다. 대개의 부사는 형용사의 최상급을 수식할 경우 the 앞에 오게 된다. 그러므로 (b)의 어순이 가장 적절하다.

3

After he was rebuked for his insensitivity, Andy treated people very __________ and with respect.

(a) difference
(b) differed
(c) differently
(d) different

그의 냉담함 때문에 비난 받고난 뒤 앤디는 사람들을 매우 다르게 존경심을 가지고 대했다.

해설 빈칸에는 with respect와 and로 대등하게 연결될 수 있는 부사구가 와야 한다.

4

(a) A: I want to go on a road trip with my friends.
(b) B: Where would you guys go?
(c) A: I'm not sure. Maybe California?
(d) B: That would be fun. I would like to do that with my friends (either → too).

(a) 친구들과 함께 여행 가고 싶어.
(b) 어디로 갈 거니?
(c) 잘 모르겠어. 아마 캘리포니아?
(d) 재미있겠다. 나도 친구들과 함께 여행 가고 싶어.

해설 either는 부정문에서 '~도 역시 (아니다)'라는 의미로 쓰이므로 긍정문에서는 too로 바꾸어야 한다.

5

(a) A: Amos, I heard you were sick!
(b) B: Yeah, my stomach's upset and I've been vomiting all day.
(c) A: Oh, no! Do you know why?
(d) B: Yeah, I think I had undercooked meat and ate it too (fastly → fast).

(a) 아모스, 너 아프다고 하던데.
(b) 응, 배가 아파. 하루 종일 토했어.
(c) 어머! 왜 그런지 알아?
(d) 내 생각엔 설익은 고기를 너무 급하게 먹었던 것 같아.

해설 fast는 형용사와 부사의 형태가 똑같다. 그러므로 fastly를 fast로 바꾸어야 한다.

Answers

1. (b) 2. (b) 3. (c) 4. (d) either → too 5. (d) fastly → fast

# Build Up 

TEPS 전 문법 요소가 모의고사 형식으로 골고루 섞인 4파트의 문제
를 골고루 풀어 본다.

Part I   Fill in the blank with the most appropriate word or phrase.

1.   A: Do you want to rest before we go back?
   B: Yes, I _______________ sleep for an hour since it's a long drive back.

   (a) would like   (b) would have liked to
   (c) would like to   (d) could like to

2.   A: Congratulations! I'm so happy to hear that _______________!
   B: Wow, thanks! How did you find out about it so fast?

   (a) you've engaged   (b) you're engaged
   (c) engaged   (d) you're engaging

3.   A: Why was the mother so sad when the paramedics arrived?
   B: Because they _________________ her child if they had arrived five minutes earlier.

   (a) could save   (b) could have saved
   (c) would save   (d) will save

4.   A: What type of bouquet would you like me to buy for your wife's dinner party?
   B: You can choose something that is elegant, but definitely choose _________ that has
     yellow roses in it.

   (a) it   (b) one
   (c) them   (d) those

▶▶ Part II   Fill in the blank with the most appropriate word or phrase.

5.   I did not understand my professor's instructions, and _____________________.

   (a) my classmates neither did
   (b) neither my classmates did
   (c) neither did my classmates
   (d) my classmates did neither

6. _________________________ his students were failing because of his unclear and complicated instructions.

(a) The professor little realized that
(b) The professor realized little that
(c) Little did the professor realize that
(d) Little did realize the professor that

7. The airline reimbursed him and apologized _________________________.

(a) for him to the late arrival of the flight.
(b) him the late arrival of the flight
(c) to him for the late arrival of the flight
(d) the late arrival of the flight to him

8. It is not ______________ to inhale gasoline fumes.

(a) safe you
(b) for you safe
(c) you are safe
(d) safe for you

▶▶ **Part III**   Identify the grammatical error in the dialogue.

9. (a) A: What did you get this present from Chanel for?
   (b) B: It's because today is your birthday! Open it.
   (c) A: You took the time and bought a present to me?
   (d) B: Of course I did. I hope you have a Happy birthday.

10. (a) A: I am so exhausted from midterms!
   (b) B: Yeah, you must be, since you had exams everyday!
   (c) A: I'm looking forward to this weekend and to catch up on some sleep.
   (d) B: Good! You definitely deserve it.

▶▶ **Part IV**   Identify the ungrammatical sentence in the passage.

11. (a) Many youth programs are being created to suggest to engage in different guidance programs. (b) Most programs that encourage abstinence and safe sex are more popular than ever. (c) Organizations that discourage drug abuse are increasing as well. (d) These programs are beneficial, especially in urban cities where sexual promiscuity and drug use are rampant.

12. (a) Arden always aspired to be a successful actress in Hollywood. (b) She participated in many talent and fashion shows and even posed for magazine covers. (c) She recently landed a role on a popular television show by, which is known as *Heroes*. (d) There is no doubt that she will make it big one day by landing a star role in a successful movie!

정답:208p

GRAMMAR
Week 3

Day 11 ▶▶ 부사

1. 부사는 보어로 쓰일 수 없음을 알아두고 Part III나 Part IV에서 부사가 보어로 쓰이지 않았는지 확인한다.
2. 형용사와 부사의 형태가 같은 것을 알아둔다.
3. 뜻이 다른 두 가지 형태의 부사를 알아둔다.

Day 12 ▶▶ 관계사

1. 선행사와 관계대명사의 수가 일치하는지 확인한다.
2. 관계대명사의 격이 제대로 쓰였는지 확인한다.
3. 관계대명사 뒤에는 불완전한 절이 와야 한다.

Day 13 ▶▶ 접속사

1. 접속사 뒤에는 절이 오고, 전치사 뒤에는 구가 온다.
2. 대등 접속사와 등위접속사에서 문법 단위가 동일한 품사끼리 병렬 구조가 되었는지 확인한다.
3. 상관접속사의 연결어구가 알맞게 연결되었는지 확인한다.

Day 14 ▶▶ 전치사

1. 기본적인 시간, 장소의 전치사를 확인해 둔다.
2. 많은 전치사의 쓰임을 알기 위해서 평소에 LC에 나오는 쓰임을 확인해 둔다.
3. 관용적인 전치사구의 쓰임을 알아둔다.

Day 15 ▶▶ 시험에 잘 나오는 문장 어순

1. 보어 자리엔 부사가 올 수 없다.
2. 목적보어를 취하는 타동사들을 알아둔다.
3. 목적보어로 to부정사를 취하는 동사들을 확인한다.

1. 관계대명사가 나오면 다음 세 단계를 확인해야 한다.

① 알맞은 선행사가 쓰였는지 확인하기
② 관계대명사의 격 확인하기
③ 선행사와 수의 일치 확인하기
④ 관계대명사는 주어 혹은 목적어 역할을 하므로 뒤에 '불완전한 절' 이 와야 한다.

This is the table which I ordered it last week. (x)
This is the table which I ordered last week. (O)
(which가 관계대명사 목적격이므로 it을 생략해야 선행사와의 중복을 피할 수 있다.)

2. what: 자체에 선행사를 포함하고 있으므로 what 앞에 선행사가 올 수 없다.

The thing what he purchased yesterday was too expensive. (X)
What he purchased yesterday was too expensive. (O)
(선행사가 있기 때문에 what을 which/that으로 바꾸든지, the thing을 생략하고 what이 이끄는 명사절로 바꿔야 한다.)

3. that의 쓰임: that 앞에 전치사를 쓸 수 없고, 계속적 용법으로 쓰이지 않는다. 선행사를 한정해주는 어구(the only/same, 최상급, some, any, no)가 있는 경우 that이 쓰인다.

관계대명사 that + 불완전한 절
접속사 that + 완전한 절

It was the most amazing moment that I have ever had. (관계대명사 that)
생애 가장 놀라운 순간이었다.
I believe that he is innocent. (접속사 that)
그가 결백하다는 것을 믿는다.
cf. 관계대명사 what도 명사절을 이끌어 '~하는 것' 이라는 의미가 있지만 뒤에 불완전한 절이 온다.
　　Do you know what I'm saying? 내가 무슨 말 하는지 아니? (say의 목적어가 없다)

4. 복합 관계대명사: 〈관계대명사+ever〉의 형태로 명사절이나 양보 부사절을 이끈다.

I will give you whichever you choose. (= anything that)
네가 무엇을 고르든지 그것을 주겠다.
Whatever happens, I will still love you. (= No matter what)
무슨 일이 일어나더라도 나는 여전히 당신을 사랑할 것입니다.

5. 관계부사

관계부사는 〈접속사+부사〉의 역할을 하며 〈전치사+관계대명사〉로 바꿔 쓸 수 있다. 그 종류에는 선행사에 따라 where, when, how, why가 있다.
This is the house where he was born.
= This is the house in which he was born.
이곳이 그가 태어난 집입니다.

Catch Up

관계사 관련 TEPS 주요 문제들을 풀어보도록 한다.

Part I Fill in the blank with the most appropriate word or phrase.

1. Wine, ___________ is one of the most popular beverages in the world, is made from the fermentation of grapes.

    (a) of which
    (b) which
    (c) that
    (d) what

2. We are planning to spend the winter in Thailand, ___________ the warm sun allows us to relax on the beach every day.

    (a) which
    (b) wherever
    (c) when
    (d) where

3. You are allowed to bring one guest to the wedding, and you may bring ___________ you choose.

    (a) whomever
    (b) whatever
    (c) whichever
    (d) whenever

Part III Identify the grammatical error in the dialogue.

4. (a) A: Did you hear that John is going to be out of town for three or four weeks?
    (b) B: No, I didn't. Does that mean we aren't going to have our weekly card game?
    (c) A: I suppose we can still play if we find someone whom we think can organize it.
    (d) B: I would do it, but my apartment is too small for that many people.

Part IV Identify the ungrammatical sentence in the passage.

4. (a) Although many people will never leave the city where they grow up, there are some who are unable to stay in one place for very long. (b) Some of these people constantly travel, others live on the road, and there are others who pack up and move to a new city every couple of years. (c) I have a friend like this, who always tried escaping to different exotic countries. (d) Ultimately, however, he has finally settled back down in the same small town which he was born.

1

Wine, __________ is one of the most popular beverages in the world, is made from the fermentation of grapes.

(a) of which
(b) which
(c) that
(d) what

세계에서 가장 유명한 음료중의 하나인 와인은 포도의 발효로 만들어진다.

해설 관계대명사와 관련된 문제이다. 빈칸에는 선행사 wine을 받는 주격 관계대명사가 와야 한다. what은 선행사를 포함하고 있는 관계대명사이므로 정답이 될 수 없고 that은 앞에 콤마가 올 수 없으므로 정답이 아니다.

어휘 fermentation 발효

2

We are planning to spend the winter in Thailand, __________ the warm sun allows us to relax on the beach every day.

(a) which
(b) wherever
(c) when
(d) where

우리는 겨울을 태국에서 보낼 계획인데 그곳은 따뜻한 태양이 매일 우리를 해변에서 쉬도록 해준다.

해설 빈칸 뒤에 완벽한 문장이 왔으므로 관계부사나 〈전치사＋관계대명사〉가 와야 한다. 선행사가 장소이므로 (d)가 정답이 된다.

3

You are allowed to bring one guest to the wedding, and you may bring __________ you choose.

(a) whomever
(b) whatever
(c) whichever
(d) whenever

결혼식에는 한 명의 손님을 데려올 수 있는데 네가 고른 누구든지 괜찮다.

해설 복합 관계대명사는 〈관계대명사＋ever〉 형태를 취하며, what과 마찬가지로 선행사를 자체적으로 포함하고 있기 때문에 선행사를 취할 수 없다. 여기서는 의미상 적절한 복합관계대명사를 골라야 하는데 choose에 대한 목적어이면서 사람을 가리키는 (a)가 정답이 된다.

4

(a) A: Did you hear that John is going to be out of town for three or four weeks?
(b) B: No, I didn't. Does that mean we aren't going to have our weekly card game?
(c) A: I suppose we can still play if we find someone (whom → who) we think can organize it.
(d) B: I would do it, but my apartment is too small for that many people.

(a) A: 존이 3주나 4주 동안 출장 갈 거라는 소식을 들었니?
(b) B: 아니. 그럼 우리 이번 주에는 카드 게임을 안 하겠네?
(c) A: 누군가 그걸 준비할 사람을 찾으면 할 수도 있을 것 같은데.
(d) B: 내가 할게. 그런데 우리집은 그렇게 많은 사람들이 모이기엔 너무 작은데.

해설 관계대명사의 용법을 묻는 문제이다. 선행사가 someone이고, can organize의 주어 역할을 하는 관계대명사가 필요하므로 who가 적절하다. 관계대명사와 동사구 사이의 we think는 삽입어구이다.

5

(a) Although many people will never leave the city where they grow up, there are some who are unable to stay in one place for very long. (b) Some of these people constantly travel, others live on the road, and there are others who pack up and move to a new city every couple of years. (c) I have a friend like this, who always tried escaping to different exotic countries. (d) Ultimately, however, he has finally settled back down in the same small town (which → in which / where) he was born.

(a) 많은 사람들은 그들이 자란 도시를 떠나려 하지 않지만 한 곳에 오래 머물 수 없는 사람들도 있다. (b) 이들 중 몇몇은 계속 옮겨 다니고, 몇몇은 길에서 지내며, 2년마다 새 도시로 짐을 싸서 이사 가는 사람들도 있다. (c) 내 친구가 이런 사람인데 그는 항상 다른 이국적인 나라들로 탈출을 시도했다. (d) 그러나 그는 결국 그가 태어난 바로 그 작은 마을에 돌아와 마침내 정착했다.

해설 관계부사 관련 문제이다. 관계대명사는 선행사를 받아 주어나 목적어 역할을 하기 때문에 뒤에 불완전한 절이 오게 된다. 그러나 여기서는 완벽한 절이 왔으므로 관계부사 where나 〈전치사 ＋관계대명사〉인 in which로 바꾸어야 한다.

Answers

1. (b) 2. (d) 3. (a) 4. (c) whom → who 5. (d) which → in which / where

 **Build Up** 

TEPS 전 문법 요소가 모의고사 형식으로 골고루 섞인 4파트의 문제
를 골고루 풀어 본다.

▶▶ **Part I**   Fill in the blank with the most appropriate word or phrase.

1. A: I hate winter, ____________________________.
B: I agree. I get scared doing it, too.

(a) driving in the snow is too difficult
(b) the snow driving is too difficult
(c) it is too difficult for my drive in the snow
(d) it is too difficult that I drive in the snow

2. A: Did you get a chance to see the Georgia O'Keeffe exhibition at the Art Museum?
B: I did, but I _______________ it because I thought it lasted another month.

(a) am nearly missing
(b) nearly didn't miss
(c) nearly missed
(d) was nearly missing

3. A: Excuse me, do you know __________ I can give my completed paperwork to?
B: I can take that from you, sir. You can just wait in the waiting room till we're ready for
  you.

(a) when
(b) what
(c) whom
(d) whomever

4. A: When can I see your band play live?
B: We __________ every weekend at a local jazz club.

(a) would perform
(b) can perform
(c) did perform
(d) perform

▶▶ **Part II**   Fill in the blank with the most appropriate word or phrase.

5. __________ that pianist tonight at the symphony has made me want to start playing
piano again.

(a) When hearing
(b) Of hearing
(c) Hearing
(d) By hearing

6. For some busy families fast food restaurants often provide many of the meals, ____________ can be harmful to any person's health.

(a) that
(b) when
(c) such
(d) which

7. If I ____________ travel cross-country, I wouldn't pack half as much baggage as you have.

(a) were to
(b) was to
(c) have to
(d) might

8. The swimmers ____________ the two sharks were hysterical and made it difficult for others to get to safety.

(a) who escape
(b) escaping
(c) for escaping
(d) to escape

▶▶ **Part III**   Identify the grammatical error in the dialogue.

9. (a) A: There is never enough work to do around the office during Christmas.
(b) B: Why do you have to work so many hours then?
(c) A: Well, I don't have to, but I definitely would use the extra money.
(d) B: Then, I guess I don't understand what you are complaining about.

10. (a) A: Hello, William! I really like your suit. Did you get a new job?
(b) B: Actually, yes. I got the job downtown that I was telling you about last week.
(c) A: But I thought you weren't able to get an interview at that company?
(d) B: I wasn't, but last Friday I just walked in and convinced to the boss to give me the job.

▶▶ **Part IV**   Identify the ungrammatical sentence in the passage.

11. (a) When I was walking home from my friend's house last night something very strange happened. (b) I didn't see any other people most of the way home, but I saw one person wearing a big wool jacket. (c) Passing my right side, I was addressed by the man. (d) Immediately I turned around to see who it was, but there was no one there!

12. (a) A friend of mine went to apply for a passport last month. (b) Once she got there she found out that she missed one of the documents needed to get her passport. (c) She went home to search for the document, but unfortunately, she does not keep her house very organized. (d) She searched and searched, and after a week of looking the missing document has located.

정답:210p

GRAMMAR
Week 3

Day 11 ▶▶ 부사

1. 부사는 보어로 쓰일 수 없음을 알아두고 Part III나 Part IV에서 부사가 보어로 쓰이지 않았는지 확인한다.
2. 형용사와 부사의 형태가 같은 것을 알아둔다.
3. 뜻이 다른 두 가지 형태의 부사를 알아둔다.

Day 12 ▶▶ 관계사

1. 선행사와 관계대명사의 수가 일치하는지 확인한다.
2. 관계대명사의 격이 제대로 쓰였는지 확인한다.
3. 관계대명사 뒤에는 불완전한 절이 와야 한다.

Day 13 ▶▶ 접속사

1. 접속사 뒤에는 절이 오고, 전치사 뒤에는 구가 온다.
2. 대등 접속사와 등위접속사에서 문법 단위가 동일한 품사끼리 병렬 구조가 되었는지 확인한다.
3. 상관접속사의 연결어구가 알맞게 연결되었는지 확인한다.

Day 14 ▶▶ 전치사

1. 기본적인 시간. 장소의 전치사를 확인해 둔다.
2. 많은 전치사의 쓰임을 알기 위해서 평소에 LC에 나오는 쓰임을 확인해 둔다.
3. 관용적인 전치사구의 쓰임을 알아둔다.

Day 15 ▶▶ 시험에 잘 나오는 문장 어순

1. 보어 자리엔 부사가 올 수 없다.
2. 목적보어를 취하는 타동사들을 알아둔다.
3. 목적보어로 to부정사를 취하는 동사들을 확인한다.

Day 13
접속사

1. 등위접속사(and, or, but)와 상관접속사 관련 문제 체크 사항 익혀두기

① 문법 단위가 동일한 품사끼리 병렬 구조가 되었는지 확인하기

② 상관접속사의 연결어구가 알맞게 연결됐는지 확인하기

③ 수의 일치 확인하기

The history class was interesting and education. (X)
The history class was interesting and educational. (O)
그 역사 수업은 흥미롭고 교육적이었다.

2. 상관접속사

both A and B A와 B 모두 (복수 취급)
either A or B A 또는 B (B에 동사 일치)
neither A nor B A도 B도 아닌
not only A but also B A 뿐만 아니라 B 도(B에 동사 일치)
Neither the boys nor Tom eats onions. 그 남자아이들도 톰도 양파를 먹지 않는다.

3. 종속접속사

시간·조건 부사절에서는 주절의 시제가 미래를 나타내거나 명령문일 때 현재시제로 미래를 대신한다.

1) 시간 접속사

after, as, before, while, when, as soon as, till, until

I will call you as soon as he comes back. 그가 돌아오자마자 너에게 전화할게.

2) 조건 접속사

if, in case, as long as, provided (that), supposing (that), as far as, unless

Why don't you get insurance in case you have an accident?

사고를 대비해서 보험을 드는 게 어때?

3) 양보 접속사

even if, even though, although, though

Although the weather was not good, they didn't cancel the game.

= Despite/In spite of the bad weather, they didn't cancel the game.

날씨가 좋지 않았지만 그들은 경기를 취소하지 않았다.

(despite, in spite of는 양보를 나타내는 전치사이므로 그 뒤에 명사(구)가 온다.)

4) 이유의 접속사

because, since, as, for, inasmuch as, seeing that, now that

Since he didn't pass the bar exam, he decided to go back to his hometown.

변호사 시험을 통과하지 못해서 그는 고향으로 돌아가기로 결정했다.

Catch Up

접속사 관련 TEPS 주요 문제들을 풀어보도록 한다.

Part I   Fill in the blank with the most appropriate word or phrase.

1. A: I can't wait until I graduate and start working!
B: You'll miss college life ___________ you start working.

(a) once
(b) before
(c) since
(d) while

2. A: Eunice is so joyful ___________ from the car accident.
B: Yeah, she says she is simply thankful to be alive.

(a) despite her bad injury
(b) even if she were badly injured
(c) though injured badly she was
(d) with the bad injury

Part II   Fill in the blank with the most appropriate word or phrase.

3. ___________ the number of incidents increased after September 11, airlines have become stricter about flying policies.

(a) Though
(b) Unless
(c) Since
(d) For

4. Jeremy is uncertain about ___________ or not he should propose to Johanna.

(a) if
(b) as
(c) neither
(d) whether

5. The movie *Transformers* is similar to the original television series ___________ the premise and characters are the same.

(a) in that
(b) provided that
(c) despite that
(d) given that

Answers 

Catch Up에서 푼 문제의 해석과 해설을 점검한다.

1

A: I can't wait until I graduate and start working!
B: You'll miss college life __________ you start working.

(a) once
(b) before
(c) since
(d) while

A: 졸업하고 어서 일을 시작했으면 좋겠어!
B: 일단 일을 시작하면 대학 생활이 그리워질 걸.

해설 선택지가 모두 접속사이기 때문에 의미상 적절한 접속사를 고르는 문제이다. once는 '일단 ~하면'이라는 조건의 접속사로 의미상 가장 적절하다.

2

A: Eunice is so joyful __________ from the car accident.
B: Yeah, she says she is simply thankful to be alive.

(a) despite her bad injury
(b) even if she were badly injured
(c) though injured badly she was
(d) with the bad injury

A: 유니스는 교통사고에서 부상을 당했음에도 불구하고 매우 쾌할해.
B: 응. 그녀는 살아있다는 것에 감사하다고 하던걸.

해설 의미상 양보의 절이나 구가 와야 한다. '~임에도 불구하고'라는 의미를 가진 전치사 despite로 이루어진 (a)가 가장 적절하다. even if는 '비록 ~일지라도'라는 조건·가정의 의미이므로 적절치 않다.

3

__________ the number of incidents increased after September 11, airlines have become stricter about flying policies.

(a) Though
(b) Unless
(c) Since
(d) For

9.11테러 이후 사고의 급증으로 항공사들은 운항 정책을 더욱 강화시켰다.

해설 부사절과 주절이 원인과 결과를 나타내므로 '이유'의 의미를 갖고 있는 접속사가 와야 한다. for는 앞 문장의 부가적인 설명이나 이유를 나타낼 때 쓰인다. 그러므로 (c)가 정답이 된다.

4

Jeremy is uncertain about __________ or not he should propose to Johanna.

(a) if
(b) as
(c) neither
(d) whether

제러미는 조안나에게 프러포즈를 해야 하는지 아닌지 확신이 서지 않는다.

해설 〈whether or not + 주어 + 동사〉의 어순으로 '~가 …인지 아닌지'라는 의미가 있다. 그러므로 (d)가 적절한 접속사가 된다.

5

The movie *Transformers* is similar to the original television series __________ the premise and characters are the same.

(a) in that
(b) provided that
(c) despite that
(d) given that

'트렌스포머'란 영화는 그 전제와 캐릭터가 똑같다는 점에서 원래의 텔레비전 시리즈와 비슷하다.

해설 in that은 '~라는 점에서, ~이므로 (= since, because)'의 의미가 있다. 그러므로 의미상 가장 적절한 답이 된다.

Answers

1. (a) 2. (a) 3. (c) 4. (d) 5. (a)

Build Up 

TEPS 전 문법 요소가 모의고사 형식으로 골고루 섞인 4파트의 문제
를 골고루 풀어 본다.

▶▶ **Part I** Fill in the blank with the most appropriate word or phrase.

1. A: Amos is really __________ about getting married next week!
B: He should be, since Alice is a wonderful woman!

(a) excited   (b) to excite   (c) exciting   (d) for excite

2. A: I have to leave town for a couple of days.
B: Okay, but I really don't understand __________ you have to do this now.

(a) why
(b) what
(c) when
(d) how

3. A: What are you looking for?
B: My cell phone! I forgot __________ it from the charger!

(a) unplug   (b) unpluging
(c) to unplug   (d) having unplugged

4. A: What kind of questions should I expect at the interview?
B: A popular one is "__________________ to apply for this job?"

(a) What make you to decide
(b) What did make you to decide
(c) What made you decide
(d) What decision you make

▶▶ **Part II** Fill in the blank with the most appropriate word or phrase.

5. How was I supposed to know __________ the store closed down and relocated?

(a) that
(b) which
(c) where
(d) who

6. Amnesty International has created many human rights programs __________ spread awareness about human rights violations in many countries.

(a) to succeed to
(b) that succeeding to
(c) succeeded to
(d) that have succeeded to

7. Among last week's guest celebrities __________ Michael Jordan of the Chicago Bulls.
(a) was
(b) is
(c) were
(d) are

8. The Thanksgiving dinner is tentatively __________ at McKinley Foundation.
(a) to hold
(b) be held
(c) holding
(d) to be held

▶▶ **Part III**   Identify the grammatical error in the dialogue.

9. (a) A: I love snacks that they provide after each service.
(b) B: Do they serve anything besides crackers?
(c) A: Yes, they serve all kinds of distinctive cheeses!
(d) B: Wow, I should stop by the snack table more often.

10. (a) A: Do you have a good trip?
(b) B: Yes, it was a wonderful experience.
(c) A: That's good to know! What happened?
(d) B: They bumped me up to first class!

▶▶ **Part IV**   Identify the ungrammatical sentence in the passage.

11. (a) The University's English department has new and interesting courses this year! (b) For example, there is a new multicultural literature class that are now being offered. (c) There is also a new course regarding the proliferation of postmodern literature in the western hemisphere. (d) I hope I can enroll in one of these courses!

12. (a) Although I was very tired, I'm grateful that I went to the informational meeting last night. (b) Initially, I didn't want to go, but my roommate, Ellie, had insisted that I went. (c) If I hadn't gone, I would've never learned about the North Korean refugees. (d) Now I'm thinking about joining the board to raise more awareness about the injustice in North Korea.

정답:212p

GRAMMAR
Week 3

Day 11 ▶▶ 부사

1. 부사는 보어로 쓰일 수 없음을 알아두고 Part III나 Part IV에서 부사
   가 보어로 쓰이지 않았는지 확인한다.
2. 형용사와 부사의 형태가 같은 것을 알아둔다.
3. 뜻이 다른 두 가지 형태의 부사를 알아둔다.

Day 12 ▶▶ 관계사

1. 선행사와 관계대명사의 수가 일치하는지 확인한다.
2. 관계대명사의 격이 제대로 쓰였는지 확인한다.
3. 관계대명사 뒤에는 불완전한 절이 와야 한다.

Day 13 ▶▶ 접속사

1. 접속사 뒤에는 절이 오고, 전치사 뒤에는 구가 온다.
2. 대등 접속사와 등위접속사에서 문법 단위가 동일한 품사끼리 병렬 구조
   가 되었는지 확인한다.
3. 상관접속사의 연결어구가 알맞게 연결되었는지 확인한다.

Day 14 ▶▶ 전치사

1. 기본적인 시간, 장소의 전치사를 확인해 둔다.
2. 많은 전치사의 쓰임을 알기 위해서 평소에 LC에 나오는 쓰임을 확인해
   둔다.
3. 관용적인 전치사구의 쓰임을 알아둔다.

Day 15 ▶▶ 시험에 잘 나오는 문장 어순

1. 보어 자리엔 부사가 올 수 없다.
2. 목적보어를 취하는 타동사들을 알아둔다.
3. 목적보어로 to부정사를 취하는 동사들을 확인한다.

Day 14
전치사

 전치사 뒤에는 명사(구)가 오게 된다.

1. 때/시간을 나타내는 전치사

at: 시간, 시점

on: 날짜, 요일

in: 월, 계절, 세기, 하루의 아침/오후/저녁(**주의** → 밤: at night, 정오: at noon, 새벽: at dawn)

at noon 정오에   **at night** 밤에   **at dawn** 새벽에   **at midnight** 한밤중에

at 10: 30 10시 30분에   **at sunset** 해질 무렵에   **at present** 현재는   **at that time** 그때에는

at this time of the year 일 년중 이맘때에는

in spring 봄에   **in 2002** 2002년에   **in the past** 과거에

in the future 앞으로, 장차   **in the 21st century** 21세기에   **in the eighties** 80년대에

in one's life 자신 생애에   **in those days** 그 당시에는   **in one's absence** 부재 중에

in one's early/mid/late twenties 20대 초/중/후반

on May 4 5월 4일에   **on Saturday** 토요일에   **on Valentine's Day** 발렌타인 데이에

on Christmas Day 크리스마스 날에 (*cf.* at Christmas 크리스마스에)

2. ~때까지: by, till, until

by: (늦어도) ~까지 (완료) → 동작, 상태가 완료를 나타냄 (1회성으로 끝나는 동작/상태)

until, till: ~까지 계속 (유지) → 동작, 상태의 계속을 나타냄.

You should hand in the report by 9 o'clock this Friday. 금요일 9시까지 레포트를 내야 한다.

The shop opens until 10 p.m. every day. 그 가게는 매일 밤 10시까지 연다.

3. ~동안: for, during

for: ~동안 (일정한 기간) – How long~?에 대한 대답

during: ~동안 (특정 기간) – When~?에 대한 대답

4. 관용적인 전치사구 표현

out of sorts 기분이 언짢은   **out of work** 실직한   **out of sight** 보이지 않는

out of stock 품절된 (*cf.* in stock 재고가 있는)   **at hand** 가까이에   **at random** 닥치는 대로

at one's own risk 자기가 책임지고   **at stake** 위태로운   **at times** 때때로

at the moment 바로 지금   **at a stretch** 단숨에   **in token of** ~의 표시로

in terms of ~의 견지에서   **on strike** 파업 중   **on leave** 휴가 중

on sale 할인판매 중 (*cf.* for sale 판매중인)   **in demand** 수요가 있는 (*cf.* on demand 청구하는 대로)

to a great extent 크게   **for the time being** 당분간

at the expense of ~의 대가를 치르고   **as a whole** 대체로   **as a result of** ~의 결과로

apart from ~은 별도로 하고   **in charge of** ~을 책임지고 있는   **in a nutshell** 한 마디로 말하자면

once in a while 이따금   **in search of** ~을 찾아서   **in this way** ~이런 식으로

thanks to ~덕분에

전치사 관련 TEPS 주요 문제들을 풀어보도록 한다.

Part I Fill in the blank with the most appropriate word or phrase.

1. A: What is the name you made the reservation __________?
B: I believe we used the name Johnston.

(a) to
(b) like
(c) on
(d) under

2. A: Doesn't it seem __________ Tina has been acting strange lately?
B: Yes, ever since she got that new boyfriend she's acted different.

(a) though
(b) about
(c) like
(d) as

3. A: When did you say you were leaving for your vacation?
B: Well, __________ everything goes smoothly at work, I'll leave next week Monday.

(a) assuming
(b) assumed
(c) to assume
(d) assume

4. A: Bill, which car do you like better, black or red?
B: If I had to choose one, I would pick the black one __________ the red one.

(a) above
(b) through
(c) about
(d) over

Part II Fill in the blank with the most appropriate word or phrase.

5. For some reason, I am always being blamed __________ the mistakes of other workers in the factory.
(a) about
(b) for
(c) to
(d) with

Answers

Catch Up에서 푼 문제의 해석과 해설을 점검한다.

1

A: What is the name you made the reservation ____________?
B: I believe we used the name Johnston.

(a) to
(b) like
(c) on
(d) under

A: 무슨 이름으로 예약을 하셨나요?
B: 존스톤이라는 이름으로 한 것 같습니다.

해설 make a reservation under~는 '~라는 이름으로 예약하다' 라는 의미이다. 그러므로 알맞은 전치사는 (d)가 된다.

2

A: Doesn't it seem ____________ Tina has been acting strange lately?
B: Yes, ever since she got that new boyfriend she's acted different.

(a) though
(b) about
(c) like
(d) as

A: 티나가 요즘 이상하게 행동하는 것 같지 않니?
B: 응. 새 남자친구를 만난 이후로 행동이 달라.

해설 빈칸 뒤에 절이 있으므로 빈칸에는 접속사가 와야 한다. 의미상 '~인 듯이' 라는 의미의 접속사 like가 적절하다.

3

A: When did you say you were leaving for your vacation?

B: Well, __________ everything goes smoothly at work, I'll leave next week Monday.

(a) assuming
(b) assumed
(c) to assume
(d) assume

A: 휴가를 언제 간다고 했지?
B: 직장에서 일이 잘 진행된다면 다음주 월요일에 떠날 거야.

해설 assuming (that)~은 '~라고 가정한다면' 이라는 의미의 독립 분사구문이다. 관용적인 표현으로 알아두도록 한다.

4

A: Bill, which car do you like better, black or red?

B: If I had to choose one, I would pick the black one __________ the red one.

(a) above
(b) through
(c) about
(d) over

A: 빌, 검정색과 빨간색 중 어떤 차가 더 마음에 들어?
B: 선택을 해야 한다면 빨간색보다 검정색을 선택할 거야.

해설 전치사 over는 '~에 비하여' 란 의미가 있다. 그러므로 (d)가 정답이 된다.

5

For some reason, I am always being blamed __________ the mistakes of other workers in the factory.

(a) about
(b) for
(c) to
(d) with

왠지 모르겠지만 나는 공장에서 다른 사람들의 실수에 대해서도 항상 비난을 받는다.

해설 blame for는 '비난하다, ~의 책임으로 돌리다' 라는 뜻이다. 여기서 for는 이유를 나타낸다.

Answers

1. (d) 2. (c) 3. (a) 4. (d) 5. (b)

Build Up

TEPS 전 문법 요소가 모의고사 형식으로 골고루 섞인 4파트의 문제
를 골고루 풀어 본다.

▶▶ **Part I**   Fill in the blank with the most appropriate word or phrase.

1. A: Something about your apartment seems different. Did you get new furniture?
B: No, all these things __________ here before.

(a) were   (b) was   (c) are   (d) will be

2. A: Which perfume did you buy for Mom's birthday present?
B: She wanted one __________ of vanilla, so I bought her Armani Mania.

(a) smells   (b) to smell   (c) smelled   (d) smelling

3. A: What happened to your hat? It looked great on you.
B: Thanks, but out of respect I __________ it when I entered the building.

(a) will remove
(b) had removed
(c) remove
(d) removed

4. A: You look as if you'd seen a ghost. Are you alright?
B: I'm fine now, but I'd ________________________________.

(a) not rather be alone tonight
(b) rather tonight be not alone
(c) rather not be alone tonight
(d) not be rather alone tonight

▶▶ **Part II**   Fill in the blank with the most appropriate word or phrase.

5. At the beginning of the year, the boss ___________________ that the factory might
have to be shut down by the end of the year.
(a) had warned to his workers
(b) had warned his workers
(c) to his workers warned
(d) has warned his workers

6. ______________ upon a more familiar subject, Jill broke the uneasy silence with a
question about Adam's family.
(a) To fallen back
(b) Fallen back
(c) Fall back
(d) Falling back

7. Many people don't realize this, but one of the most physically strenuous activities for the body __________ swimming.

(a) is
(b) was
(c) are
(d) be

8. The organization's new headquarters will be built and __________ with the help of donations from its large number of benefactors.

(a) financing
(b) finance
(c) financed
(d) finances

▶▶ **Part III**   Identify the grammatical error in the dialogue.

9. (a) A: Are there any more people coming? Or is this all of them?
(b) B: I don't know for sure. We will have to wait and see.
(c) A: We don't have any more time waiting right away. We need to start the presentation.
(d) B: Go ahead and start then, it shouldn't be a problem.

10. (a) A: Did you enjoy your summer vacation?
(b) B: I did. It was very rewarding.
(c) A: Why was it rewarding? What did you do?
(d) A: I spent two months down south to helping rebuild damaged houses.

▶▶ **Part IV**   Identify the ungrammatical sentence in the passage.

11. (a) Koalas are some of the longest sleepers in the animal kingdom. (b) Actually, most of their lives are spent sleeping. (c) On average, a koala sleeps for 22 hours a day, which helps their bodies to conserve energy. (d) In turn, koalas do not need to consume very much vegetations for food, because their bodies do not need much energy.

12. (a) Deep sea fishing has been a favorite pastime of seaside peoples for thousands of years. (b) Over time, navigational and fishing tools have increased in proficiency, the activity less challenging. (c) Besides this, other concerns have been raised in recent years. (d) The increase in seafood consumption and pollutants in the water has seriously threatened the future of many aquatic animals worldwide.

정답:214p

<table>
<tr><td>

Day 11

</td><td>

▶▶ 부사

1. 부사는 보어로 쓰일 수 없음을 알아두고 Part III나 Part IV에서 부사가 보어로 쓰이지 않았는지 확인한다.
2. 형용사와 부사의 형태가 같은 것을 알아둔다.
3. 뜻이 다른 두 가지 형태의 부사를 알아둔다.

</td></tr>
<tr><td>

Day 12

</td><td>

▶▶ 관계사

1. 선행사와 관계대명사의 수가 일치하는지 확인한다.
2. 관계대명사의 격이 제대로 쓰였는지 확인한다.
3. 관계대명사 뒤에는 불완전한 절이 와야 한다.

</td></tr>
<tr><td>

Day 13

</td><td>

▶▶ 접속사

1. 접속사 뒤에는 절이 오고, 전치사 뒤에는 구가 온다.
2. 대등 접속사와 등위접속사에서 문법 단위가 동일한 품사끼리 병렬 구조가 되었는지 확인한다.
3. 상관접속사의 연결어구가 알맞게 연결되었는지 확인한다.

</td></tr>
<tr><td>

Day 14

</td><td>

▶▶ 전치사

1. 기본적인 시간, 장소의 전치사를 확인해 둔다.
2. 많은 전치사의 쓰임을 알기 위해서 평소에 LC에 나오는 쓰임을 확인해 둔다.
3. 관용적인 전치사구의 쓰임을 알아둔다.

</td></tr>
<tr><td>

Day 15

</td><td>

▶▶ 시험에 잘 나오는 문장 어순

1. 보어 자리엔 부사가 올 수 없다.
2. 목적보어를 취하는 타동사들을 알아둔다.
3. 목적보어로 to부정사를 취하는 동사들을 확인한다.

</td></tr>
</table>

Day 15
시험에 잘 나오는 문장 어순

▶▶ 목적격 보어로 to부정사를 취하는 타동사가 시험에 잘 나온다. 목적격 보어를 to부정사로 취하는 동사류를 암기하도록 한다.

1. 보어를 필요로 하는 불완전자동사

keep, remain, stay, become, get, go, grow, look, feel, smell, sound, taste, seem, appear

보어 자리에 부사는 올 수 없다.
It sounds strangely. (X)
It sounds strange. (O) 이상하게 들린다.

2. 목적격 보어를 취하는 타동사: V+O+OC

목적격 보어 자리에도 부사는 올 수 없다.
1) find, make, think, believe+ it(가목적어)+형용사 +to V
   I found it difficult to solve the problem.
   나는 그 문제를 푸는 것이 어렵다는 것을 알았다.
   The noise made it impossible to hear her talking.
   그 소음 때문에 그녀가 이야기하는 것을 듣는 것은 불가능했다.

2) 목적격 보어로 to부정사를 취하는 타동사: V+ O + to V
   allow, urge, encourage, enable, cause, force, help, get, forbid

   It is obvious that the new test system encourages students to study hard.
   새 시험 제도가 학생들을 열심히 공부할 수 있게 한다는 것은 명백하다.

Catch Up 

시험에 잘 나오는 문장 어순 관련 TEPS 주요 문제들을 풀어보도록
한다.

Part I Fill in the blank with the most appropriate word or phrase.

1. A: Don't worry, Ms. Kim. I take ______________ that Raymond is turning in all of his
homework and projects.
B: Thank you, but do you think he can raise his grade to at least a B?

(a) a sign is good
(b) it a good sign
(c) good signs
(d) it as a good sign

2. A: Was Danny's mom hospitable when you visited for the holidays?
B: Yes, she even prepared ______________ in Danny's sister's old room.

(a) myself a room
(b) a room to me
(c) mine room
(d) a room for me

3. A: Jacob can bend his fingers all the way back!
B: Not only is that disgusting, but I find __________________.

(a) that hard to believe
(b) hard to believe that
(c) believing that hard to be
(d) that hard to believe it

Part II Fill in the blank with the most appropriate word or phrase.

4. The school hallways remain __________ when there is no one in the building.

(a) silence
(b) silenced
(c) silent
(d) silently

5. I'm still waiting to see if ______________________ because Esther said it was hilarious.

(a) proves the TV program silly or not to be
(b) the TV program proving to be silly or not
(c) the TV program proves to be silly or not
(d) silly or not the TV program proves

Catch Up에서 푼 문제의 해석과 해설을 점검한다.

1

A: Don't worry, Ms. Kim. I take ___________ that Raymond is turning in all of his homework and projects.

B: Thank you, but do you think he can raise his grade to at least a B?

(a) a sign is good
(b) it a good sign
(c) good signs
(d) it as a good sign

A: 걱정하지 마세요. 저는 레이몬드가 그의 모든 숙제와 과제물들을 낸 것을 좋은 징조로 보고 있습니다.

B: 고맙습니다. 그런데 그 아이의 점수가 적어도 B까지 오를 수 있을 것 같나요?

해설　〈take + 목적어 + as + 보어〉는 '~을 …라고 생각하다, 여기다' 라는 의미이다. 그러므로 (d)가 정답이 된다.

2

A: Was Danny's mom hospitable when you visited for the holidays?

B: Yes, she even prepared ___________ in Danny's sister's old room.

(a) myself a room
(b) a room to me
(c) mine room
(d) a room for me

A: 휴가 때 대니의 어머님이 잘해 주셨어?

B: 응, 나를 위해 대니 누나의 오래된 방에 숙소까지 준비해 주셨어.

해설　prepare는 '~을 준비하다' 라는 의미의 타동사로 목적어를 필요로 한다. 그리고 목적어 뒤에 또 다른 목적어가 오기 위해서는 전치사가 필요한데 의미상 for가 적절하다. 〈prepare + 목적어 + for〉는 '~을 위해 …을 준비하다' 라는 뜻이다.

3

<table>
<tr><td>

A: Jacob can bend his fingers all the way back!
B: Not only is that disgusting, but I find

_______________.

(a) that hard to believe
(b) hard to believe that
(c) believing that hard to be
(d) that hard to believe it

</td><td>

A: 제이콥은 손가락을 뒤로 구부릴 수도 있어!
B: 그건 역겨울 뿐 아니라 믿기도 어려워.

</td></tr>
</table>

 not only A but also B는 'A뿐만 아니라 B 역시' 라는 의미다. not only가 문두에 오게 되면 도치가 이루어진다. 여기서 find는 5형식 동사로 쓰여져서 〈find＋목적어＋목적격 보어〉의 어순이 되어야 한다. (d)는 believe의 목적어가 that이므로 it을 없애야 한다. 그러므로 (a)가 정답이 된다.

4

<table>
<tr><td>

The school hallways remain __________ when there is no one in the building.

(a) silence
(b) silenced
(c) silent
(d) silently

</td><td>

건물 내에 아무도 없을 때면 학교 복도는 침묵 속에 잠겨 있다.

</td></tr>
</table>

해설 remain은 형용사를 보어로 취하는 2형식 동사이다. 그러므로 (c)가 정답이 된다.

5

<table>
<tr><td>

I'm still waiting to see if ______________ because Esther said it was hilarious.

(a) proves the TV program silly or not to be
(b) the TV program proving to be silly or not
(c) the TV program proves to be silly or not
(d) silly or not the TV program proves

</td><td>

에스더가 이 TV 프로그램이 재미있다고 해서 우스운지 아닌지 아직 보고 있는 중이야.

</td></tr>
</table>

해설 if는 접속사로 뒤에 〈주어＋동사〉의 절을 취해야 한다. 또한 동사 prove는 〈prove＋(to be)＋보어〉의 형태가 된다. 그러므로 (c)가 정답이 된다.

Answers

1. (d) 2. (d) 3. (a) 4. (c) 5. (c)

Build Up

TEPS 전 문법 요소가 모의고사 형식으로 골고루 섞인 4파트의 문제를 골고루 풀어 본다.

▶▶ **Part I** Fill in the blank with the most appropriate word or phrase.

1. A: I read in the tabloids that Reese Witherspoon and Ryan Phillippe _______________ after all.
B: Wow! That's so sad considering they were one of Hollywood's cutest couples.

(a) should be divorced
(b) had got divorced
(c) did get divorced
(d) has been divorcing

2. A: Do you know _______________ for dinner?
B: I think Caroline said it's at 6:30 p.m., so we should probably leave at 6 p.m.

(a) what time to leave
(b) to leave what time
(c) what time leaving
(d) of leaving what time

3. A: Nathan told me _________ him, but I lost his number.
B: Oh, I think Emily has it!

(a) calling
(b) called
(c) to call
(d) to be called

4. A: Ben is a huge Chicago Bears fan, but not as _________ fanatic as Eddie.
B: Yeah, Eddie paints his face blue and orange for every game!

(a) a much
(b) much of a
(c) much of
(d) of a much

▶▶ **Part II** Fill in the blank with the most appropriate word or phrase.

5. I wouldn't have survived senior year _______________ my friends' daily support.

(a) haven't it been for
(b) had it not been for
(c) weren't it for
(d) was it not for

6. Josh takes working out consistently as seriously __________ Joel does.

(a) because
(b) since
(c) while
(d) as

7. The two children, ______________ in the cave, were rescued and taken to safety.

(a) to be discovered
(b) discovering
(c) discovered
(d) having discovered

8. __________ that Jane would appreciate his gesture, Eddie bought her a dozen roses and had it delivered to her workplace.

(a) To think
(b) Thinking
(c) Thought
(d) Think

▶▶ **Part III** Identify the grammatical error in the dialogue.

9. (a) A: What happened after the party this weekend?
(b) B: Not only is my house trashed from the party, but I also crashed my parents' car!
(c) A: Oh, no! Sound like you're going to be in big trouble.
(d) B: That's for sure. They're coming back from vacation tomorrow!

10. (a) A: Where did you get your two puppies from?
(b) B: I brought them from the shelter. They were rescued from an abandoned building.
(c) A: Wow, what luck! Who knows what would have happened to them?
(d) B: Yeah, they won't be alive if it weren't for the animal rescue team.

▶▶ **Part IV** Identify the ungrammatical sentence in the passage.

11. (a) With the increase of standards to enter a top University for high school students, it has become increasingly difficult to become an all-around high school student. (b) There are just too many students competing for the same University, but not enough spots to give away to each one. (c) So what should a perfect student do to get in to a top University? (d) It seems there's no choice, but to hope for the best.

12. (a) There has been a huge increase in HIV/AIDS victims in Africa in the past decade. (b) However, because of the lack of HIV/AIDS education, the statistics aren't decreasing. (c) African governments are trying to provide an information about HIV/AIDS and abstinence to prevent the spread of the disease. (d) They believe that this will help people make the right decisions to protect themselves from contracting the disease.

정답:216p

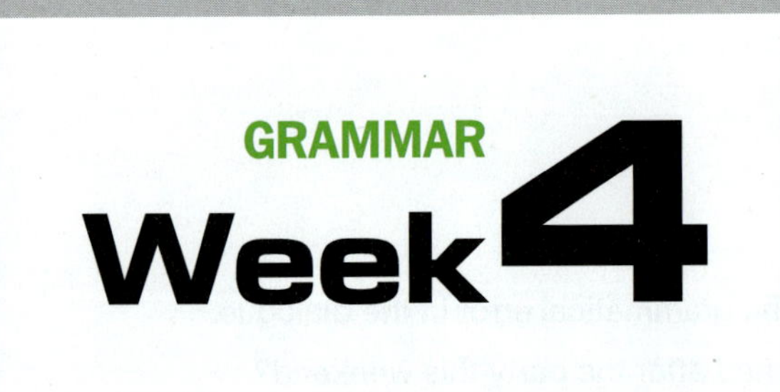
GRAMMAR
Week 4

<table>
<tr><td>Day 16</td><td>▶▶ 어순</td></tr>
</table>

1. 사역동사의 쓰임을 알아둔다.
2. 사역동사는 목적격 보어로 현재분사가 올 수 없다.
3. 간접의문문의 순서를 파악해 둔다.

<table>
<tr><td>Day 17</td><td>▶▶ 일치</td></tr>
</table>

1. 명사와 대명사의 수 일치를 확인한다.
2. 선행사와의 수 일치를 확인한다.
3. 시험에 잘 나오는 수 일치 관련 표현을 익혀둔다.

<table>
<tr><td>Day 18</td><td>▶▶ 도치 구문을 잡아라</td></tr>
</table>

1. 부정부사가 문두에 오게 되면 도치가 일어난다.
2. so와 such의 어순을 익혀둔다.
3. so 뒤에 문장이 올 때 도치가 되는 경우를 알아둔다.

<table>
<tr><td>Day 19</td><td>▶▶ Part III를 바로잡자</td></tr>
</table>

1. Part III는 대화체이므로 LC에서 Part I과 III의 대화체를 자주 따라 읽고 익혀둔다.
2. Part III에서 동사 위주로 틀린 곳을 찾아본다.
3. Part III에서 자주 출제되는 포인트를 알아둔다.

<table>
<tr><td>Day 20</td><td>▶▶ Part IV가 고득점의 관문이다</td></tr>
</table>

1. Part IV는 하나의 글이기 때문에 전체적인 시제의 일치를 보아야 한다.
2. 자동사가 수동태로 쓰이지 않았는지 확인한다.
3. Part IV에 자주 출제되는 포인트를 알아둔다.

Day 16
어순

사역동사의 어순은 시험에 잘 나오므로 알아두도록 한다. 사역동사의 목적격 보어로는 현재분사는 올 수 없고 동사원형이나 과거분사만 올 수 있다.

1. 사역동사

목적격 보어로 동사원형이나 과거분사를 취한다.

1) 사역동사 + 목적어 + 동사원형 (목적어와 목적격 보어가 능동의 의미)

2) 사역동사 + 목적어 + 과거분사 (목적어와 목적격 보어가 수동의 의미)

I had him repair my radio. 그에게 내 라디오를 고치게 했다.
I had my radio repaired by him.

2. 준사역동사 get의 용법

1) get + 목적어 + to부정사 → 능동
I got him to mend my watch. 나는 그에게 시계를 수선하게 했다. (능동의 의미)

2) get + 목적어 + 과거분사 → 수동
I got my watch mended. 나는 시계를 수선시켰다. (수동의 의미)

3. 의문문의 순서

1) 직접의문문: 의문사 + 동사 + 주어
What did you buy for Jane? 제인을 위해 무엇을 샀니?

2) 간접의문문: 의문사 + 주어 + 동사
Do you know where the post office is? 우체국이 어디 있는지 아세요?

3) 의문사와 함께 think, suppose, believe, imagine, say가 동사로 쓰일 때 의문사가 문두에 오게 된다.
Who do you think his new girlfriend is? 누가 그의 새 여자친구인 것 같니?
Which do you think is better on me? 어떤 것이 나에게 더 어울리는 것 같니?

Catch Up 

어순 관련 TEPS 주요 문제들을 풀어보도록 한다.

Part I Fill in the blank with the most appropriate word or phrase.

1. A: How did it feel to see your son on the stage last night?
B: It felt really great. I _____________________ such a successful performer.

(a) never expected him to become
(b) could never expect him to become
(c) expected never him to become
(d) never expected to become

2. A: Aren't John and Simon in the band as well?
B: No, not anymore. But they _________.

(a) used to
(b) used to be
(c) used
(d) used to being

3. A: This book looks good. Do you know what it's about?
B: It tells the story of farmers forced by the government __________ their land.

(a) to evacuate
(b) evacuating
(c) to evacuation
(d) evacuated

Part II Fill in the blank with the most appropriate word or phrase.

4. Unfortunately, the study shows that there are dangerously low numbers of white rhinoceros __________ safely in the wild.

(a) survived
(b) survival
(c) surviving
(d) survives

5. Excessive amounts of loud music causes _____________________.

(a) the hearing deterioration
(b) deterioration of hear
(c) hearing to be deteriorating
(d) hearing to deteriorate

Answers 

Catch Up에서 푼 문제의 해석과 해설을 점검한다.

1

A: How did it feel to see your son on the stage last night?
B: It felt really great. I _________________ such a successful performer.

(a) never expected him to become
(b) could never expect him to become
(c) expected never him to become
(d) never expected to become

A: 지난밤에 무대에서 당신의 아들을 본 기분이 어땠어요?
B: 정말 좋았어요. 난 그가 그렇게 훌륭한 연기자가 될 줄 몰랐어요.

해설　expect는 목적어 뒤에 to부정사를 취하는(expect+목적어+to부정사) 5형식 동사이다. 부정부사 never는 일반동사 앞에 위치하므로 (a)가 정답이 된다. (b)가 정답이 되려면 could never have expected him to become이 되어야 한다.

2

A: Aren't John and Simon in the band as well?
B: No, not anymore. But they __________.

(a) used to
(b) used to be
(c) used
(d) used to being

A: 존과 시몬도 밴드에 있지 않니?
B: 아니. 더 이상은 아니야. 예전에는 그랬지만.

해설　used to V는 '~하곤 했다' 라는 과거의 습관적인 행동을 표현하는 의미이다. 여기서 to는 to부정사로 뒤에 동사원형이 와야 한다. 원래는 they used to be in the band라는 문장이었다. 여기서는 (a)처럼 be동사를 생략하면 의미가 명확하지 않기 때문에 (b)와 같은 형태로 사용해야 한다.

3

A: This book looks good. Do you know what it's about?

B: It tells the story of farmers forced by the government __________ their land.

(a) to evacuate
(b) evacuating
(c) to evacuation
(d) evacuated

A: 이 책 좋아 보인다. 무엇에 관한 책인지 아니?
B: 정부에 의해 강제로 그들의 땅을 내줘야 했던 농부들에 관한 이야기야.

해설 force는 목적어 다음에 목적격 보어로 to부정사를 취하는 동사이다. 그러므로 (a)가 정답이 된다.

4

Unfortunately, the study shows that there are dangerously low numbers of white rhinoceros __________ safely in the wild.

(a) survived
(b) survival
(c) surviving
(d) survives

불행히도 이 연구는 야생에서 안전하게 살아 남은 흰코뿔소의 수가 위험할 정도로 적다는 것을 보여 준다.

해설 survive는 '생존하다' 는 의미의 자동사로 여기서는 앞에 있는 명사를 수식하는 역할을 한다. 그러므로 능동의 진행형인 (c)가 정답이 된다.

5

Excessive amounts of loud music causes __________.

(a) the hearing deterioration
(b) deterioration of hear
(c) hearing to be deteriorating
(d) hearing to deteriorate

과도하게 시끄러운 음악은 청력을 악화시킨다.

해설 cause는 목적어 다음에 목적격 보어로 to부정사를 취하는 동사이다. 또한 여기서는 의미상 진행형이 될 이유가 없으므로 (d)가 정답이 된다. (a)가 정답이 되려면 the가 빠져야 한다.

Answers

1. (a) 2. (b) 3. (a) 4. (c) 5. (d)

Build Up

TEPS 전 문법 요소가 모의고사 형식으로 골고루 섞인 4파트의 문제
를 골고루 풀어 본다.

▶▶ **Part I**   Fill in the blank with the most appropriate word or phrase.

1. A: How many people _______________________ for this seminar?
B: I expect at least 350 people will attend the lecture portion.

(a) will you think actually show up
(b) will actually show up you think
(c) do you think will actually show up
(d) do you actually show up will think

2. A: Hello, Ma'am. Are you finding everything satisfactory with your meal this evening?
B: Oh, yes. You said the salmon would be an excellent choice and __________.

(a) so it is
(b) so is it
(c) so doe it
(d) so it does

3. A: There's nothing better than a good massage, _______________?
B: Actually, I prefer to relax in a sauna when I can.
(a) wouldn't you think
(b) didn't you think
(c) can you think
(d) don't you think

4. A: Are you glad that the coach chose you to be the team captain?
B: Not really, I don't know if I can handle ____________.

(a) a position
(b) position
(c) that position
(d) those positions

▶▶ **Part II**   Fill in the blank with the most appropriate word or phrase.

5. A local wildlife conservation group has decided that ______________ must be relocated
to a northwestern national park.

(a) herd of purebred bison
(b) a herd of purebred bison
(c) herds of purebred bisons
(d) a herd of purebred of bisons

6. I can't stand having to drive ____________ snowy winter days.

   (a) about
   (b) in
   (c) for
   (d) on

7. I think it's funny that Jenny is so humble about her appearance, because she really is as beautiful ______________.

   (a) as they come
   (b) as she comes
   (c) as she is
   (d) as they be

8. My leg has felt one hundred percent better ____________ I had that surgery done.

   (a) although
   (b) whenever
   (c) ever since
   (d) why

▶▶ **Part III**　Identify the grammatical error in the dialogue.

9. (a) A: It will be quicker to get there if we take a taxi, won't it?
    (b) B: I don't think it will be at this time of day. Didn't you see all cars on the road?
    (c) A: Oh yeah, I guess you're right.
    (d) B: We should probably just take the subway, or else we'll be really late.

10. (a) A: Hi, I'm here to drop some children off for Children's Day.
    (b) B: Okay, great. You just have to sign all their names and leave a contact number.
    (c) A: Sure. Will the children wait out here until I've finished?
    (d) B: No, they can go in now. Just make sure they each get a nametag.

▶▶ **Part IV**　Identify the ungrammatical sentence in the passage.

11. (a) Blue prints are extremely important and useful tools for homeowners. (b) The architects, when designing the house, create a drawing from a bird's eye view to scale. (c) Utilized this map during construction, the electrical engineers add marks to the drawing showing where and how they have installed the house's electrical wiring. (d) This communication by means of the blue prints proves to be a necessity when modifications are made years down the road.

12. (a) Although my real name is Nicholas, I've always preferred to call Tim. (b) Most of the time people get confused when I tell them this; however, it goes all the way back to my early childhood, and it seems more normal to me. (c) My cousin would always call me Tim as a joke, and I always did so many things with him. (d) The name engrained itself in my impressionable head and I learned to like it.

정답:218p

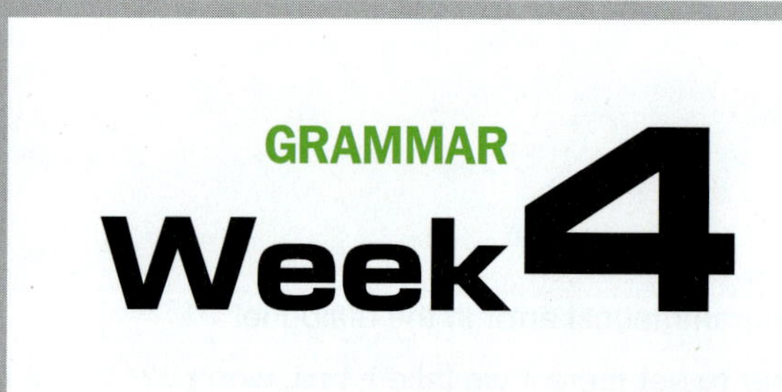
GRAMMAR
Week 4

Day 16	▶▶ 어순

1. 사역동사의 쓰임을 알아둔다.
2. 사역동사는 목적격 보어로 현재분사가 올 수 없다.
3. 간접의문문의 순서를 파악해 둔다.

Day 17	▶▶ 일치

1. 명사와 대명사의 수 일치를 확인한다.
2. 선행사와의 수 일치를 확인한다.
3. 시험에 잘 나오는 수 일치 관련 표현을 익혀둔다.

Day 18	▶▶ 도치 구문을 잡아라

1. 부정부사가 문두에 오게 되면 도치가 일어난다.
2. so와 such의 어순을 익혀둔다.
3. so 뒤에 문장이 올 때 도치가 되는 경우를 알아둔다.

Day 19	▶▶ Part III를 바로잡자

1. Part III는 대화체이므로 LC에서 Part I과 III의 대화체를 자주 따라 읽고 익혀둔다.
2. Part III에서 동사 위주로 틀린 곳을 찾아본다.
3. Part III에서 자주 출제되는 포인트를 알아둔다.

Day 20	▶▶ Part IV가 고득점의 관문이다

1. Part IV는 하나의 글이기 때문에 전체적인 시제의 일치를 보아야 한다.
2. 자동사가 수동태로 쓰이지 않았는지 확인한다.
3. Part IV에 자주 출제되는 포인트를 알아둔다.

Day 17
일치

대명사의 수 일치, 주어와 동사의 수 일치, 선행사의 수 일치 등은 시험에 자주 나온다. 특히 Part Ⅲ나 Part Ⅳ에서 수 일치 문제가 자주 등장하니 주의하도록 한다.

1. 수 일치에서 확인해야 할 것

① 대명사의 수를 확인해야 한다.
② 동사와 멀리 떨어져 있는 주어의 수가 일치하는지 확인해야 한다.
③ 선행사의 수와 일치하는지 확인한다.

2. 시험에 잘 나오는 수의 일치

1) 기간, 거리, 가격, 무게를 나타내는 복수 명사가 '하나의 단위'를 나타내는 경우 단수 취급을 한다.
   Twenty pounds is all I've got. 20파운드가 내가 가진 전부이다.

2) 복수 취급하는 표현
   both A and B: A와 B 둘 다
   the + 형용사 = 복수 보통 명사

3) 동사 가까이에 있는 명사에 수를 일치시키는 표현들
   Either A or B A 또는 B
   Neither A nor B A도 B도 아닌
   Not only A but also B A뿐만 아니라 B 역시
   일부를 나타내는 표현 most of~, the majority of ~, the rest of ~, half of ~, 분수 of ~
   Neither the students nor the driver was responsible for the accident.
   학생들이나 운전자는 그 사고에 책임이 없다.

4) **the number of** ~의 숫자(단수취급)
   a number of 많은(복수취급)

   The number of people attending the fashion show decreases every year.
   그 패션쇼에 참석하는 사람의 숫자는 매년 줄어든다.

3. 주어와 동사의 수 일치

The students in this room are watching the movie _Hero_.
이 교실에 있는 학생들은 영화 '히어로'를 보고 있다.
〈선행사 + 주격 관계대명사 + 동사〉의 수 일치
Julie isn't the only girl that/who has a laptop. 줄리가 노트북을 가지고 있는 유일한 소녀는 아니다.

4. 명사와 대명사의 수 일치

I met Jane and Tom and had some fun with them. 나는 제인과 탐을 만나서 재미있게 놀았다.

# Catch Up 

일치 관련 TEPS 주요 문제들을 풀어보도록 한다.

Part I Fill in the blank with the most appropriate word or phrase.

1. A: __________ there enough seats for all of us?
B: I think we're going to need at least three more chairs.

(a) Is
(b) Was
(c) Are
(d) Were

Part II Fill in the blank with the most appropriate word or phrase.

2. King Crab Legs __________ one of the area's culinary specialties.

(a) are
(b) is
(c) were
(d) was

3. A species of reptile __________ to be extinct, but a specimen has been found in the Brazilian rain forests.

(a) thought
(b) were thought
(c) was thought
(d) was thinking

4. Either grilled cheese or tacos __________ served for lunch today.

(a) is being
(b) be
(c) have been
(d) are being

Part IV Identify the ungrammatical sentence in the passage.

5. (a) Many people have always promoted education as a way to guarantee one's success. (b) However, in the modern world a university degree doesn't always cut it anymore. (c) A majority of employers looks for other qualities nowadays, including work experience and networking skills. (d) It has become increasingly important for young job seekers to acquire strong communication and interpersonal qualities.

Answers 

Catch Up에서 푼 문제의 해석과 해설을 점검한다.

1

A: __________ there enough seats for all of us? B: I think we're going to need at least three more chairs. (a) Is (b) Was (c) Are (d) Were	A: 우리 모두를 위해 충분한 좌석이 있니? B: 내 생각엔 적어도 의자가 세 개 더 필요할 것 같은데.

해설 〈there+동사〉 문장은 동사를 뒤에 나온 주어인 명사의 수에 일치시킨다. 여기서는 주어가 seats이므로 복수 동사가 와야 한다.

2

King Crab Legs __________ one of the area's culinary specialties. (a) are (b) is (c) were (d) was	킹크랩 레그스는 그 지역의 요리 특산품 중 하나이다.

해설 King Crab Legs는 고유명사로 게 종류의 하나이므로 단수 취급해야 한다. 그러므로 (b)가 정답이 된다.

3

A species of reptile __________ to be extinct, but a specimen has been found in the Brazilian rain forests.

(a) thought
(b) were thought
(c) was thought
(d) was thinking

파충류 종은 멸종되었다고 여겨졌는데 표본이 브라질의 열대우림에서 발견되었다.

해설 species는 '(분류상의) 종'의 의미로 단수 취급한다. 그러므로 단수 동사가 와야 하며 의미상 '여겨졌다'는 수동이 되어야 하므로 (c)가 정답이 된다.

4

Either grilled cheese or tacos __________ served for lunch today.

(a) is being
(b) be
(c) have been
(d) are being

구운 치즈나 타코가 오늘 점심에 나올 예정이다.

해설 either A or B는 'A 혹은 B'라는 의미로 B에 오는 명사의 수에 동사의 수를 일치시킨다. tacos라는 복수 명사가 왔으므로 (d)가 정답이 된다.

5

(a) Many people have always promoted education as a way to guarantee one's success. (b) However, in the modern world a university degree doesn't always cut it anymore. (c) A majority of employers (looks for → look for) other qualities nowadays, including work experience and networking skills. (d) It has become increasingly important for young job seekers to acquire strong communication and interpersonal qualities.

(a) 많은 사람들은 항상 그들의 성공을 확실히 하는 방법으로 교육을 장려해왔다. (b) 그러나 현대 사회에서 대학 졸업장은 더 이상 언제나 효과적이지는 않다. (c) 요즘 고용주의 대부분은 일의 경험과 네트워크 실력 등 다른 특성을 찾는다. (d) 젊은 취업생들에게는 대화나 대인 관계를 잘 이해하는 능력을 키우는 것이 더욱 더 중요하게 되었다.

해설 〈a majority of + 명사〉는 of 이하의 명사의 수에 동사의 수를 일치시킨다. 명사 employers가 복수이므로 look for로 고치는 것이 적절하다.

어휘 quality 특성　interpersonal 대인 관계의

Answers

1. (c)　2. (b)　3. (c)　4. (d)　5. (c) looks for → look for

Build Up 

TEPS 전 문법 요소가 모의고사 형식으로 골고루 섞인 4파트의 문제
를 골고루 풀어 본다.

▶▶ **Part I**   Fill in the blank with the most appropriate word or phrase.

1. A: Honey, should I wear the black dress __________ the red one?
B: I think the red one looks fabulous.

(a) or
(b) either
(c) as much as
(d) and

2. A: I am so excited about the wedding tomorrow.
B: So am I. I'm sure it __________ be a great event.

(a) should
(b) would
(c) might
(d) will

3. A: Should we drive home Saturday night or Sunday morning?
B: I think Saturday night is better, but __________ is fine with me since you're driving.

(a) neither
(b) both
(c) every
(d) either

4. A: Eddie's taco dip wasn't __________ delicious.
B: I disagree! It was the best taco dip I've ever tasted.

(a) that
(b) much
(c) far
(d) such

▶▶ **Part II**   Fill in the blank with the most appropriate word or phrase.

5. Tracy's room is a lot more organized than her little brother __________.

(a) Jimmy's is
(b) Jimmy is
(c) Is Jimmy
(d) Jimmy

6. I have always wanted to know ________________ to be a Hollywood movie star.

(a) what is it like
(b) what was it like
(c) what it was like
(d) what it is like

7. I had no idea that Dad had so much __________ about Iranian history.

(a) insights
(b) an insight
(c) insight
(d) the insight

8. The more I study and prepare myself for the exam, __________ I will do well on it.

(a) likely
(b) likelier
(c) more likely
(d) the more likely

▶▶ **Part III**   Identify the grammatical error in the dialogue.

9. (a) A: What's the most difficult part about having a husband who travels a lot?
(b) B: One thing that is hard is being alone with the kids.
(c) A: Is there anything else that makes it difficult?
(d) B: Yes, I just miss him and want to speak him.

10. (a) A: Mina, I just need a break! My boss has been driven me crazy!
(b) B: Oh, no! Work's been that tough, huh?
(c) A: Yes! Not only do we have multiple deadlines, but my boss is so demanding!
(d) B: I' m sorry. Is there anything I can do to help you?

▶▶ **Part IV**   Identify the ungrammatical sentence in the passage.

11. (a) My parents are very overprotective and caring about everything I do. (b) They call me every other day because they concerned about my health and wellbeing. (c) My mom sends me cookies and snacks at the beginning of each month. (d) Also, even though I work, my dad makes sure that I have enough money in my checking account at all times.

12. (a) HIV/AIDS is a deadly disease that has been on the rise in the past decade. (b) The problem with HIV/AIDS, however, is that drastic symptoms appear much later in the sickness. (c) Therefore, many people live without knowing that they have the deadly disease and can consequently spread it to the others. (d) That is why it is important for people to receive proper HIV/AIDS education.

정답:221p

GRAMMAR
Week 4

Day 16 ▶▶ 어순
1. 사역동사의 쓰임을 알아둔다.
2. 사역동사는 목적격 보어로 현재분사가 올 수 없다.
3. 간접의문문의 순서를 파악해 둔다.

Day 17 ▶▶ 일치
1. 명사와 대명사의 수 일치를 확인한다.
2. 선행사와의 수 일치를 확인한다.
3. 시험에 잘 나오는 수 일치 관련 표현을 익혀둔다.

Day 18 ▶▶ 도치 구문을 잡아라
1. 부정부사가 문두에 오게 되면 도치가 일어난다.
2. so와 such의 어순을 익혀둔다.
3. so 뒤에 문장이 올 때 도치가 되는 경우를 알아둔다.

Day 19 ▶▶ Part III를 바로잡자
1. Part III는 대화체이므로 LC에서 Part I과 III의 대화체를 자주 따라 읽고 익혀둔다.
2. Part III에서 동사 위주로 틀린 곳을 찾아본다.
3. Part III에서 자주 출제되는 포인트를 알아둔다.

Day 20 ▶▶ Part IV가 고득점의 관문이다
1. Part IV는 하나의 글이기 때문에 전체적인 시제의 일치를 보아야 한다.
2. 자동사가 수동태로 쓰이지 않았는지 확인한다.
3. Part IV에 자주 출제되는 포인트를 알아둔다.

Day 18
도치 구문을 잡아라

동사와 주어의 위치가 바뀌는 도치 구문을 주의해야 한다. TEPS에는 부정 부사 관련 도치와 so와 such의 어순이 잘 나온다.

1. 강조의 도치

부정부사가 문두에 오는 경우 → 일반 동사일 경우 조동사가 주어 앞으로 도치되고, be동사일 경우는 be동사 자체가 주어 앞으로 도치된다.

부정부사 **hardly, scarcely, rarely, barely, little, no sooner, not only, only** 부사구

Not only is she pretty, but she is also smart.

그녀는 예쁠 뿐 아니라 똑똑하기도 하다.

Little did they know that he would become such a great singer.

그들은 그가 이렇게 위대한 가수가 될 줄 전혀 몰랐다.

Only on weekends is Mary able to visit her parents.

메리는 주말에만 그녀의 부모님을 방문할 수 있다.

only는 외형적으로는 부정형이 아니지만 의미상으로는 부정적인 요소를 가지고 있다. only가 문두에 오면 도치가 일어날 수 있지만 꼭 그런 것은 아니다. 하지만 시험에 나올 경우 대부분은 도치로 쓰이므로 도치의 형식으로 알아두도록 한다.

2. so와 such의 어순

1) such, many, quite, what+ a/an+형용사+명사

   The meeting lasted for half an hour. 그것은 30분 동안 계속되었다.

   It's quite a horrible story. 그것은 아주 무서운 이야기이다.

2) so , too+형용사+ a/an+ 명사

   He is so clever a boy. 그는 너무 영리한 소년이다.

   I'm not as good a storyteller as you are. 나는 당신처럼 이야기를 잘 하지 못한다.

   It's too small a T-shirt for me. 그것은 내게는 너무 작은 티셔츠다.

3) 〈so+주어+동사〉의 어순: so는 yes의 뜻이 되어 '정말 그래'의 뜻.

   〈so+동사+주어〉의 어순: so는 also의 뜻이 되어 '~도 역시 그래'의 뜻.

   Julie has a laptop and so do I. 줄리는 노트북이 있고 나도 그렇다.

Catch Up 

도치 관련 TEPS 주요 문제들을 풀어보도록 한다.

Part I   Fill in the blank with the most appropriate word or phrase.

1.   A: I'm sorry we're running late! Jeremy was _______________! He forgot to bring the files!
B: It's okay. I have some time.

(a) in such a hurry
(b) in a such hurry
(c) in so hurry
(d) in so a hurry

2.   A: Jenny is going to the hospital right now to visit her sister and her newborn baby.
B: __________, but I'll probably arrive after her.

(a) I go too
(b) So am I
(c) So I do
(d) So do I

Part II   Fill in the blank with the most appropriate word or phrase.

3.   Daniel is very young, but he is _____________ child!

(a) a so mature
(b) as so a mature
(c) so mature
(d) so mature a

4.   ______________________ a great basketball player, he is also a wonderful coach.

(a) Not only is Michael Jordan
(b) Not only Michael Jordan is
(c) It is not only Michael Jordan
(d) It is Michael Jordan not only

5.   Only if everyone gets above a 90% on the test, _____________________ a pizza party.

(a) will Mrs. Madden give
(b) will give Mrs. Madden
(c) Mrs. Madden will give
(d) Mrs. Madden be giving

Catch Up에서 푼 문제의 해석과 해설을 점검한다.

1

A: I'm sorry we're running late. Jeremy was
______________. He forgot to bring the files.
B: It's okay. I have some time.

(a) in such a hurry
(b) in a such hurry
(c) in so hurry
(d) in so a hurry

A: 늦어서 죄송해요. 제러미가 서둘러서 파일을
가져오는 것을 잊었어요.
B: 괜찮아요. 시간이 있어요.

해설 in a hurry는 '급하게, 조급하게' 라는 의미이다. such가 올 경우 〈such + a/an + (형용사) + 명사〉의 어순이 된다. 그러므로 (a)가
정답이 된다.

2

A: Jenny is going to the hospital right now to visit
her sister and her newborn baby.
B: ______________, but I'll probably arrive after her.

(a) I go too
(b) So am I
(c) So I do
(d) So do I

A: 제니는 지금 그녀의 여동생과 동생의 아기를
보기 위해 병원에 가고 있어.
B: 나도 마찬가지야. 그런데 아마 그녀보다 늦게
도착할 것 같아.

해설 〈so + 동사 + 주어〉의 어순이 될 때 so는 also의 뜻이 되어 '~도 역시 그래' 의 의미이다. 여기에서는 동사구 is going to~를 받고
있으므로 be동사 am이 되어야 한다.

3

Daniel is very young, but he is ________________ child!

(a) a so mature
(b) as so a mature
(c) so mature
(d) so mature a

다니엘은 매우 어리지만 정말 성숙한 아이이다.

해설 〈so + 형용사 + a/an + 명사〉의 어순이다. 그러므로 (d)가 정답이 된다.

4

________________ a great basketball player, he is also a wonderful coach.

(a) Not only is Michael Jordan
(b) Not only Michael Jordan is
(c) It is not only Michael Jordan
(d) It is Michael Jordan not only

마이클 조던은 뛰어난 농구 선수일 뿐만 아니라 훌륭한 코치이기도 하다.

해설 not only A but also B는 'A뿐만 아니라 B도 역시' 라는 의미로 not only가 문두에 오게 되면 문장의 도치가 이루어진다. 그러므로 (a)의 어순이 정답이 된다.

5

Only if everyone gets above a 90% on the test, ________________ a pizza party.

(a) will Mrs. Madden give
(b) will give Mrs. Madden
(c) Mrs. Madden will give
(d) Mrs. Madden be giving

모든 사람이 그 테스트에서 90% 이상을 받을 때에만 매든 선생님은 모두에게 피자를 사 주실 것이다.

해설 only는 외형적으로는 부정형이 아니지만 의미상으로 부정적인 요소를 포함하고 있다. 다시 말해 모든 사람이 테스트에서 90% 이상 받을 때만 Madden 선생님이 피자를 사주실 것이란 이야기는 모두가 90% 이상을 받지 않으면 피자를 못 먹게 된다는 것이다. 따라서 부정 도치 구문으로 이때 문장의 도치가 이루어진다. 그러므로 (a)의 어순이 가장 적절하다.

Answers

1. (a) 2. (b) 3. (d) 4. (a) 5. (a)

Build Up

TEPS 전 문법 요소가 모의고사 형식으로 골고루 섞인 4파트의 문제를 골고루 풀어 본다.

▶▶ Part I Fill in the blank with the most appropriate word or phrase.

1. A: What kind of restaurant do you want to take your parents to tonight?
B: _______________ they feel like eating, I'll be happy with their decision.

(a) Whichever
(b) Whatever
(c) When
(d) What

2. A: I don't think we can make it to the movie, the hour has become late.
B: That's okay. We can see it _______________.

(a) another time
(b) the other time
(c) other time
(d) for the time

3. A: I think we might get stuck in heavy traffic.
B: I _______________. We can't be late today.

(a) hope not it
(b) hope no
(c) don't hope
(d) hope not

▶▶ Part II Fill in the blank with the most appropriate word or phrase.

4. The success of the golf outing depends _______________ the weather next weekend.

(a) about
(b) for
(c) of
(d) on

5. My grandfather likes to tell me that he only had to pay a nickel for a coke when he _______________ a kid.

(a) had been
(b) was
(c) is
(d) could be

6. _______________ since she was ten years old, Amber has high expectations about competing in the Olympics next year.

(a) Training
(b) Having trained
(c) To train
(d) To have trained

7. Many health concerns ____________ to cigarettes, for smokers and nonsmokers alike.

(a) are attributed
(b) have attributed
(c) attribute
(d) were attributing

8. David began ____________ during class for no reason at all.

(a) to laughing
(b) of laughing
(c) laughing
(d) laughter

▶▶ **Part III** Identify the grammatical error in the dialogue.

9. (a) A: I hiked that mountain last year. It's a great hike.
(b) B: That one too? Are there any mountains you haven't hiked?
(c) A: Well, I have yet to climb tall mountain in the state.
(d) B: Maybe I'll come with you when you finally do.

10. (a) A: Where have you been for the past three weeks?
(b) B: I was vacationing on an island in the South Pacific.
(c) A: That sounds like fun. Who did you go with?
(d) B: I went by myself. I just wanted to relax for few weeks.

▶▶ **Part IV** Identify the ungrammatical sentence in the passage.

11. (a) Recently there have been complaints that food and beverages are being brought into the library. (b) I would like to remind all students that absolutely anyone is not allowed to bring either food or beverages inside the building. (c) The remnants of snacks have been attracting insects and rodents, both of which are great hazards to a library. (d) Not only can these pests disturb students and faculty, but they can also cause irreparable damage to our books.

12. (a) Thomas Jefferson is widely known as the third President of the United States of America, he was also successful in many other areas of study. (b) Many people don't know that Jefferson had a great knowledge and talent in the study of architecture. (c) He helped to make the Neo-Palladian style of architecture popular in America, and he designed his own home in Virginia, the now-famous Monticello. (d) On top of that, he invented multiple modern amenities, such as the swivel chair, for his home.　　정답 : 223p

GRAMMAR
Week 4

Day 16	▶▶ 어순

1. 사역동사의 쓰임을 알아둔다.
2. 사역동사는 목적격 보어로 현재분사가 올 수 없다.
3. 간접의문문의 순서를 파악해 둔다.

Day 17	▶▶ 일치

1. 명사와 대명사의 수 일치를 확인한다.
2. 선행사와의 수 일치를 확인한다.
3. 시험에 잘 나오는 수 일치 관련 표현을 익혀둔다.

Day 18	▶▶ 도치 구문을 잡아라

1. 부정부사가 문두에 오게 되면 도치가 일어난다.
2. so와 such의 어순을 익혀둔다.
3. so 뒤에 문장이 올 때 도치가 되는 경우를 알아둔다.

Day 19	▶▶ Part III를 바로잡자

1. Part III는 대화체이므로 LC에서 Part I과 III의 대화체를 자주 따라 읽고 익혀둔다.
2. Part III에서 동사 위주로 틀린 곳을 찾아본다.
3. Part III에서 자주 출제되는 포인트를 알아둔다.

Day 20	▶▶ Part IV가 고득점의 관문이다

1. Part IV는 하나의 글이기 때문에 전체적인 시제의 일치를 보아야 한다.
2. 자동사가 수동태로 쓰이지 않았는지 확인한다.
3. Part IV에 자주 출제되는 포인트를 알아둔다.

Day 19

Part Ⅲ를 바로잡자

▶▶ Part III는 대화문이다. 관용적인 표현은 LC 스크립트를 많이 따라 읽음으로써 자연스럽게 표현을 익히도록 한다. 동사 위주로 찾아보고, 시험에 자주 출제 되었던 부분들을 점검하도록 한다.

1. 관사의 missing을 찾아라.

관용적인 부정관사가 빠지지 않았는지 확인한다.

Have good time. (X) → Have a good time. (O)
(time 앞에는 보통 관사가 붙지 않지만 형용사가 오게 되면 부정관사가 붙는다.)

2. 수의 일치

대명사의 수 일치, 주어와 동사의 수 일치, 선행사와 동사의 수 일치를 확인한다.

3. 대부정사 문제가 아닌지 확인한다.

대부정사는 to부정사를 취하는 동사에서 동사구의 반복을 피하기 위해 to만 쓰는 것을 의미한다.

4. 관사의 쓰임이 제대로 되었는지 확인한다.

부정관사(불특정한 단수 명사를 수식함)와 정관사(특정한 단수/복수의 명사를 수식함)의 차이를 알아두자.

5. 조동사의 의미가 제대로 쓰였는지 확인한다.

조동사 관련 문제는 보통 해석을 통해 오류를 찾아야 하므로 문맥을 해석하여 오류를 찾아본다.

6. 어순

도치: 부정부사(hardly, scarcely, rarely, barely, little, no sooner, not only, only 부사구)가 문두에 오면 도치가 이루어진다.
　　간접의문문(의문사＋주어＋동사)
　　동사＋대명사＋부사

Check out it. (X) → Check it out. (O) (동사와 부사 사이에 대명사는 가운데 위치한다.)

7. 전치사 to와 to부정사를 구별한다.

〈자동사＋전치사 to〉의 표현을 알아둔다.

8. 보어로 부사가 올 수 없다.

It makes the culture uniquely. (X)
It makes the culture unique. (O)
그것이 그 문화를 독특하게 만든다.

# Catch Up 

Part III   Identify the grammatical error in the dialogue.

1. (a) A: You're going to the Aerosmith concert tomorrow, right?
(b) B: Actually, I won't be able because my boss called a last-minute meeting.
(c) A: What a shame! What did you do with your ticket?
(d) B: Well, it worked out. I gave it to my sister because she loves Aerosmith.

2. (a) A: Michael Jackson's new song went from top of the charts to number seven.
(b) B: Wow! His new song was number one?
(c) A: Yeah, it was up there for three weeks.
(d) B: That's quite a comeback.

3. (a) A: What are you doing for your parents' fiftieth anniversary?
(b) B: My siblings and I bought them an all expense paid trip to New Zealand.
(c) A: Wow! Have they ever been there?
(d) B: No, and it'll be in years the first time that they have traveled outside of the country.

4. (a) A: Were you scared while you were home alone?
(b) B: Yes! I heard loud sounds at the door.
(c) A: What did they sound like? Was it like a scratching sound?
(d) B: No, it was more of pounding noise, as if someone was trying to break the door.

5. (a) A: Have you seen my keys?
(b) B: I thought I saw them on top of the kitchen table.
(c) A: Oh, boy! I'm in a rush. I'd look for it there first.
(d) B: Let me know if you need any help!

1

(a) A: You're going to the Aerosmith concert tomorrow, right?
(b) B: Actually, I won't (be able → **be able to**) because my boss called a last-minute meeting.
(c) A: What a shame! What did you do with your ticket?
(d) B: Well, it worked out. I gave it to my sister because she loves Aerosmith.

(a) A: 너 내일 에어로스미스 콘서트 갈 거지?
(b) B: 아니. 사장이 막바지에 회의를 소집해서 못 갈 것 같아.
(c) A: 안됐다! 티켓은 어떻게 했니?
(d) B: 해결됐어. 내 여동생에게 줬어. 에어로스미스를 좋아하거든.

해설 대부정사 문제이다. 대부정사는 to부정사를 취하는 동사에서 동사구의 반복을 피하기 위해 to만 쓰는 것을 의미한다. be able to는 '~할 수 있다' 는 의미로 to를 생략해서는 안 된다.

2

(a) A: Michael Jackson's new song went from (top → **the top**) of the charts to number seven.
(b) B: Wow! His new song was number one?
(c) A: Yeah, it was up there for three weeks.
(d) B: That's quite a comeback.

(a) A: 마이클 잭슨의 새 노래가 차트 1위에서 7위로 내려갔대.
(b) B: 와! 새 노래가 1위였어?
(c) A: 응, 3주간이나 했는 걸.
(d) B: 근사한 컴백인 걸.

해설 관사 문제이다. top은 '수석, 일등, 최고' 의 의미가 있을 때 the와 함께 쓰인다. 여기서는 the charts 중에서 제일 위에 있는 '1위 (the top)' 를 뜻하므로 the가 같이 쓰여야 한다.

3

(a) A: What are you doing for your parents' fiftieth anniversary?
(b) B: My siblings and I bought them an all expense paid trip to New Zealand.
(c) A: Wow! Have they ever been there?
(d) B: No, and it'll be (in years the first time → **the first time in years**) that they have traveled outside of the country.

(a) A: 부모님 50주년 결혼기념일에 넌 뭘 해드릴 거니?
(b) B: 형제들과 함께 경비가 모두 포함된 뉴질랜드 여행 티켓을 사 드렸어.
(c) A: 와! 거기 가 보신 적이 있으셔?
(d) B: 아니, 이번이 연세드신 후에 외국으로 가시는 첫 번째 여행이 되실 거야.

해설 문장의 어순과 관련된 문제이다. 의미상 be동사의 보어로 the first time이 와야 하고 in years는 전치사구로서 부사의 역할을 하므로 그 뒤에 위치하는 것이 옳다.

4

<table>
<tr><td>

(a) A: Were you scared while you were home alone?

(b) B: Yes! I heard loud sounds at the door.

(c) A: What did they sound like? Was it like a scratching sound?

(d) B: No, it was more of (pounding noise → a punding noise), as if someone was trying to break the door.

</td><td>

(a) A: 집에 혼자 있을 때 무서웠니?

(b) B: 응! 문에서 큰 소리를 들었어.

(c) A: 무슨 소리였는데? 뭔가 긁는 소리였어?

(d) B: 아니, 시끄럽게 두드리는 소리 같았어. 마치 누군가 문을 부수려고 한 것처럼 말이야.

</td></tr>
</table>

해설 more of에서 more은 대명사로 '그 이상의 것' 이라는 의미가 있다. noise는 '소음' 이라는 일반적인 의미일 때에는 불가산명사이지만 여기서는 '어떤' 소리의 의미로 사용되었다. 그러므로 a와 함께 쓰여야 한다.

5

<table>
<tr><td>

(a) A: Have you seen my keys?

(b) B: I thought I saw them on top of the kitchen table.

(c) A: Oh, boy! I'm in a rush. (I'd look → I'll look) for it there first.

(d) B: Let me know if you need any help!

</td><td>

(a) A: 내 열쇠 봤니?

(b) B: 부엌 테이블 위에서 본 것 같은데.

(c) A: 이런, 급한데. 거기를 먼저 찾아볼게.

(d) B: 도움이 필요하면 얘기해!

</td></tr>
</table>

해설 조동사 관련 문제이다. 여기서는 의미상 바로 열쇠를 찾아보겠다는 의미가 되므로 주어의 의지를 강하게 나타내는 미래 조동사 will이 적절하다.

Answers

1. (b) be able → be able to 2. (a) top → the top 3. (d) in years the first time → the first time in years
4. (d) pounding noise → a pounding noise 5. (c) I'd look → I'll look

Build Up 

TEPS 전 문법 요소가 모의고사 형식으로 골고루 섞인 4파트의 문제를 골고루 풀어 본다.

Part I Fill in the blank with the most appropriate word or phrase.

1. A: Where is the new sushi restaurant located?
B: It's ___________ the street from the pizzeria.

(a) under
(b) across
(c) through
(d) beyond

2. A: Does John know that the concert has been rescheduled?
B: I will tell him that the concert has been delayed when he ___________.

(a) will come
(b) comes
(c) was coming
(d) came

3. A: ___________________ to get an A$^+$ on the paper when she is busy with two jobs?
B: She is very studious and manages her time well.

(a) How do you think did Janice manage
(b) How do you think did manage Janice
(c) How do you think Janice manage
(d) How do you think Janice managed

4. A: Nathan ___________ run six miles every morning until he tore his Achilles' heel.
B: Oh, so that's why he doesn't run anymore.

(a) ought to
(b) used to
(c) will
(d) did

Part II Fill in the blank with the most appropriate word or phrase.

5. ___________________________ continue to fight and delay every group project.

(a) It is the two employees who
(b) The two employees who
(c) When the two employees who
(d) Which are the two employees who

6. Not all of the students were doing well, ______________, since some of them were failing the tests.

    (a) it seems
    (b) it seeming
    (c) seemed
    (d) seeming

7. The dinner included many types of foods, most of which ______________ my favorite to eat.

    (a) is
    (b) have
    (c) are
    (d) has

8. Michael, ______________ lovingly at his sleeping daughter, whispered "good night."

    (a) smiles
    (b) smiled
    (c) smiling
    (d) was smiling

▶▶ **Part III**   Identify the grammatical error in the dialogue.

9. (a) A: Henry bought Sony laptop from Circuit City.
    (b) B: He always wanted it. How much was it.
    (c) A: It was on sale for $400.
    (d) B: He got very lucky.

10. (a) A: The troops need more medical assistance and resources as soon as possible!
    (b) B: They'll receive some soon since the president sent medical teams over.
    (c) A: Yes, but that must have been done sooner before hundreds of soldiers died.
    (d) B: It's better late than never.

▶▶ **Part IV**   Identify the ungrammatical sentence in the passage.

11. (a) The YMCA recently developed a new community outreach program for the impoverished youth in this area. (b) They provide practical lessons about life. (c) The lessons cover a broad range of topics like drugs, gangs, abuse, family, and even poverty. (d) The program not only gives general information about these topics, but they also teach children how can they deal with such issues.

12. (a) Sometimes, cancer can be completely eliminated if treatment began in its early stages. (b) If cancer is detected in its early stages, doctors can remove cancerous cells before they spread to other parts of the body. (c) However, it is almost impossible to get rid of cancerous cells once they spread throughout the body, especially to vital organs. (d) That is why it is extremely important to get yearly health checkups.

정답:225p

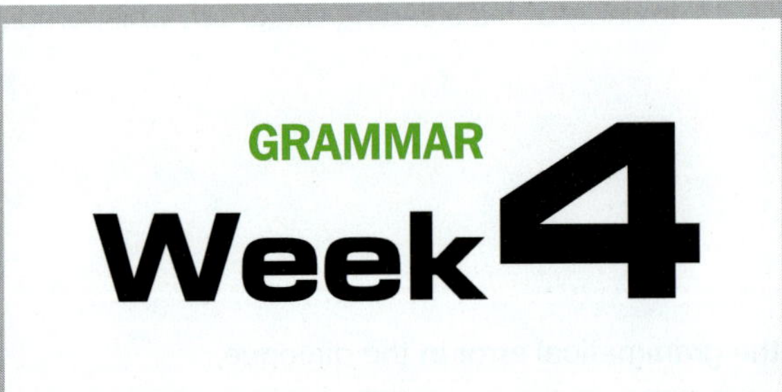

Day 16 ▶▶ 어순

1. 사역동사의 쓰임을 알아둔다.
2. 사역동사는 목적격 보어로 현재분사가 올 수 없다.
3. 간접 의문문의 순서를 파악해 둔다.

Day 17 ▶▶ 일치

1. 명사와 대명사의 수 일치를 확인한다.
2. 선행사와의 수 일치를 확인한다.
3. 시험에 잘 나오는 수 일치 관련 표현을 익혀둔다.

Day 18 ▶▶ 도치 구문을 잡아라

1. 부정부사가 문두에 오게 되면 도치가 일어난다.
2. so와 such의 어순을 익혀둔다.
3. so 뒤에 문장이 올 때 도치가 되는 경우를 알아둔다.

Day 19 ▶▶ Part III를 바로잡자

1. Part III는 대화체이므로 LC에서 Part I과 III의 대화체를 자주 따라 읽고 익혀둔다.
2. Part III에서 동사 위주로 틀린 곳을 찾아본다.
3. Part III에서 자주 출제되는 포인트를 알아둔다.

Day 20  ▶▶ Part IV가 고득점 관문이다

1. Part IV는 하나의 글이기 때문에 전체적인 시제의 일치를 보아야 한다.
2. 자동사가 수동태로 쓰이지 않았는지 확인한다.
3. Part IV에 자주 출제되는 포인트를 알아둔다.

동사 위주로 오류를 먼저 찾아본다. 한 문장을 따로 떼어 놓았을 때의 오류뿐 아니라 전체 문맥 내의 시제 불일치 문제도 있으니 전체 단락을 파악한다.

1. 시제가 일치하는지 확인한다.

전체적인 내용이 일반적인 사실을 나타내고 있어서 현재시제로 나타내고 있는데 한 문장만 과거시제를 썼다면 의심해야 한다.

2. 수동태를 주목하라.

수동태의 동사 뒤에 목적어가 있으면 4형식 수여동사가 아닌 이상 오류이다. 또한 자동사(arrive, become, remain, appear, disappear, fall, come, occur)가 수동태가 되어 있지 않은지 확인하라.

3. 접속사

의미상 적절한 접속사가 쓰였는지 확인하고, 접속사 없이 두 개의 문장이 있으면 접속사를 넣어야 한다.

He loves Mary so much, but he popped the question to her. (X)
He loves Mary so much, so he popped the question to her. (O)

그는 메리를 사랑해서 청혼을 했다.

4. 분사와 분사구문을 주목하라.

분사구문의 주어와 주절의 주어가 논리적으로 연결되는지 확인한다.

Looking at the evidence, a decision was made. (X)
Looking at the evidence, they made a decision. (O)

증거를 보고 그들은 결정했다.

5. 관계대명사를 확인하라.

관계대명사 뒤에 완벽한 문장이 있다면 이것이 범인이다. 단, 접속사 that 뒤에는 완벽한 문장이 올 수 있다.

There is a famous spot which hundreds of tourists come every year in the city. (X)
There is a famous spot in which/where hundreds of tourists come every year in the city. (O)

그 도시에는 매년 수백 명의 관광객이 오는 유명한 장소가 있다.

6. 수의 일치

주어와 동사, 선행사와 동사의 수 일치, 대명사의 수일치, 수식어와 피수식어의 일치 등을 확인한다.

Part IV Identify the ungrammatical sentence in the passage.

1. (a) Graphs have long been one of the most effective visual aids available when given presentations. (b) There are many different types of graphs, such as bar graphs, pie charts, and line graphs, each having their own benefits to particular situations. (c) The visual aspect of a graph can attract attention as well as relate a large amount of information in an easy-to-understand manner. (d) Furthermore, modern computer technology has reduced the amount of work required to create a visually appealing graph.

2. (a) Washington High School of the Arts is now accepting applications for the upcoming school year. (b) An application may be submitted by any student who will be beginning ninth grade in the fall. (c) However, the students who would be accepted to the school must show an already developed talent and a dedication to the further development of their art. (d) We would like to discourage any student from applying if he or she cannot provide references capable of confirming the student's excellence and experience in the chosen artistic field.

3. (a) City hall has announced a meeting, scheduled for next Wednesday evening, which will address the issue of the intersection at Main Street and Murray Avenue. (b) For many years this intersection has been notorious for the large number of car accident which occur there. (c) The meeting will begin with a discussion of the problem and a number of civil engineers proposing solutions. (d) There will then be an open floor debate, at which citizens of the city may give their opinions regarding the different solutions that are presented.

4. (a) There are many situations in our daily lives in which we find ourselves vulnerable as pedestrians. (b) With the number of cars on the street continually rising, how we can expect to safely cross or walk near a busy street? (c) Learning to look both ways before crossing a street must be taught to children at an early age if we want to be sure that they will grow to be conscious of the extreme danger involved in stepping onto a street. (d) The most important lesson they can learn is to be always aware of their surroundings, and especially of automobiles on the streets.

5. (a) Mozart is one of the most well known musicians to have ever lived. (b) He is considered by many to be the greatest composer in the history of western music. (c) Even today, students who began to study music are required to examine his compositions closely in order to recognize the revolutionary techniques that he applied. (d) More than three hundred years after his death, he continues to be a great influence and teacher to students all over the world.

Answers

Catch Up에서 푼 문제의 해석과 해설을 점검한다.

1

(a) Graphs have long been one of the most effective visual aids available when (given → **giving**) presentations. (b) There are many different types of graphs, such as bar graphs, pie charts, and line graphs, each having their own benefits to particular situations. (c) The visual aspect of a graph can attract attention as well as relate a large amount of information in an easy-to-understand manner. (d) Furthermore, modern computer technology has reduced the amount of work required to create a visually appealing graph.

(a) 그래프는 프레젠테이션을 보여 줄 때 가장 효과적인 시각 도구 중의 하나가 되어 왔다. (b) 그래프에는 각각의 특별한 상황에 맞는 막대 그래프, 원 그래프, 그리고 선 그래프 같은 많은 다양한 종류들이 있다. (c) 그래프의 시각적인 면은 많은 양의 정보를 쉽게 이해할 수 있는 방법으로 연관시키고 주의를 끌 수 있다. (d) 게다가 현대 컴퓨터 기술은 시각적으로 눈길을 끄는 그래프를 만들기 위해 필요한 일의 양을 줄여 왔다.

해설 분사구문 용법에 관한 문제이다. 분사구문에서는 주어가 일반인일 경우 생략이 가능하다. 여기서 의미상 원래 문장은 when you give presentations이다. 그러므로 능동 형태의 분사구문으로 바꾸는 것이 적절하다.

2

(a) Washington High School of the Arts is now accepting applications for the upcoming school year. (b) An application may be submitted by any student who will be beginning ninth grade in the fall. (c) However, the students who (would → **will**) be accepted to the school must show an already developed talent and a dedication to the further development of their art. (d) We would like to discourage any student from applying if he or she cannot provide references capable of confirming the student's excellence and experience in the chosen artistic field.

(a) 워싱턴 예술 고등학교는 내년 학기의 지원서를 받고 있습니다. (b) 가을에 9학년이 되는 학생이라면 누구나 지원서를 제출할 수 있습니다. (c) 그러나 학교에 합격되는 학생들은 이미 개발된 재능과 그들의 예술을 더욱 발전시킬 수 있는 헌신을 보여 주어야 합니다. (d) 학생의 능력과 선택 예술 분야의 경험을 확인할 수 있는 추천서를 보여줄 수 없다면 지원을 권하지 않습니다.

해설 조동사 관련 문제이다. 이 문장에서는 '학교에 합격되는 학생들은 그들의 재능과 헌신을 보여 주어야 할 것이다'라는 의미가 되어야 하므로 불확실한 추측의 would가 아닌 미래의 조동사 will이 적절하다. 합격이 불확실한 학생들이 그들의 재능과 헌신을 보여야만 한다는 것은 논리적으로 맞지 않기 때문이다.

3

(a) City hall has announced a meeting, scheduled for next Wednesday evening, which will address the issue of the intersection at Main Street and Murray Avenue. (b) For many years this intersection has been notorious for the large number of car (accident → accidents) which occur there. (c) The meeting will begin with a discussion of the problem and a number of civil engineers proposing solutions. (d) There will then be an open floor debate, at which citizens of the city may give their opinions regarding the different solutions that are presented.

(a) 시청은 다음주 수요일 저녁 메인 거리와 머리가의 교차로 문제를 다루기 위한 회의를 발표했습니다. (b) 수년 동안 이 교차로는 그곳에서 발생되는 많은 교통사고로 악명이 높았습니다. (c) 이 회의는 그 문제에 대한 토론 및 민간 기술자들이 제시하는 많은 해결책들과 함께 시작할 것입니다. (d) 그리고 제시된 다른 해결책들과 관련해서 시민들이 그들의 의견을 발표할 수 있는 공개 토론도 있을 예정입니다.

해설 수의 일치 문제이다. 관계대명사 which 앞의 선행사와 동사 occur가 일치해야 한다. 동사가 복수 취급됐으므로 앞의 선행사도 복수 명사가 와야 해서 car accidents로 바꾸어야 한다.

4

(a) There are many situations in our daily lives in which we find ourselves vulnerable as pedestrians. (b) With the number of cars on the street continually rising, (how we can expect to → how can we expect to) to safely cross or walk near a busy street? (c) Learning to look both ways before crossing a street must be taught to children at an early age if we want to be sure that they will grow to be conscious of the extreme danger involved in stepping onto a street. (d) The most important lesson they can learn is to be always aware of their surroundings, and especially of automobiles on the streets.

(a) 일상생활 속에서 우리는 보행자로서 다칠 수 있는 상황이 많다. (b) 거리에서 차의 수가 계속적으로 증가하는데 바쁜 거리에서 어떻게 안전하게 길을 건너거나 걷는 것을 기대할 수 있는가? (c) 아이들이 거리에 발을 내딛는다는 것이 매우 위험한 일이라는 것에 대한 의식을 갖기를 원한다면 길을 건너기 전에 양쪽을 모두 보는 것을 배우는 것이 어릴 때부터 가르쳐져야 한다. (d) 그들이 배울 수 있는 가장 중요한 교훈은 그들의 주변과 특히 길거리의 자동차들에 대해서 항상 인식하는 것이다.

해설 이 문장에서는 간접의문문이 아닌 직접의문문이므로 의문사 뒤의 주어와 (조)동사의 위치가 바뀌어야 한다.

어휘 vulnerable 공격받기 쉬운 pedestrian 보행자

5

(a) Mozart is one of the most well known musicians to have ever lived. (b) He is considered by many to be the greatest composer in the history of western music. (c) Even today, students who (began → **begin**) to study music are required to examine his compositions closely in order to recognize the revolutionary techniques that he applied. (d) More than three-hundred years after his death, he continues to be a great influence and teacher to students all over the world.

(a) 모짜르트는 생존했던 음악가 들 중 가장 잘 알려진 사람의 하나이다. (b) 그는 서구 음악 역사에 있어서 가장 위대한 작곡가로 많은 이들에게 알려졌다. (c) 심지어 오늘날에도 음악을 배우는 학생들은 그가 적용한 혁신적인 기술들을 알기 위해서 그의 작품을 면밀히 검토해야만 한다. (d) 그의 사후 삼백년 이상 그는 전 세계의 학생들에게 지대한 영향을 주었으며 스승이 되었다.

해설 시제 일치에 관한 문제이다. 이 문장에서는 의미상 '음악 공부를 시작했던 학생들' 이 아니라 '음악 공부를 시작하는 학생들' 을 의미하므로 과거형이 아닌 현재시제가 되어야 한다. 그러므로 현재시제 begin으로 고치는 것이 올바르다.

Answers

1. (a) given → giving 2. (c) would → will 3. (b) accident → accidents
4. (b) how we can expect to → how can we expect to 5. (c) began → begin

Build Up

TEPS 전 문법 요소가 모의고사 형식으로 골고루 섞인 4파트의 문제
를 골고루 풀어 본다.

▶▶ **Part I**   Fill in the blank with the most appropriate word or phrase.

1. A: Did you know that Tom doesn't know how to ride a bicycle?
B: Really? _____________ learn how to ride when they are children.

(a) Most of the people
(b) The most people
(c) Most people
(d) People most

2. A: Have you been to New York?
B: Yes. I _____________ there by myself soon after I graduated from college.

(a) went
(b) have been
(c) had gone
(d) have gone

3. A: When do you want to go shopping?
B: In a little while. I'm _____________________ by the neighbor kids right now.

(a) having my washed car
(b) having my car washed
(c) having my car wash
(d) washing my car

4. A: Did you have fun at the reunion?
B: It was a lot of fun, actually. There were _____________________________.

(a) 100 people we thought more than
(b) 100 more people than we thought
(c) we thought more than 100 people
(d) more than 100 people we thought

▶▶ **Part II**   Fill in the blank with the most appropriate word or phrase.

5. His principal made his options very clear: either he starts doing his homework _______
he doesn't graduate.

(a) or
(b) nor
(c) but
(d) and

6. Jeff needed to have his birth certificate in order to obtain a passport, but he couldn't find
______________ .

    (a) an original   (b) original
    (c) the original   (d) one original

7. After years of hard work and training, Alex is golfing ______________ an equal level with the
professionals.

    (a) with   (b) in
    (c) as   (d) on

8. Even though Bill ______________ his car at the moment, he still made time to play with
his children before bed.

    (a) had repaired
    (b) was repairing
    (c) has repaired
    (d) had been repairing

▶▶ **Part III**   Identify the grammatical error in the dialogue.

9. (a) A: Is it true that they will implement a new testing system next year at school?
    (b) B: Yes, it is, and it will not be for us, only for the new freshman.
    (c) A: That's a relief. I was not looking forward to an unfamiliar testing system.
    (d) B: Well, it wouldn't be fair for them to change our testing program.

10. (a) A: I don't think we should eat Italian tonight, I don't really like spaghetti.
    (b) B: You don't have to get spaghetti. How about lasagna?
    (c) A: No, I don't like neither spaghetti nor lasagna.
    (d) B: But you like pizza, right? I will split a pizza with you.

▶▶ **Part IV**   Identify the ungrammatical sentence in the passage.

11. (a) Recent studies show that the number of Americans suffering from vision loss or
blindness is increasing at a rapid rate. (b) Eye diseases most common affect middle-
aged and elderly people. (c) As the children of the baby-boomer era grow up and
technological advances allow people to live longer, the number of elderly people
increases by great strides. (d) Studies project that nearly six-million Americans could
suffer from eye diseases by the year 2020, thus increasing the burden upon both local
and national governments.

12. (a) Recently, voices around the community have been calling for the conservation of our
countryside. (b) The natural beauty of the town attracts developers who want to destroy
the land by building both residentially and commercially lucrative structures. (c)
However, these developments remain unwanted by local citizens. (d) A bill is in the
works, which, if passed, will be warded off the developers by officially recognizing our
surrounding lands as a state park.

정답:227p

FINAL CHECK

GRAMMAR

DIRECTIONS

The part of the exam tests your grammar skills. You will have 25 minutes to complete the 50 questions. Be sure to follow the directions given by the proctor.

1. A: Before I hire you, _____________
   me a list of references to do a
   background check.
   B: That's not a problem. I have all of the
   information with me.
   (a) I'd like to give
   (b) I'd like you to give
   (c) I'd like that you gave
   (d) I'd like you give

2. A: Have you heard what is happening
   with Jerry and his business?
   B: Yes, he's _________ attack from a
   group of animal rights activists.
   (a) under   (b) about
   (c) in   (d) by

3. A: I thought the speaker gave a really
   nice speech today.
   B: I didn't think so. In fact, a lot of the
   things he said _________ offended
   me.
   (a) all kinds of   (b) a kind of
   (c) kinds of   (d) kind of

4. A: I'm getting sick of having such long
   hair.
   B: It's probably about time that you had
   _________.
   (a) cut it   (b) the cut
   (c) it cut   (d) cutting it

5. A: Is there anyone here who wants to
   pick up Bill from the airport?
   B: Here. I _________ do it.
   (a) had to   (b) will
   (c) may   (d) would

6. A: If I _________ facing the same
   situation as you, I would get a new
   job.
   B: Thanks for your advice; I know I can
   always trust you.
   (a) was   (b) were
   (c) could be   (d) am

7. A: Hello, my truck needs _________ by
   tomorrow. Can you help me?
   B: I don't know, sir. I'll have to take a
   look at it first.
   (a) to repair
   (b) repairing
   (c) repaired
   (d) repair

8. A: How did the football team play in
   their game last weekend?
   B: _________ by the size of the other
   team's players, they didn't play very
   well.
   (a) Intimidating
   (b) To intimidate
   (c) Intimidated
   (d) Intimidation

9. A: The boss wanted me to tell you not to
   organize things that way.
   B: I know this job better than he does. I
   couldn't care _________ what he
   thinks.
   (a) any   (b) less
   (c) a little   (d) some

10. A: Did your son enjoy his first
   Christmas in a cold climate?
   B: He loved it. I can't explain to you
   ______________ to see snow for the
   first time.
   (a) how excited he was
   (b) how he was excited
   (c) how excited was he
   (d) how was excited he

11. A: Will you be able to finish your
   project before the weekend?
   B: I'm expecting ________, but I'll have
   to have complete concentration all
   week.
   (a) that   (b) about
   (c) to   (d) to do

12. A: Were you able to join the writing
   group you wanted to join?
   B: No, by the time I applied the
   committee had objected
   __________ any new members.
   (a) acceptance   (b) to accepting
   (c) to accept   (d) accepting

13. A: Did Amy go with you to the
   symphony?
   B: She _________ about going, but in
   the end decided not to.
   (a) would think
   (b) had thought
   (c) has thought
   (d) would have thought

14. A: How was the winter in Maine this
   year?
   B: We had ___________ weather. The
   snow was beautiful, but it wasn't too
   cold.
   (a) such an amazing
   (b) amazing such
   (c) an amazing such
   (d) such amazing

15. A: How ___________________
   to get to Phoenix?
   B: It's going to take at least thirteen
   hours. You might as well take a nap.
   (a) do you think it is going to take
   (b) long do you think it is going to take
   (c) long do you think is it going to take
   (d) do you think it is going to take long

16. A: Has the museum decided to build the
   addition yet?
   B: No. It was only yesterday _________
   they had the meeting, and they
   haven't reached a decision yet.
   (a) where   (b) of which
   (c) when   (d) about

17. A: Okay, kids, every _________
   person will be on the defensive team.
   B: Teacher, what happens if the teams
   are uneven?
   (a) double   (b) two
   (c) again   (d) second

18. A: Will you try to get into the advanced
   math class next year?
   B: No way. Math tests are _________
   difficult for me to get a passing grade
   in that class.
   (a) a lot   (b) far too
   (c) so much   (d) some

19. A: Jenny was thinking of bringing her
   dog along on the trip. Do you mind?
   B: Honestly, I would rather she
   _________. I'm allergic to dog hair.
   (a) couldn't   (b) can't
   (c) hadn't   (d) didn't

20. A: This is just a trial copy, right?
   B: Correct. _________ you not approve
   of the software, there will be no
   charge to your account.
   (a) Until   (b) When
   (c) Should   (d) Unless

21. The hurricane hit the southern coast of Florida hard, __________ the destruction of many homes and businesses.
(a) resulted in
(b) resulting in
(c) as a result of
(d) having resulted

22. The mountain pass rose __________ steeply that my old truck overheated on the way up.
(a) much
(b) very
(c) quite
(d) so

23. The company will remain in its current location for the holidays, __________ we are searching for a better suited location for after the New Year.
(a) however,
(b) then
(c) unless
(d) because

24. The judge demanded that all reporters and media correspondents __________ from the court room.
(a) were removed
(b) to be removed
(c) be removed
(d) are removed

25. I've always thought seeing music performed __________ to be more satisfying than listening to a record at home.
(a) alive
(b) to live
(c) live
(d) lively

26. To earn the promotion to chief inspector, you must build a reputation for examining the products __________ than others.
(a) more thoroughly
(b) most thoroughly
(c) more thorough
(d) a lot thorough

27. Before beginning the tour, there is __________ to store your coats and other belongings just inside the doors and to your left.
(a) the place
(b) a placement
(c) any place
(d) a place

28. __________________________, this university has one of the most intensive application processes in the country.
(a) All the requirements given
(b) The given all requirements
(c) Given all the requirements
(d) Giving all the requirements

29. Anyone caught trespassing on the premises after operating hours __________ immediately reported to the authorities.
(a) was
(b) were
(c) will be
(d) has been

30. A university study shows that a reevaluation of residential planning __________ many people, should another hurricane evacuation be required.
(a) can benefit
(b) can have benefited
(c) could benefit
(d) could have benefited

31. There were reports of wildlife mysteriously __________ in the area long before the disease was known to have reached this part of the world.
(a) dead   (b) dying
(c) has died   (d) died

32. Music industry experts __________ that the industry is on the verge of some major changes.
(a) are believed
(b) were believed
(c) are to believe
(d) believe

33. The defendant admitted __________ at the hotel on December 6th, but said he was having dinner at the time the crime was committed.
(a) to be stayed
(b) to stay
(c) to staying
(d) to being stayed

34. My brother is turning forty next week, but I can't imagine __________ because he still has the energy of a twenty years old.
(a) he is that old
(b) he was that old
(c) his being that old
(d) his having been that old

35. Alan became __________ musician that he was able to quit the office job he had always hated.
(a) such successful
(b) so successful a
(c) so a successful
(d) very successful

36. Ted and Mary O'Conner traveled the world for years, __________ in New Zealand.
(a) finally settling down
(b) to settle finally down
(c) finally settled down
(d) and finally settling down

37. Ted moved away from home when he was eighteen, but __________ that he would never return to his hometown again.
(a) little he knew
(b) little did he know
(c) little had he known
(d) he little knew

38. Marilyn no longer believes in love at first sight since she __________ her husband.
(a) will divorce   (b) divorces
(c) has divorced   (d) divorced

39. The company's new line of environmentally-friendly cars __________ better than any of their other models.
(a) are sold   (b) is sold
(c) are selling   (d) is selling

40. The concert is supposed to start in half an hour, so it's about time we __________ for the theater.
(a) left   (b) will leave
(c) have left   (d) did leave

Identify the option that contains an awkward expression or an error in grammar.

41. (a) A: Do you find it appropriately to question the decisions of your president?
(b) B: Of course! We are supposed to challenge the decisions of our government.
(c) A: I guess you have a point. It just seems disrespectful to me.
(d) B: It's disrespectful not to ask questions. That's our duty as citizens of a democracy.

42. (a) A: Hello. Can I purchase those two sofas in the corner?
(b) B: Absolutely, sir. Do you want us to deliver them for you as well?
(c) A: Yes, please. I'd like to deliver them by Friday, if that's possible.
(d) B: I don't think that will be a problem.

43. (a) A: Is there anything I can help you with today?
(b) B: Yes, I need to buy the truck.
(c) A: Do you know what kind of truck you're looking for?
(d) B: I don't know anything about trucks, that's why I need your help.

44. (a) A: How has your leg been feeling?
(b) B: It's been feeling a lot better before last week.
(c) A: Are you going to be able to play in the soccer game this weekend?
(d) B: Unfortunately, no. The doctor says I should stay off of it for three more weeks.

45. (a) A: What would you like me to do with this coffee table?
(b) B: You can move in it next to the sofa in the living room.
(c) A: I don't think it will fit in there right now.
(d) B: Oh, you're right. Just leave it for now while I clean out the living room.

Part IV **Questions 46-50**

Identify the option that contains an awkward expression or an error in grammar.

46. (a) Last night I introduced my two good friends, Dave and Mike, for the first time. (b) I knew they would get along fine, but I may have underestimated how much they have in common. (c) Once they were begun talking about music they never stopped. (d) Also, they are both very knowledgeable when it comes to music, so it made for an interesting conversation to listen to.

47. (a) Frank Johnston created a convincing world and strong characters in his classic novel *Powercrash*. (b) The future world that he created is actual not only convincing, but prophetic, as his predictions for the future were correct. (c) Although he wrote the book twenty-five years ago, he was able to predict and successfully implement many of the technological advances that we now take for granted. (d) Ideas such as the internet, modern video games, video cell phones, and high-tech navigation equipment are each described perfectly in the story, which was written long before their time.

48. (a) Besides the application process, the most competitive universities often require an interview process as well. (b) The interviews are similar to job interviews, and they are conducted in order to find the best students for the school. (c) Selective schools like to have outgoing, and social students among their student body. (d) The interviews are useful because it gives the schools a glimpse at the personalities of the prospective students.

49. (a) The Regional Performance Arts Competition will accept submissions until the end of August. (b) At that time, ten applicants will be chosen to perform their pieces live before a panel of judges. (c) One winner will be announced on September 30th, after which he or she will be flown to Chicago for the national finals. (d) The contestant is allowed to bringing one friend or family member, and all flight and hotel expenses will be provided.

50. (a) In recent years, many middle-class families have been adopted children from less fortunate foreign nations. (b) This has proven to be beneficial to both parties. (c) Families unable to bear children naturally get a healthy young son or daughter, and the children are given a chance to grow up in a prosperous and safe environment. (d) Also, in the coming decades this will create a new and interesting dynamic in the ethnic make-up of our society.

This is the end of the Grammar section. Do NOT move on to the next section until instructed to do so. You are NOT allowed to turn to any other section of the test.

ANSWERS
정답과 해설

Day 1

Build Up
20p

1. (a)	**2.** (b)	**3.** (b)	**4.** (c)	**5.** (b)	**6.** (b)
7. (a)	**8.** (d)	**9.** (d)	**10.** (d)	**11.** (d)	**12.** (c)

1.

A: What did the witness say?

B: The witness testified that she __________ the convicted murderer in the alleyway behind the diner at 9:13 p.m.

(a) saw   (b) see

(c) have seen   (d) had seen

| 해석 |

A: 목격자가 뭐라고 말했어?

B: 그 목격자는 오후 9시 13분에 식당차 뒤 골목길에서 살인자를 보았다고 말했어.

| 해설 |

알맞은 시제를 고르는 문제이다. 여기서는 과거를 나타내는 시점 부사구 at 9:13 p.m.과 함께 과거의 한 시점에 일어났던 일을 말하고 있으므로 단순 과거인 (a)가 정답이 된다. 과거완료 (d)는 과거의 한 시점을 기준으로 그 이전부터 그 과거 시점까지를 아우르는 기간의 개념이므로 여기서는 적절치 않다.

| 어휘 |

alleyway 골목길   **diner** 식당차

2.

A: Hurry! I need to stop by the gas station before I go __________ the airport.

B: OK. I will be ready in a minute.

(a) at   (b) to

(c) for   (d) from

| 해석 |

A: 빨리 해. 공항 가기 전에 주유소에 들러야 돼.

B: 알았어. 금방 준비돼.

| 해설 |

알맞은 전치사를 고르는 문제이다. 여기서는 공항으로 향한다는 의미의 방향의 전치사 to가 가장 적절하다.

3.

A: The waitress asked us what we __________ like to drink.

B: I want a Coke. What about you?

(a) should   (b) would

(c) could   (d) can

| 해석 |

A: 종업원이 무엇을 마실 건지 물어봤어.

B : 난 콜라. 너는?

| 해설 |

알맞은 조동사를 고르는 문제이다. would like to V는 '~하고 싶다' 라는 의향을 나타내는 관용적인 표현으로 여기서는 조동사 would가 정답이 된다.

4.

A: __________ the basketball team wins this game, will they compete in the playoffs?

B: Yes, they will.

(a) To assume   (b) Assumed

(c) Assuming   (d) Assume

A: 그 농구팀이 이 경기를 이긴다고 가정한다면 그들이 결승 경기에 나갈까?

B: 응, 그럴 거야.

| 해설 |

assuming (that)~은 '~을 가정한다면' 이라는 뜻의 독립분사구문이다. 그러므로 주절의 주어와 상관없이 하나의 관용적인 표현으로 알아두어야 한다.

| 어휘 |

playoff (무승부, 동점일 때) 결승 시합

5.

Alcohol __________ people's cognitive processes; therefore, they make bad decisions.

(a) influenced   (b) influences

(c) is influenced   (d) is influencing

| 해석 |

알코올은 사람의 인지 과정에 영향을 미친다. 그래서 그들은 잘못된 결정을 한다.

| 해설 |

알코올이 사람의 인지 과정에 영향을 미친다는 '사실(fact)' 을 말하고 있으므로 현재형이 가장 적절한 시제가 된다. 현재진행은 현재 진행되는 일시적인 행동을 나타내므로 (d)는 정답과 거리가 멀다.

6.

Joshua ordered the laptop two weeks ago, but he hasn't received it __________.

(a) still   (b) yet

(c) already   (d) then

| 해석 |

조슈아는 2주 전에 노트북을 주문했지만 아직 받지 못했다.

| 해설 |

의미상 알맞은 부사를 고르는 문제이다. yet은 부정문에서 '아직 ~하지 못하다' 라는 의미로 문장의 끝에 위치한다. still도 의미상 쓰일 수 있으나 위치가 맞지 않아 답이 될 수 없다. still이 쓰이려면 he still hasn't received it.이 되어야 한다.

7.

College applicants are expected __________ four years of high school English courses.

(a) to have completed   (b) to completing

(c) to have completion   (d) to be completing

| 해석 |

대학 지원자들은 4년간의 고등학교 영어 과정을 마쳐야 한다.

| 해설 |

to have p.p.는 주절의 시제보다 한 시제 앞선 시제를 나타낼 때 쓰인다. 대학을 지원할 때 이미 4년간의 고등학교 영어 과정을 마쳐야 하므로 to have p.p.로 나타내는 것이 가장 적절하다. be expected to V는 '~하기로 되어 있다, 예정되어 있다' 라는 의미로 시험에 자주 출제되는 유형이다.

8.

Very __________ people lack credit cards because they are easier to carry.

(a) little   (b) a little

(c) a few   (d) few

| 해석 |

가지고 다니기 편하기 때문에 신용카드 없는 사람이 거의 없다.

| 해설 |

people은 셀 수 있는 가산명사이므로 a few나 few가 와야 한다. a little과 little은 셀 수 없는 불가산명사에 쓰인다. a few는 '약간은' 이라는 의미고 few는 '거의 없는' 이라는 의미다. 여기에선 '신용카드는 가지고 다니기 쉽기 때문에 그것을 가지지 않은 사람은 거의 없다' 라는 의미가 되어야 하므로 few가 적절하다.

| 어휘 |

lack ~이 없다

9.

(a) A: How did you do on your exam?

(b) B: Horribly, but let's not talk about it.

(c) A: I thought you did well since you studied a week in advance!

(d) B: I (think → thought) so, too! I don't understand it.

| 해석 |

(a) A: 시험 어떻게 쳤니?

(b) B: 망했어. 시험에 대해서 말하지 말자.

(c) A: 난 네가 일주일이나 먼저 공부해서 잘 볼 줄 알았는데.

(d) B: 나도 그렇게 생각했어. 이해가 가질 않아.

| 해설 |

(d)에서 B는 A의 말에 동의하고 있다. 그러므로 의미상 '그렇게 생각했다' 라는 의미가 자연스러우므로 과거형으로 말해야 한다.

10.

(a) A: What's wrong, Tina?

(b) B: It's my daughter. She wants to move out and live on her own.

(c) A: That's great! She's growing up.

(d) B: Yes, she is, but (I am → it is) hard to accept that she's growing up.

| 해석 |

(a) A: 무슨 일이니, 티나?

(b) B: 내 딸 문제야. 따로 나가서 혼자서 살기를 원해.

(c) A: 잘됐다. 그 아이도 자라고 있잖아.

(d) B: 맞아. 그런데 그 아이가 자라고 있다는 사실을 받아들이기 힘들어.

| 해설 |

I am hard~가 되면 I의 상태가 hard하다는 의미가 되므로 적절치 않다. 가주어 it을 쓰는 것이 적절하고 여기서 it은 to accept that she's growing up을 나타낸다. it is hard 뒤에 의미상의 주어 for me가 생략됐음도 알아두자.

11.

(a) There are several different theories regarding losing weight. (b) Some people believe that there are supplements that can help increase their metabolism to lose weight. (c) Today, many believe that the best way to lose weight is to exercise and eat in small portions. (d) Although there is no solid evidence (support → to support / supporting) the supplement theory, it seems that it is becoming more and more popular these days.

| 해석 |

(a) 몸무게를 줄이는 것에 대해 몇 가지 다양한 이론들이 있다. (b) 어떤 사람들은 몸무게를 줄이기 위해 그들의 신진대사를 증가시키는 데 도움이 되는 보충제가 있다고 생각한다. (c) 오늘날 많은 사람들은 몸무게를 줄이는 가장 좋은 방법은 운동을 하고 적은 양을 먹는 것이라고 생각한다. (d) 보충 이론을 뒷받침하는 확실한 증거는 없지만 그것은 오늘날 더욱 더 인기가 느는 것 같다.

| 해설 |

주어가 evidence이므로 support는 evidence를 수식하는 형태가 되어야 한다. 그러므로 to부정사나 -ing 형태로 앞에 있는 evidence를 수식해야 한다.

| 어휘 |

metabolism 신진대사   supplement 보충

12.

(a) There are over 100 children at the new pre-school. (b) Because there are so many children, it is difficult to give each child the proper attention that they need. (c) In order to accommodate this problem, they (must divide → **must be divided**) into smaller groups. (d) By doing this, the teacher-to-student ratio is much better.

| 해석 |

(a) 새 보육학교에 100명이 넘는 아이들이 있다. (b) 아이들이 너무 많아서 각각의 아이들에게 그들이 필요한 관심을 주기가 힘들다. (c) 이 문제를 해결하기 위해서 아이들은 소규모 그룹으로 분리되어야 한다. (d) 이렇게 하면 학생 대 교사의 비율이 훨씬 낫다.

| 해설 |

divide는 '나누다, 쪼개다'라는 의미의 타동사인데 여기서는 동사 뒤에 목적어도 없고 의미상 '분리되다'라는 수동의 의미가 적절하다. 그러므로 수동의 형태인 must be divided가 되어야 한다.

| 어휘 |

accommodate 적응하다, 조정하다   ratio 비율

Day 2

Build Up
28p

> **1.** (b)　**2.** (c)　**3.** (d)　**4.** (a)　**5.** (c)　**6.** (b)
> **7.** (c)　**8.** (d)　**9.** (b)　**10.** (c)　**11.** (b)　**12.** (c)

1.

A: How does Sarah like her new job?
B: She hasn't decided yet, __________ there for three days.
(a) she'll only work
(b) she's only worked
(c) she only worked
(d) she'd only worked

| 해석 |

A: 사라는 새 일을 어떻게 생각해?
B: 아직 결정하지 못했어. 거기서 일한 지 겨우 3일 됐잖아.

| 해설 |

현재완료는 과거에서 현재까지 이어지는 기간의 개념이다. 이 문장에서는 그녀가 3일 전부터 새로운 일을 시작했고 아직까지 일을 하고 있으므로 현재까지 이어지는 기간의 개념으로 표현한 현재완료 (b)가 가장 적절한 시제가 된다. (b)에서 she's는 she has의 줄임말로 부사인 only는 조동사 has 뒤에 위치하게 된다.

2.

A: Roger ruined the party yesterday.
B: You're right, he __________ have ever come.
(a) wouldn't
(b) can't
(c) shouldn't
(d) won't

| 해석 |

A: 로저는 어제 파티를 망쳤어.
B: 맞아. 그는 오지 말았어야 했어.

| 해설 |

shouldn't have p.p.는 '~을 하지 말았어야 했다'라는 과거 일에 대한 유감을 나타내는 표현이다. 파티를 망친 로저에 대한 A의 말에 대한 가장 적절한 반응이라고 볼 수 있다. 그러므로 (c)가 정답이다.

3.

A: Are you going to perform at the concert tomorrow?
B: No, I __________ able to practice at all.
(a) weren't
(b) hadn't been
(c) don't
(d) wasn't

| 해석 |

A: 내일 콘서트에서 공연할 거니?
B: 아니, 연습을 전혀 할 수 없었어.

| 해설 |

시제를 묻는 문제이다. B는 연습을 전혀 할 수 없었기 때문에 내일 공연을 하지 않을 거라고 말하고 있다. 단순 과거시제를 사용하여 과거의 단순 사실을 서술하므로 (d)가 가장 적절한 시제가 된다. (b)의 과거완료는 기준 시점이 과거가 되어 그 이전의 일에 대해 언급할 때 쓰이므로 여기서는 적절하지 않다.

4.

A: I love watching the firework show __________ the city puts on every Independence Day.
B: Me, too. They are very pretty.
(a) that
(b) when
(c) whichever
(d) how

| 해석 |

A: 매년 독립일마다 시에서 하는 불꽃 축제가 좋아.
B: 나도. 정말 예뻐.

| 해설 |

적절한 관계대명사를 찾는 문제이다. the firework show를 선행사로 하는 관계대명사를 찾아야 하므로 사람이나 사물 모두를 선행사로 취할 수 있는 that이 가장 적절하다.

5.

Certain species of parrots are known for their extremely long lifespans, though there are __________ very short lifespans.

(a) some have

(b) those have

(c) some having

(d) none having

| 해석 |

짧은 수명을 갖고 있는 앵무새들도 있지만 앵무새들 중에 어떤 종들은 상당히 긴 수명으로 알려져 있다.

| 해설 |

존재를 나타내는 there is 형태의 문장으로 there이 형식상 주어로 취급되고 동사 뒤에 진짜 주어가 오게 된다. 그러므로 빈칸에는 진짜 주어가 와야 하므로 〈주어＋동사〉의 형태인 (a)와 (b)는 적절치 않으며 (c)가 정답이 된다. some having에서 having은 능동 형태의 분사로 사용됐다.

6.

This is a difficult experiment because you have no __________ for error.

(a) the room

(b) room

(c) rooms

(d) a room

| 해석 |

실수의 여지가 없으므로 이것은 어려운 실험이다.

| 해설 |

명사 room의 의미와 성격을 파악하는 문제이다. room이 '방' 의 의미로 쓰이면 셀 수 있는 가산명사가 되지만 여기처럼 '여지, 여유, 기회 (＋for)' 의 의미로 사용되면 불가산명사가 된다. 또한 여기서는 특정한 것을 가리키는 경우가 아니므로 the와 a도 정답이 될 수 없다. 그러므로 정답은 (b)가 된다.

7.

We can throw everything in the trash, except for those photo albums __________ are piled in the corner.

(a) who

(b) for whom

(c) which

(d) where

| 해석 |

구석에 쌓인 사진 앨범을 제외하고 모든 것을 쓰레기통에 버려도 된다.

| 해설 |

관계대명사의 용법을 묻는 질문이다. 여기서는 선행사 those photo albums(사물)을 취할 수 있는 관계 대명사를 골라야 한다. 그러므로 which가 정답이 되며 여기서 which는 관계대명사 주격으로 사용되었다.

8.

A dental analysis proved that the skeleton found in the tomb __________ a female pharaoh between the years B.C. 300 and B.C. 100.

(a) should be

(b) should not have been

(c) would not be

(d) must have been

| 해석 |

치아 분석에 의하면 그 무덤에서 발견된 해골은 B.C. 300년과 B.C. 100년 사이의 여성 파라오였음에 틀림없다.

| 해설 |

must have p.p.는 과거 일에 대한 추정을 나타내어 '~이었음[했음]에 틀림없다' 라는 의미로 사용된다. 여기서는 해골이 B.C. 300년과 B.C. 100년 사이에 존재했던 여성 파라오라고 추측하고 있으므로 '과거의 추측' 을 나타내는 표현인 (d)가 정답이 된다.

| 어휘 |

skeleton 해골

9.

(a) A: How did the dinner with your parents go?

(b) B: Awful! It was nice to see my parents, but we ate at (such horrible a restaurant → such a horrible restaurant).

(c) A: I'm glad you told me that because I have a reservation there for tonight.

(d) B: I would cancel it if I were you. I am never going back there again.

| 해석 |

(a) A: 부모님과 함께 한 저녁 식사 어땠어?

(b) B: 끔찍했어! 부모님을 뵙는 것은 좋았지만 정말 끔찍한 레스토랑에서 먹었거든.

(c) A: 말해줘서 고맙다. 오늘밤 거기에다 예약을 했거든

(d) A: 내가 너라면 취소하겠어. 다시는 거기 가지 않을 거야.

| 해설 |

such는 〈형용사＋명사〉 앞에서 부사적으로 '그렇게, 이렇게, 매우' 등의 의미로 쓰이며 이의 어순을 묻는 문제가 TEPS에는 자주 출제된다. 〈such, many, quite, what＋a/an＋형용사＋명사〉의 어순도 알아두도록 한다.

10.

(a) A: How did you do on your calculus exam?

(b) B: I don't have the exam until next period. How did you do?

(c) A: I think I did really well. I should have since (I and Wendy → Wendy and I) studied all weekend.

(d) B: Well, I didn't have much time to study so I hope it's not too difficult.

(a) A: 미적분학 시험 어떻게 봤어?

(b) B: 다음 수업 시간에 봐. 너는?

(c) A: 꽤 잘 본 것 같아. 잘 봤어야 돼. 웬디하고 난 주말 내내 공부했거든.

(d) B: 난 공부할 시간이 없었는데. 너무 어렵지 않으면 좋겠다.

| 해설 |

인칭 관련 어순을 묻는 문제이다. 3인칭과 1인칭이 등위접속사로 연결돼 있을 때 3인칭을 먼저 말하고 1인칭을 말하는 것이 올바른 어순이다. 그러므로 (c)의 I and Wendy를 Wendy and I로 바꾸어야 한다.

| 어휘 |

calculus 미적분학 **period** 수업 시간

11.

(a) Many people read literature for leisure. (b) of these people, a great number prefer to purchase their books, (as opposing to → as opposed to) borrowing them. (c) They enjoy the close proximity of a useful book. (d) Once they have read a book, it can be quite a pleasure to glance back at the pages or to reference the book freely at a later time.

| 해석 |

(a) 많은 사람들이 여가 시간에 문학 작품을 읽는다. (b) 이들 중 많은 사람들이 책을 빌리기보다는 구입하는 것을 더 선호한다. (c) 그들은 유용한 책을 가까이 두는 것을 좋아한다. (d) 일단 책을 읽고 나서 다시 훑어보거나 나중에 자유롭게 그 책을 인용하는 것이 상당한 즐거움일 수 있다.

| 해설 |

as opposed to~는 '~에 반대하여, 대립함으로써' 라는 의미의 관용적인 표현이다. 그러므로 as opposing to를 as opposed to로 바꾸어야 한다. 또한 (b)의 a great number에서 a number는 '많은 수(many)' 의 의미가 있으므로 복수 취급한다.

| 어휘 |

proximity 근접, 인접 **reference** 인용하다

12.

(a) In modern times technology has taken incredible strides. (b) For thousands of years science and technology evolved very slowly, taking hundreds of years at a time for any major changes to occur. (c) However, as human knowledge of the physical world continues to grow, we (gained → gain) the ability to push our technology even further. (d) Advances in communication, for instance, have allowed this rapid growth to continue its acceleration.

| 해석 |

(a) 현대 사회에서 과학 기술은 엄청난 발전을 이루었다. (b) 수천 년 동안 과학과 과학 기술은 주요한 발전이 일어나는 데 한 번에 수백 년이 걸리면서 매우 천천히 진화했다. (c) 그러나 물질 세계에 대한 인간의 지식이 계속 성장할 때 우리는 우리의 과학 기술을 더욱 더 발전시킬 능력을 갖게 된다. (d) 예를 들어, 통신 발달은 빠른 성장이 계속해서 가속화되게 했다.

| 해설 |

여기서는 물질 세계에 대한 인간의 지식이 계속 성장할 때 우리의 과학 기술이 더욱 발전한다는 사실(fact)를 말하고 있으므로 과거형(gained)이 아닌 현재형으로(gain) 써야 한다.

| 어휘 |

stride 큰 걸음

Day 3

Build Up 36p

1. (a)	**2.** (d)	**3.** (c)	**4.** (b)	**5.** (b)	**6.** (b)
7. (a)	**8.** (a)	**9.** (b)	**10.** (d)	**11.** (c)	**12.** (b)

1.

A: I can't believe smoking is still allowed in restaurants!

B: Why don't we petition ___________________________?

(a) the government to do something about it

(b) to the government to do something about it

(c) for the government to stop

(d) for a stop to the government

| 해석 |

A: 아직도 레스토랑에서 흡연이 가능하다니 믿을 수가 없어!

B: 그것에 대해 뭔가 조치를 취하게끔 정부에 청원하자.

| 해설 |

〈petition+목적어+to V〉는 '~에게 …하도록 간청(청원)하다' 라는 의미가 있다. 그러므로 (a)의 어순이 정답이 된다. Why don't we V~? 는 '우리 ~하는 게 어때?' 라는 제안의 의미가 있다.

2.

A: Why do you watch so many cooking shows?

B: I enjoy learning the art of making __________.

(a) the meal

(b) meal

(c) the meals

(d) meals

| 해석 |

A: 넌 왜 그리 많은 요리 프로그램을 보니?

B: 나는 음식 만드는 법을 배우는 것이 좋아.

| 해설 |

관사에 관한 문제이다. meal은 가산명사이며, 정관사 the가 쓰인 the meal과 the meals는 '특정한 그 음식'을 의미한다. 여기서는 불특정한 음식을 만드는 것을 의미하므로 (d)가 정답이 된다.

3.

A: Do you recognize anyone in this picture?
B: I think I remember ___________ the woman in the purple shirt.
(a) saw
(b) to see
(c) seeing
(d) seen

| 해석 |
A: 이 사진에서 알아보는 사람이 있습니까?
B: 제 생각에는 보라색 셔츠를 입은 여자를 본 것 같은데요.

| 해설 |
remember는 to부정사와 동명사를 모두 취할 수 있는 동사이다. 〈remember＋to부정사〉는 '(앞으로 할 것을) 기억하다' 라는 의미이고 〈remember＋-ing(동명사)〉는 '(이미 한 것을) 기억하다' 라는 의미이다. 그러므로 여기서는 이미 본 것을 기억한다는 의미가 되므로 (c)가 정답이 된다.

4.

A: Slow down! There's an injured dog over there!
B: Oh, no! I ___________ that!
(a) don't see
(b) didn't see
(c) hadn't seen
(d) have seen

| 해석 |
A: 천천히 가! 저기 부상당한 개가 있어.
B: 어머. 난 못 봤어.

| 해설 |
알맞은 시제를 고르는 문제이다. 여기서는 의미상 과거의 한 시점을 말하고 있으므로 단순 과거시제가 적절하다. (a)의 현재시제는 '사실, 습관, 진리' 등의 뜻이 되므로 적절하지 않다.

5.

___________ Richard was in an accident was given to his wife.
(a) A message is that
(b) The message that
(c) The message which
(d) From the message

| 해석 |
리처드가 사고 당했다는 소식이 그의 부인에게 전달되었다.

| 해설 |
이 문장에서 본동사는 was given이 된다. 그러므로 빈칸에는 주어가 와야 한다. 본동사 was given 앞에 완벽한 절(Richard was in an accident)이 있으므로 관계대명사 which는 앞에 쓰일 수 없다. 여기서

that은 동격 명사절을 이끌어서 〈the＋추상명사(fact/news/rumor/proof)＋that＋완벽한 문장〉이 오게 된다.

6.

As the war continued and the number of injured soldiers grew, ___________ for medical supplies and bigger facilities.
(a) so the need did
(b) so did the need
(c) such was the need
(d) as such was the need

| 해석 |
전쟁이 계속되고 부상당한 군인의 숫자도 늘어나면서 의약품과 더 큰 시설의 필요성도 늘어났다.

| 해설 |
부사 so의 용법을 고르는 문제이다. 〈so＋동사＋주어〉로 도치되는 경우 so는 '～도 역시(also)'의 의미이다. 〈so＋주어＋동사〉가 되는 경우에는 앞서 말한 내용을 강하게 긍정하여 '틀림없이, 정말로'라는 yes의 의미가 된다. 여기서는 so가 also의 의미로 쓰였으므로 (b)가 정답이 된다.

7.

Contrary to popular belief, ___________ most crimes occur.
(a) at dawn is when
(b) dawn is at when
(c) when is at dawn
(d) when at is dawn

| 해석 |
대부분이 믿는 것과 반대로 대부분의 범죄는 새벽에 일어난다.

| 해설 |
도치와 생략이 일어난 문장이다. 원래의 문장을 보면 The time when most crimes occur is at dawn.이다. 이 문장에서 부사구 at dawn을 강조하여 도치한 문장으로 관계부사(when) 앞에 있는 선행사(the time)이 생략된 문장이다.

8.

Dr. James came ___________ as the leading authority on the subject because he conducted studies on it for 33 years.
(a) to be recognized
(b) to recognize
(c) recognized to be
(d) to recognized be

| 해석 |
제임스 박사는 33년 동안 그 주제에 관해 연구해서 그 분야의 주요 권위자로 인정받게 되었다.

| 해설 |
come to V는 '～하게 되다'라는 의미이다. recognize는 '～을 인정하다, 알아보다'라는 타동사이다. 여기서는 '인정받다'라는 수동의 의미가

되어야 하므로 to부정사의 수동 형태인 (a)가 정답이 된다.

9.

(a) A: Do you have any pets?

(b) B: I have a cat, but (most of time → **most of the time**) it wanders outside of my home.

(c) A: Is your cat hard to take care of?

(d) B: Not really. It seems that my cat is very well trained.

| 해석 |

(a) A: 애완동물 키우니?
(b) B: 고양이가 하나 있는데 대부분의 시간을 집 밖에서 돌아다녀.
(c) A: 네 고양이는 돌보기 힘드니?
(d) B: 아니. 내 고양이는 잘 훈련된 것 같아.

| 해설 |

most of the time은 '대체로, 보통' 이라는 뜻으로 쓰이는 숙어이다. 그러므로 정관사 the를 time 앞에 붙여야 한다.

10.

(a) A: What do you plan on doing after graduating?

(b) B: I plan on opening a business, but I need a partner.

(c) A: Are you talking about the bakery you talked about?

(d) B: That's (which → **what**) I want to discuss with you.

| 해석 |

(a) A: 졸업 후에 무엇을 할 거니?
(b) B: 사업을 할 계획인데 파트너가 필요해.
(c) A: 전에 말했던 빵집 말이니?
(d) B: 그게 바로 너와 얘기하고 싶은 거야.

| 해설 |

관계대명사의 용법을 묻는 문제이다. 관계대명사 which 앞에 선행사가 없으므로 선행사를 포함한 관계대명사 what이 적절하다. 관계대명사 what은 선행사를 포함하여 '~하는 것(the thing that)' 이라는 의미가 있다.

11.

(a) Many supporters of the Chicago Cubs tend to be fair-weather fans. (b) More fans are eager to switch sides when the Chicago White Sox are doing well. (c) However, when both teams are doing well, they try to (prevent from cheering → **prevent themselves from cheering**) for the wrong team by staying with the Chicago Cubs. (d) That is what happened during the 2002-2003 regular baseball season.

| 해석 |

(a) 시카고 컵스의 많은 지지자들은 성적이 좋을 때만 팬인 경향이 있다.

(b) 시카고 화이트 삭스가 잘할 때에 편을 바꾸는 팬들이 더 많다. (c) 그러나 두 팀이 다 잘할 때에는 시카고 컵스에 있으면서 잘못된 팀을 응원하지 않으려 한다. (d) 이것이 2002-2003년 정기 야구 시즌에 벌어진 일이다.

| 해설 |

prevent A from B는 'A가 B하는 것을 막다' 라는 의미가 있다. prevent 뒤에 목적어가 와야 하므로 의미상 적절한 themselves가 와야 한다.

| 어휘 |

fair-weather 유리할 때만의

12.

(a) Many kinds of dinosaurs roamed the earth thousands of years ago. (b) There (is → **are**) fossils that prove that they existed. (c) Many of these fossils have been excavated and placed as display in museums. (d) People can go to museums and see what dinosaurs looked like.

| 해석 |

(a) 많은 종류의 공룡들이 수천 년 전에 지구에 존재했다. (b)그들이 존재했다는 화석이 이것을 증명한다. (c) 많은 화석들이 발굴되어 박물관에 전시되었다. (d) 사람들은 박물관에 가서 공룡들이 어떻게 생겼는지 볼 수 있다.

| 해설 |

there 뒤에 오는 동사의 수 일치는 동사 뒤의 명사, 즉 의미상의 주어에 달려 있다. 여기서는 fossils가 의미상의 주어가 되므로 복수 동사가 와야 한다. 그러므로 is를 are로 바꾸어야 한다.

| 어휘 |

roam 방랑하다, 거닐다   **excavate** 발굴하다

Day 4

Build Up   44p

| 1. (d) | 2. (c) | 3. (c) | 4. (a) | 5. (b) | 6. (b) |
| 7. (a) | 8. (b) | 9. (d) | 10. (c) | 11. (c) | 12. (d) |

1.

A: You should really take your dog to the veterinarian.

B: I know, I __________, but I don't have enough money to pay the bill.

(a) want it to do

(b) want to do it

(c) want

(d) want to

A: 네 강아지를 수의사에게 데리고 가야 돼.
B: 알아, 그러고 싶어. 그렇지만 치료비를 낼 돈이 충분치 않아.

| 해설 |
대부정사 관련 문제이다. 명사의 반복을 피하기 위해서 대명사를 쓰고, 동사의 반복을 피하기 위해서 대동사를 쓰듯이 같은 to부정사의 동사구의 반복을 피하기 위해서 동사구를 생략하고 to까지만 쓰는 것을 대부정사라고 한다. 원래는 I want to take my dog to the veterinarian의 문장이었다.

2.

A: Tom and I are getting married next month, and you are invited.
B: Wow, congratulations! I __________ there.
(a) was
(b) must have been
(c) will be
(d) could be

| 해석 |
A: 탐과 나는 다음달에 결혼해. 널 초대할게.
B: 와, 축하해! 꼭 갈게.

| 해설 |
will은 1인칭과 함께 쓰여 말하는 사람의 의지를 나타내기도 한다. 여기서도 주어의 의지를 나타내는 의미로 쓰였다. must have p.p.는 과거에 대한 확실한 추측을 나타내는 표현으로 '~했음에 틀림없다'라는 의미가 있다.

3.

A: I thought you were planning to move away from Chicago.
B: I was, but over the last year I've grown __________ the city.
(a) with love
(b) loving for
(c) to love
(d) loving

| 해석 |
A: 난 네가 시카고에서 떠날 거라고 생각했는데.
B: 그랬지. 근데 지난 1년간 이 도시를 사랑하게 됐어.

| 해설 |
〈grow+to+동사원형〉은 '~하게 되다'라는 의미가 있다. 그러므로 여기서는 to부정사를 취한 (c)가 정답이 된다.

4.

A: Have you ever seen __________ of the seven natural wonders of the world?
B: I've only seen the Grand Canyon.
(a) any
(b) those
(c) some
(d) every

| 해석 |
A: 세계 7대 불가사의를 본 적 있니?
B: 그랜드 캐년만 봤어.

| 해설 |
적절한 대명사를 고르는 문제이다. 긍정문에서 any of ~는 '무엇이든지, 누구든지, 어느 것이든지'라는 의미이다. 여기서 해석상 가장 적절한 대명사는 any가 된다.

5.

Passing the bar exam __________ than I had expected.
(a) was difficult
(b) was more difficult
(c) were difficult
(d) were more difficult

| 해석 |
변호사 시험을 통과하는 것은 생각보다 어려웠다.
| 해설 |
동명사는 단수 취급을 하므로 동사는 was가 되어야 한다. 또한 뒤에 형용사나 부사의 비교급과 함께 쓰이는 접속사 than이 있으므로 difficult의 비교급 more difficult가 와야 한다. 그러므로 (b)가 정답이다.

6.

Five miles __________ the longest I had ever run before I ran in the marathon this afternoon.
(a) has been
(b) was
(c) were
(d) have been

| 해석 |
오늘 오후에 마라톤을 뛰기 전까지 5마일이 내가 뛰어본 가장 긴 거리였다.

| 해설 |
기간, 거리, 가격, 무게를 나타내는 복수 명사가 '하나의 단위'를 나타내는 경우에는 단수 취급한다. 그러므로 단수 동사인 (b)가 적절하다.

7.

When we were children, we learned __________ to protect ourselves in the case of fire.
(a) how
(b) when
(c) what
(d) why

| 해석 |
우리는 어렸을 때 화재시 우리를 어떻게 보호해야 하는지 배웠다.

| 해설 |
〈의문사+to부정사〉는 명사적 용법으로 사용되어 문장에서 주어, 목적어, 보어로 쓰인다. 여기서는 의미상 가장 적절한 의문사를 고르는 문제이다. 이 문장에서는 자신을 지키는 방법(how)에 대해서 배웠다는 의미가 되기 때문에 how가 가장 적절한 의문사가 된다. 의문사 what은 동

사(protect)의 목적어(ourselves)가 있으므로 적절치 않다.

8.

__________ all their money at the casino, the Smiths had to end their vacation early and head home.
(a) Wasting
(b) Having wasted
(c) To have wasted
(d) Wasted

| 해석 |
스미스 부부는 카지노에서 돈을 다 썼기 때문에 휴가를 일찍 마치고 집으로 향해야 했다.

| 해설 |
분사구문 문제이다. 분사구문을 만들 때에는 주절의 주어와 종속절의 주어가 일치할 때 주어를 없애므로 the Smiths가 분사구문의 주어가 된다. 이때 waste의 목적어인 all their money가 있으므로 능동 형태의 분사구문을 골라야 한다. 그런데 주절의 시제보다 종속절의 시제가 앞서야 의미상 적절하므로 여기서는 (a)가 아닌 (b)가 적절한 분사구문의 형태가 된다.

9.

(a) A: Tonight is the final night that the Munich Symphony will be in town.
(b) B: I know. I'm very excited for the performance.
(c) A: You're going, too? After the show we are all going out to dinner. Can you come?
(d) B: I wish I could, but I must (go for home → go home) afterwards so I can finish some paperwork.

| 해석 |
(a) A: 오늘밤이 뮌헨 심포니가 여기서 공연을 하는 마지막 날이야.
(b) B: 알아. 공연이 너무 기대돼.
(c) A: 너도 가니? 공연 끝나고 우리 모두 저녁 식사를 하러 가는데, 너도 올 수 있니?
(d) B: 그랬으면 좋겠어. 그런데 끝나고 집에 가야 해. 그래야지 서류 일을 끝낼 수 있어.

| 해설 |
go는 자동사로 뒤에 방향의 전치사를 취할 수 있다. 그러나 home이 부사이므로 방향의 전치사를 붙이지 않아도 된다. 따라서 for가 없어져야 한다. 참고로 afterwards는 부사로 '그 후에, 나중에'라는 의미가 있다.

10.

(a) A: Hello, can we check in for flight 402 here?
(b) B: You sure can, sir. Can I see your boarding passes and photo IDs'?
(c) A: Sure. Also, I want to make sure that my wife and I (are seating → are seated / sit) next to each other.

(d) B: I'll see what I can do, Mr. Park, but it might be difficult. This flight is filled to capacity.

| 해석 |
(a) A: 안녕하세요? 402편 수속을 여기서 할 수 있나요?
(b) B: 물론이죠. 탑승권과 신분증을 볼 수 있나요?
(c) A: 그럼요. 또한 저와 제 아내가 서로 옆에 앉게 해주세요.
(d) B: 알아는 보겠습니다만 어려울 수도 있습니다. 정원이 꽉 차서요.

| 해설 |
seat은 타동사로 '착석시키다, 앉히다'라는 뜻이 있다. 그러므로 여기서는 의미상 수동태가 되거나 자동사 sit으로 바꾸어 능동의 형태로 만들어야 한다.

| 어휘 |
capacity 수용 인원, 정원

11.

(a) No one had ever taught Jeff how to swim, but he very much wanted to learn. (b) He had nothing to do this weekend, so he decided to drive to nearby Lake Wikoma. (c) (Entering the water → As Jeff was entering the water), the wind grew strong and the waves became too large for a novice swimmer. (d) Jeff was disappointed that he would have to wait for another day, but he knew it was dangerous for him to be in the lake in those conditions.

| 해석 |
(a) 아무도 제프에게 수영하는 법을 가르친 적이 없지만 제프는 매우 배우고 싶어 했다. (b) 그는 이번 주말에 할 일이 없었다. 그래서 위코마 호수 근처로 가기로 했다. (c) 제프가 물로 들어갈 때 바람이 강해졌고 물결은 초보 수영자에겐 너무 거셌다. (d) 제프는 다른 날을 기다려야 하는 것이 실망스러웠지만 그러한 상황에서 호수에서 수영하는 것은 위험하다는 것을 알고 있었다.

| 해설 |
생략된 분사구문의 주어와 주절의 주어가 일치하지 않아 생긴 비논리적인 분사구문 문제이다. 주절의 주어가 the wind인데 the wind가 물에 들어간다(enter the water)는 것은 비논리적이다. 그러므로 종속절의 주어 Jeff를 생략하지 않고 As Jeff was entering the water로 바꾸어야 한다.

| 어휘 |
novice 풋내기

12.

(a) The following is a reminder to all returning students. (b) There has been a great increase in the number of new students who have joined our institution this coming semester. (c) Many of them will be confused and will require your patient assistance in order to help get their bearings here. (d) Please be willing to offer directions, advice, and any other sort of aid, should you

come across any students (appeared →
appearing) lost or disoriented.

| 해석 |

(a) 모든 재학생들에게 알립니다. (b) 이번 학기에 우리 학원에 등록한 신입생의 숫자가 증가했습니다. (c) 그들 중 많은 학생들이 혼란스러워할 것이고 여기 환경에 익숙해지는 데 여러분의 도움을 필요로 할 것입니다. (d) 누구든지 길을 잃거나 혼란스러워하는 듯한 학생을 만난다면 방향이나 충고, 다른 도움을 기꺼이 주시길 바랍니다.

| 해설 |

appear는 자동사로 과거분사의 형태(appeared)가 되면 완료의 의미가 된다. 그러므로 능동의 현재분사 형태가 되어야 한다. (d)에서 should you come across any students는 가정법 if가 생략되어 도치된 구문이다. 원래는 if you should come across any students이다.

| 어휘 |

get one's bearings 환경에 익숙해지다

Day 5
Build Up
52p

1. (c)	2. (b)	3. (b)	4. (a)	5. (c)	6. (a)
7. (c)	8. (a)	9. (a)	10. (d)	11. (a)	12. (c)

1.

A: Who's the fastest runner on the track team?
B: Jordan is definitely the fastest. He runs
___________ the second fastest runner.
(a) faster than three times as
(b) as three times fast as
(c) three times as fast as
(d) as three times faster than

| 해석 |

A: 육상부에서 가장 빠른 선수가 누구니?
B: 조단이 당연히 가장 빠르지. 그는 두 번째로 빨리 달리는 선수보다 3배 빨리 달려.

| 해설 |

배수 비교의 표현으로는 〈배수사+as+형용사/부사 원급+as〉와 〈배수사+비교급+than〉이 주로 쓰이므로 알아두도록 한다. 그러므로 여기서는 (c)가 정답이다.

2.

A: Which candidate did you vote for?
B: I voted for George Bush ___________ my wife
did.
(a) although

(b) as
(c) as if
(d) when

| 해석 |

A: 어떤 후보를 뽑았니?
B: 내 아내처럼 조지 부시를 뽑았어.

| 해설 |

알맞은 접속사를 고르는 문제이다. 여기서는 '~처럼'이란 의미가 가장 적절하므로 as가 답이 된다. vote for는 '~에게 투표하다'라는 의미이다.

3.

A: Everyone failed the chemistry midterm!
B: I know. ___________ how difficult it would be, I
would've studied more!
(a) I could've known
(b) Had I known
(c) Have I known
(d) If I knew

| 해석 |

A: 모두가 화학 중간고사에 낙제했대.
B: 알아. 얼마만큼 어려울지 알았더라면 나는 더 공부했을 거야.

| 해설 |

가정법 과거완료 형태의 문제이다. 가정법 과거완료는 과거의 상황에 반대되는 것을 가정하는 것으로 〈if+주어+had p.p.~, 주어+would/could/might/should+have p.p.〉로 나타낸다. 여기서는 if 절에서 if가 생략되어 도치가 된 구문이다. 그러므로 정답은 (b)가 된다.

4.

A: John is ___________ in the attic.
B: Oh! I thought he was studying downstairs in
the basement!
(a) up
(b) down
(c) back
(d) around

| 해석 |

A: 존은 다락방에 올라가 있어.
B: 어! 나는 그애가 아래층 지하실에서 공부하는 줄 알았는데.

| 해설 |

attic은 '지붕과 천장 사이의 공간, 다락방'을 의미하므로 의미상 '올라가'라는 의미의 부사 up과 어울린다.

5.

Being able ___________ music takes a lot of
dedication and understanding of music.
(a) to composing
(b) to be composed of
(c) to compose
(d) to have composed

| 해석 |

음악을 작곡할 수 있으려면 많은 헌신과 음악에 대한 이해가 필요하다.

| 해설 |

compose는 '작곡하다'라는 의미이다. be able to V는 '~할 수 있다'는 의미로 여기서 to는 to부정사이므로 뒤에 동사원형이 와야 한다. 그런데 be composed of~는 '~으로 구성되다'라는 의미이다. 여기서는 '음악을 작곡할 수 있는 것'이라는 의미가 되어야 하므로 능동의 형태가 와야 한다.

6.

It is _______________ decent housing in the south side of Chicago.

(a) likely to find
(b) to find it likely
(c) to find likely
(d) likely to find it

| 해석 |

시카고 남쪽에서 괜찮은 집을 찾을 수 있을 것 같다.

| 해설 |

be likely to~는 '~하기가 쉽다/있음직하다'라는 의미가 있다. (d)는 find의 목적어 decent housing이 있기 때문에 it이 있으면 안 되므로 정답이 될 수 없다. 그러므로 정답은 (a)가 된다.

7.

Although Ms. Franzen has a strict restroom policy, she _______________ let you go to the restroom during class if it is an emergency.
(a) might have
(b) used to
(c) may
(d) did

| 해석 |

프랜젠 선생님은 엄격한 화장실 규칙을 가지고 계시지만 급한 상황일 경우에는 수업 시간에 화장실을 가도록 허락해 줄 것이다.

| 해설 |

알맞은 조동사를 고르는 문제이다. although가 양보 접속사이므로 주절에는 반대의 내용이 오게 된다. 그러므로 여기서 의미상 가장 알맞은 조동사는 불확실한 추측을 나타내는 조동사 may가 적절하다. (a)의 might have p.p.는 과거 일에 대한 추측이므로 알맞지 않고, (b)의 used to는 '과거에 ~하곤 했다'는 의미이다.

8.

Nobody really knows _______________________.

(a) for sure where the movie theater is
(b) for sure the movie theater is there
(c) how for sure the movie theater is
(d) how for sure the movie theater was

| 해석 |

극장이 어디에 있는지 확실히 아는 사람이 아무도 없다.

| 해설 |

know의 목적어로 간접의문문 where the movie theater is가 왔다. 간접의문문의 순서는 〈의문사＋주어＋동사〉이다. 여기서 for sure는 '확실하게'라는 의미의 부사구로 간접의문문 앞이나 뒤에 모두 위치할 수 있다.

9.

(a) A: (Are → **Were**) you nervous when you took the exam?
(b) B: Not at all! I was as cool as a cucumber.
(c) A: Wow! Most people were panicking right before the exam!
(d) B: Yeah, but I felt very prepared since I attended every lecture and studied a lot.

| 해석 |

(a) A: 시험 볼 때 떨었니?
(b) B: 아니 전혀! 아주 침착했어.
(c) A: 와! 대부분 사람들이 시험 직전에 긴장하고 있었는데.
(d) B: 맞아. 근데 나는 모든 수업을 다 듣고 공부도 많이 해서 매우 준비된 느낌이었어.

| 해설 |

시간 부사절의 시제가 과거(took)이므로 과거형으로 시제를 일치시켜 주어야 한다.

| 어휘 |

as cool as a cucumber 침착하여, 냉정하여

10.

(a) A: How are your golf lessons?
(b) B: The lessons helped me improve my backswing.
(c) A: How long have you been taking lessons?
(d) B: (Since → **For**) over two months.

| 해석 |

(a) A: 골프 수업은 어떠니?
(b) B: 백스윙이 향상되는 데 도움이 되었어.
(c) A: 얼마 동안 수업을 받았니?
(d) B: 2달 넘게.

| 해설 |

for 다음에는 기간을 나타내는 명사가 나와 '~동안'이란 의미를 가진다. since 다음에는 '특정 시점'을 나타내는 명사나 절이 나와서 '(그 시점) 이후로'라는 의미를 가진다. over two months는 기간이므로 전치사 for가 와야 한다.

11.

(a) In the United States, a bill must be approved (with → **by**) Congress before it becomes a law. (b) The bill is read and reviewed at a legislative meeting. (c) Members of Congress may debate the bill and offer amendments. (d) Members then vote on the bill and the bill becomes a law if the majority of Congress approves it.

(a) 미국에서 법안은 그것이 법이 되기 전에 의회의 승인을 받아야 한다. (b) 그 법안은 입법부 회의에서 낭독되고 검토된다. (c) 국회의원들은 그 법안을 논의하고 수정안을 제시할 것이다. (d) 의원들이 그 법안을 표결해서 그 법안을 의회 대다수가 승인하면 법이 된다.

| 해설 |

approve는 '~을 승인하다, 찬성하다' 라는 의미의 3형식 동사로 수동태가 되면 뒤에 목적어가 올 수 없다. 이에 수동태가 될 때 전치사가 오게 되는데 approve는 with와 함께 쓰이지 않기 때문에 'by+행위자' 로 나타내는 것이 옳다.

| 어휘 |

legislative 입법부의
amendment 수정

12.

(a) All college students participating in any athletics will be tested for drugs. (b) From next year, each athlete will need to go through proper testing including a personal interview. (c) The fine for (a first positive test → the first positive test) will result in a suggestion to be treated. (d) After their second positive test, players will receive a full season suspension.

| 해석 |

(a) 어떠한 스포츠에든 참여하는 모든 대학생들은 약물 테스트를 받게 될 것이다. (b) 다음 연도부터는 각 선수들은 개인 면접을 포함한 적절한 테스트를 통과해야 할 것이다. (c) 처음 양성 반응이 나오면 치료가 권고될 것이다. (d) 두 번째 양성반응 후에는 전 시즌에 참가하지 못하게 될 것이다.

| 해설 |

서수사 앞에는 정관사 the가 와야 한다. 그러므로 the first positive test로 고친다.

| 어휘 |

athletics 스포츠, 운동 경기   suspension 정지

Day 6
Build Up
60p

| 1. (c) | 2. (b) | 3. (c) | 4. (a) | 5. (b) | 6. (d) |
| 7. (d) | 8. (a) | 9. (d) | 10. (c) | 11. (b) | 12. (d) |

1.

A: I won the tennis match.
B: Good for _________!
(a) them
(b) him
(c) you
(d) her

| 해석 |

A: 테니스 경기를 이겼어.
B: 잘됐다!

| 해설 |

Good for you!는 '잘됐다' 라는 의미로 축하의 의미를 전하는 관용적인 표현어구이다. for의 목적어로는 축하의 대상이 되는 대명사 목적격이 온다. 예를 들어 '그에게 잘된 일이다' 라는 의미일 때에는 Good for him!이라고 하면 된다.

2.

A: Do you have any _________ classes this semester?
B: Yes, I'm taking a really great history class.
(a) to interest
(b) interesting
(c) interested
(d) interest

| 해석 |

A: 이번 학기에 재미있는 수업 듣는 거 있니?
B: 응, 아주 재미있는 역사 수업을 들어.

| 해설 |

interest는 '흥미를 일으키다' 라는 타동사로 분사의 형태가 될 때 interesting은 상대의 관심을 불러일으키는 성질을 지니고 interested는 어떤 것에 관심을 갖게 된 것을 의미하므로 여기서는 interesting이 정답이 된다.

3.

A: How long until you have to pay the bill?
B: It _________ by July 19th.
(a) paid
(b) must pay
(c) has to be paid
(d) is paid

| 해석 |

A: 그 청구서 언제까지 내야 하니?
B: 7월 19일까지 내야 돼.

| 해설 |

A의 원래 문장은 How long will it be until you have to pay the bill?로 will it be가 편의상 생략된 구문이다. 그러므로 '언제 ~하는 것인가' 라는 의미가 된다. 여기서 pay는 '~을 치루다' 라는 타동사로 의미상 수동태가 되어야 하므로 to부정사의 수동태로 쓰인 (c)가 가장 적절하다.

4.

A: Is there anything wrong with your dog?
B: Not at all. _________ is to be petted.
(a) All she wants
(b) She all wants

(c) she needs all
(d) All wants it

| 해석 |

A: 네 강아지 뭐 잘못됐니?
B: 아니 전혀. 귀여움 받고 싶어서 그래.

| 해설 |

pet은 '귀여워하다, 총애하다' 라는 뜻이다. 빈칸은 주어 자리이므로 주어가 될 구문을 골라야 한다. 여기서 all은 대명사로 '~하는 모든 것' 이라는 의미로 단수 취급한다.

5.

_______________ made a more important contribution to psychiatry than Sigmund Freud.
(a) All psychiatrists
(b) No other psychiatrist has
(c) Any psychiatrist has
(d) Any other psychiatrists have

| 해석 |

다른 어떤 정신의학자도 지그문트 프로이드보다 정신의학에 중요한 기여를 한 사람은 없다.

| 해설 |

other는 보통 복수 명사를 수식하지만 no, any, some, one, the와 함께 단수 명사를 수식하기도 한다. 여기는 비교급과 함께 쓰여 의미상 '다른 어떤 정신의학자도 없다' 라는 의미가 되어야 자연스러우므로 (b)가 정답이다.

6.

After __________ hard for months, Alex was able to buy a brand-new car.
(a) worked
(b) he working
(c) his work
(d) working

| 해석 |

몇 달 열심히 일한 후에, 알렉스는 신형 차를 살 수 있었다.

| 해설 |

분사구문을 만들 때에는 주절의 주어와 종속절의 주어가 일치할 때 종속절의 주어를 없앤다. 그리고 난 뒤 종속절의 동사를 -ing 형태로 만들며 접속사는 때에 따라 없애기도 하고 그냥 두기도 한다. 그러므로 여기서는 working이 적절한 답이 된다. 원래는 After he worked hard for months이었다.

7.

The organization receives many donations _________ local citizens.
(a) by
(b) with
(c) to
(d) from

| 해석 |

그 기관은 지역 시민들에게 많은 기부를 받는다.

| 해설 |

적절한 전치사를 고르는 문제이다. 여기서는 '출처' 의 의미를 가진 from이 의미상 가장 자연스러우므로 정답이 된다.

8.

We can perform this entire experiment without _________ materials at all.
(a) any
(b) the
(c) some
(d) no

| 해석 |

우리는 어떤 다른 물질 전혀 없이 전체 실험을 할 수 있다.

| 해설 |

의미상 가장 적절한 한정어를 고르는 문제이다. 〈any+가산명사 단수형〉은 '하나(한 사람이)라도' 라는 의미로 any의 뜻이 강하고, 〈any+가산명사 복수형〉은 '어떤 ~라도' 라는 의미로 명사의 뜻에 중점이 있다. 여기서는 후자의 경우로 쓰인 any가 정답이 된다.

9.

(a) A: You seem really sick! You should just stay in bed today.
(b) B: I think I will. Could you get me a glass of water?
(c) A: Of course. Do you need anything else?
(d) B: Maybe some chicken soup (either → too), if you don't mind.

| 해석 |

(a) A: 너 정말 아파 보인다! 오늘은 그냥 누워 있어.
(b) B: 그래야 될 것 같아. 물 한 잔 좀 줄래?
(c) A: 물론이지. 다른 거 필요 없어?
(d) B: 괜찮다면 약간의 치킨 스프도.

| 해설 |

either는 부정문에서 '~도 역시' 라는 의미를 가진다. (e.g. I don't like eggs either. 나도 달걀이 싫어.) too는 보통 문미에 와서 문장 전체를 수식하여 긍정문에서 '~도 또한(also)' 의 의미를 지닌다. 그러므로 여기서는 either가 아닌 too가 적절하다.

10.

(a) A: It's so nice to see you, Kelly! I thought you couldn't come to the party.
(b) B: I wouldn't miss your birthday party for the world.
(c) A: Well, I'm glad you're here, but how was the work you (have to → had to) do?
(d) B: I've worked very hard for the past week, so I was able to finish it all in time.

(a) A: 켈리, 반갑다. 난 네가 못 오는 줄 알았어.
(b) B: 네 생일은 무슨 일이 있어도 안 빠지지.
(c) A: 와줘서 기뻐. 그런데 해야 한다는 일은 어떡하고?
(d) B: 지난주에 열심히 해서. 그래서 시간 모두 일을 끝낼 수 있었지.

| 해설 |
'네가 해야 했던 일은 어떻냐' 는 의미가 되어야 하므로 수식하는 어구의
동사(have to)를 과거시제로 바꾸어야 한다.

11.

(a) Wendy, congratulations on your promotion at work. (b) I just stopped by (to be given to → **to give**) you these flowers, but you weren't here. (c) It's been a long time since we've been able to spend any quality time together, but I understand how busy you must be with all your new responsibilities. (d) Good luck with everything and call me soon, so we can have lunch.

| 해석 |
(a) 웬디, 직장에서 승진한 거 축하해. (b) 너에게 이 꽃을 주려고 잠깐 들렀는데 자리에 없네. (c) 우리가 좋은 시간을 함께 보낸 게 꽤 오래됐지. 그러나 네가 새로 맡게 된 일로 얼마나 바쁜지 이해해. (d) 너의 모든 것에 행운이 있길 바라고 점심 같이 하게 전화줘.

| 해설 |
to부정사의 태를 묻는 문제이다. 여기서는 to be given이 수동으로 쓰였으나 의미상 꽃을 '주러' 온 것이므로 능동의 형태인 to give로 바꾸어야 한다.

12.

(a) Rock climbing ranks high among outdoor enthusiasts as one of the most rewarding outdoor activities. (b) However, it is also one of the most physically demanding and dangerous activities. (c) Without proper training and steady understanding of safety procedures, you risk serious injury, or even death. (d) Rock climbing without proper certification is prohibited in all national parks, so you (might → **must**) complete a training course before you begin.

| 해석 |
(a) 암벽 등반은 야외 활동 애호가들 사이에서 가장 보람된 야외 활동 중 하나로 상위를 차지한다. (b) 그러나 이것은 육체적으로 가장 힘들고 위험한 운동 중에 하나이기도 하다. (c) 적절한 훈련과 안전 절차에 대한 확실한 이해 없이는 심한 부상이나 죽음까지도 당할 위험이 있다. (d) 적합한 증명서 없이 암벽을 등반하는 것은 모든 국립공원에서 금지되어 있다. 그래서 암벽 등반을 시작하기 전에 훈련 과정을 마쳐야 한다.

| 해설 |
암벽 등반을 할 수 있는 증명서 없이는 암벽 등반이 금지되어 있으므로 훈련 코스를 '이수해야만 한다' 는 의무의 조동사가 적절하다. 그러므로 불확실한 추측의 조동사 might를 must로 고쳐야 한다.

| 어휘 |
rank ~에 위치하다 **enthusiast** 광팬, 애호가 **prohibit** 금지하다

| **1.** (d) | **2.** (b) | **3.** (b) | **4.** (a) | **5.** (c) | **6.** (a) |
| **7.** (b) | **8.** (d) | **9.** (c) | **10.** (c) | **11.** (a) | **12.** (b) |

1.

A: Is Mary not feeling well?
B: No. She __________ when I got home.
(a) slept
(b) is sleeping
(c) has slept
(d) was sleeping

| 해석 |
A: 메리가 몸이 안 좋니?
B: 안 좋아. 내가 집에 왔을 때 자고 있었어.

| 해설 |
시간 부사절의 시제가 과거시제이므로 현재진행이나 현재완료인 (b)와 (c)는 제외된다. 과거의 한 시점 상황을 말하고 있으므로 과거진행으로 표현하는 것이 적절하다.

2.

A: Thank you for the dinner, William.
B: It was my pleasure. I would like __________ again.
(a) to seeing you
(b) to see you
(c) of you seeing
(d) you to see

| 해석 |
A: 저녁 식사 고마워요. 윌리엄.
B: 천만에요. 다시 보고 싶어요.

| 해설 |
would like to~는 '~을 하고 싶다' 라는 의향을 나타내는 표현으로 여기서의 to는 to부정사로서 뒤에 동사원형이 와야 하므로 (b)가 정답이 된다.

3.

A: Dinosaurs __________ once the largest creatures to roam the earth.
B: Neat! What happened to them?
(a) was
(b) were
(c) have been
(d) had been

| 해석 |

A: 공룡이 한때 지구에 존재했던 가장 큰 동물이었대.
B: 굉장하다! 그들에게 무슨 일이 벌어진 거래?

| 해설 |

once는 '한때' 라는 의미의 부사로 과거의 시점을 나타내고 있으므로 과거형인 (b)가 정답이 된다.

4.

A: Why were you late to the board meeting?
B: ____________ to drop off my sister at the airport, but then I got stuck in traffic.

(a) I had
(b) I had had
(c) I have had
(d) I have

| 해석 |

A: 이사회 회의에 왜 늦었니?
B: 여동생을 공항에 데려다 줘야 했는데 그러고 나서 교통이 막혔어.

| 해설 |

시제 문제이다. 여기서는 과거의 사실을 이야기하고 있으므로 단순 과거 시제로 표현하는 것이 적절하다. (b)와 같은 과거완료는 과거의 한 시점을 기준으로 그 이전부터 그 시점까지의 행동이나 상태를 나타내는 것이므로 여기서는 적절치 않다.

5.

The computer manufacturer recommends ____________ the battery every 2 years.

(a) for changing
(b) for change
(c) changing
(d) to change

| 해석 |

컴퓨터 제조업자는 2년마다 건전지를 바꾸라고 권한다.

| 해설 |

recommend는 동명사를 취하는 동사이다. 그러므로 (c)가 정답이 된다.

6.

I will go to the barbeque ____________ it doesn't rain.

(a) if
(b) although
(c) unless
(d) while

| 해석 |

비가 내리지 않는다면 바비큐 파티에 갈 거야.

| 해설 |

적절한 접속사를 고르는 문제이다. 여기서는 조건의 의미를 나타내는 if가 가장 적절하다. although는 '비록 ~하지만' 이라는 양보 접속사로 적합하지 않다. unless 역시 if ~ not(만약 ~하지 않는다면)이란 의미로

의미상 적절치 않다.

7.

The company ____________ once the leading producer of soy products.

(a) is
(b) was
(c) have
(d) has

| 해석 |

그 회사는 한때 콩 제품에서 최고 업체였다.

| 해설 |

적절한 시제를 고르는 문제이다. once는 '한때' 라는 의미를 지니고 있다. 이것을 통해 과거 시제가 적절하다는 것을 알 수 있다.

8.

Many great writers emerged from the Harlem Renaissance ____________ Langston Hughes was one of the most talented and well-known.

(a) that
(b) what
(c) whose
(d) of which

| 해석 |

많은 위대한 작가들이 할렘 르네상스 기간에 나왔는데 랭스턴 휴즈는 가장 재능 있고 잘 알려진 이들 중 한 명이었다.

| 해설 |

빈칸 뒤에 완벽한 절이 왔으므로 빈칸 뒤에는 접속부사나 〈전치사＋관계대명사〉 등이 와야 한다. 의미상 '할렘 르네상스 기간에' 가 되므로 (d)가 정답이 된다.

9.

(a) A: I went to Olive Garden with Jim.
(b) B: Wow! They serve big portions. Did you have any leftovers?
(c) A: Yes, I brought some back with me. (I → I'll) probably eat them later. Do you want some?
(d) B: Sure! I'll be happy to share them with you!

| 해석 |

(a) A: 짐하고 올리버 가든에 갔었어.
(b) B: 와! 거기 양이 많은데. 남은 음식 싸왔어?
(c) A: 응, 좀 가져왔지. 이따가 먹을 것 같은데. 좀 줄까?
(d) B: 물론이지! 같이 나눠 먹으면 너무 좋지.

| 해설 |

later라는 시간 부사를 통해서 현재형이 아니라 미래형이 되어야 함을 알 수 있다. 그러므로 시제를 미래형으로 바꾼다.

10.

(a) A: Did you hear that someone left a newborn baby outside of Dr. Thornton's clinic?

(b) B: Really? What did he do?

(c) A: He tried finding the parents of the baby who couldn't (find → **be found**).

(d) B: Wow, that is very sad to hear.

| 해석 |

(a) A: 손튼 병원 밖에 누군가 신생아를 버려 두고 갔다는 소식 들었어?

(b) B: 정말? 그래서 어떻게 했대?

(c) A: 아기 부모를 찾으려고 시도했는데 찾을 수가 없었대.

(d) B: 어머, 정말 안됐다.

| 해설 |

관계대명사 who의 선행사는 the parents이므로 부모가 능동적으로 찾을 수 없다는 것은 의미상 맞지 않다. 그러므로 수동의 형태인 couldn't be found로 바꾸어야 한다.

11.

(a) I need (to speak to → **to tell**) John about his failing grade. (b) He was doing well in class for a while, especially in the beginning of the year. (c) However, he stopped doing his homework and his attendance was far from being acceptable. (d) His test scores also dropped drastically, which affected his grade a lot.

| 해석 |

(a) 존에게 그의 낙제 점수에 대해서 말해야 한다. (b) 그는 특히 학기 초에 잠시 동안 수업 시간에 잘 했었다. (c) 그러나 숙제를 하지 않기 시작했고, 출석률은 인정되기 어려워졌다. (d) 그의 시험 점수 역시 급격히 떨어지게 됐고 그것은 점수에 많은 영향을 미쳤다.

| 해설 |

〈speak to+사람〉은 '~에게 말하다' 라는 의미다. 그러나 그 뒤에 전치사 about이 올 수 없다. 그러므로 여기서는 tell이라는 동사를 쓰는 것이 적절하다. 〈tell+목적어+about~〉은 '~에게 …에 대해서 말하다' 라는 의미이다.

12.

(a) Relationships, whether they are business, romantic, or platonic, are important in life. (b) It is difficult, however, to (maintain of → **maintain**) them. (c) Many people do not understand that relationships take commitment and compromise. (d) Both parties must be willing to commit and sacrifice in order to make things work.

| 해석 |

(a) 사람 관계는 그것이 사업상이건 연인 관계이건 정신적이건 상관없이 삶에서 중요하다. (b) 그러나 그것을 유지하는 것은 어렵다. (c) 많은 사람들은 사람 관계가 의무와 양보가 필요하다는 것을 이해하지 못한다. (d) 일이 제대로 되게 하기 위해서는 양쪽 모두 기꺼이 감수하고 희생해야 한다.

| 해설 |

maintain은 타동사이므로 뒤에 전치사 of를 수반하지 않는다. 그러므로 전치사 of를 제거해야 한다.

Day 8

Build Up 76p

1. (b)	**2.** (b)	**3.** (d)	**4.** (c)	**5.** (a)	**6.** (d)
7. (a)	**8.** (d)	**9.** (b)	**10.** (d)	**11.** (c)	**12.** (d)

1.

A: My parents have invited you over for dinner. Can you come?

B: Enough __________. You know I could never turn down their invitation.

(a) to say

(b) said

(c) says

(d) saying

| 해석 |

A: 우리 부모님이 너를 저녁식사에 초대했어. 올 수 있니?

B: 알았어. 너도 내가 그 초대를 거절할 수 없다는 것을 알잖아.

| 해설 |

Enough said.는 '더 말 안 해도 안다, 잘 알았다' 라는 관용적인 표현이다. 그러므로 (b)가 정답이 된다.

2.

A: How long has the search for the missing girl been going on?

B: I think they've been __________ for a few weeks.

(a) searched

(b) searching

(c) being searched

(d) search

| 해석 |

A: 실종된 아이를 찾는 조사가 얼마나 오랫동안 진행되고 있니?

B: 그들이 몇 주 동안 찾고 있는 것 같아.

| 해설 |

없어진 과거 시점부터 지금까지 진행되고 있으므로 현재완료 진행으로 표현하는 것이 적절하다. 그러므로 (b)가 정답이 된다.

3.

A: What do you plan to do on vacation?

B: I am going to hike the mountain __________ camp near the peak.

(a) but

(b) so

(c) also

(d) and

| 해석 |

A: 방학 때 무엇을 할 계획이니?
B: 산에 올라가 정상 근처에서 캠프를 할 거야.

| 해설 |

의미상 적절한 접속사를 고르는 문제이다. 두 문장이 시간적인 순서로 대등하게 나열되므로 접속사 and가 가장 적절하다.

4.

A: Have you and Tom ever done this __________?
B: No, we have never been scuba diving.
(a) long
(b) ago
(c) before
(d) since

| 해석 |

A: 너와 탐은 전에 이거 해본 적 있니?
B: 아니, 스쿠버 다이빙은 해본 적 없어.

| 해설 |

의미상 적절한 부사를 고르는 문제이다. ago와 before 모두 '~전에'라는 의미를 가지고 있지만 ago는 과거시제와 함께 쓰여 현재를 기준으로 '그 이전'을 의미하고 before는 과거 · 현재완료에서 '그 이전'을 의미한다. 그러므로 여기서는 before가 적절하다.

5.

Jason said he had never seen __________ at the symphony before.
(a) such a small attendance
(b) such small an attendance
(c) such small attendance
(d) such attendance small

| 해석 |

제이슨은 음악회에 그렇게 적은 사람이 참석한 것을 본 적이 없다고 말했다.

| 해설 |

such의 용법을 묻는 문제이다. 〈such+(a/an)+형용사+명사〉의 어순으로 이와 관련된 문제가 TEPS에 자주 나오므로 반드시 알아두도록 한다. a small attendance는 '소수 참석자'라는 의미가 있다.

6.

Small fish are easy to catch, __________ larger fish aren't.
(a) besides
(b) rather than
(c) otherwise
(d) whereas

| 해석 |

작은 고기는 잡기 쉽지만 반면에 큰 고기는 그렇지 않다.

| 해설 |

두 개의 문장이 있으므로 빈칸에는 접속사가 들어가야 한다. 두 개의 문장이 대조를 이루므로 대조의 의미를 가진 whereas(그런데, 반면에)가 가장 적절하다. otherwise는 부사로 '그렇지 않다면'이라는 의미가 있다.

7.

The Industrial Revolution __________________,
starting in the England in the late 1700s.
(a) lasted over 150 years
(b) has lasted over 150 years
(c) over 150 years lasted
(d) did 150 years last over

| 해석 |

산업혁명은 1700년대 후반 영국에서 시작해 150년 넘게 지속됐다.

| 해설 |

알맞은 시제를 고르는 문제이다. in the late 1700s를 통해 과거의 사실에 대해서 이야기하고 있음을 알 수 있으므로 과거시제인 (a)가 정답이 된다. (c)는 전치사구가 뒤에 와야 하므로 바른 어순이 아니다.

8.

Some people claim that a cellphone __________ radiation that affects the user's brain.
(a) producing
(b) has produced
(c) is producing
(d) produces

| 해석 |

어떤 사람들은 휴대전화가 사용자의 뇌에 영향을 끼치는 방사선이 나온다고 주장한다.

| 해설 |

현재형은 습관적으로 반복되는 일, 사실, 변하지 않는 진리 등을 나타낼 때 쓴다. 여기서는 사실(fact)을 말하고 있으므로 현재형으로 나타내는 것이 가장 적절하다.

9.

(a) A: Your cat's still ill? Didn't you take her to the veterinarian?
(b) B: I did, last week. And (I took → I've been taking) care of her just like the vet told me.
(c) A: Well, it will take a little time for her to be cured.
(d) B: I know, but I am starting to get a little worried.

| 해석 |

(a) A: 네 고양이 여전히 아프니? 수의사한테 데리고 가지 않았니?
(b) B: 지난주에 데리고 갔어. 그리고 수의사가 말한 대로 돌보고 있어.
(c) A: 치료가 되기 전까지 시간이 좀 걸릴 거야.
(d) B: 알아, 그런데 좀 걱정이 되기 시작해.

| 해설 |

과거형(took)은 현재까지 영향이 미치지 않으므로 여기서는 적절치 않다. 수의사가 처방한 대로 지금도 돌보고 있다는 의미가 되어야 하므로

현재완료 진행(I've been taking)으로 표현하는 것이 적절하다.

10.

(a) A: I missed Anna's wedding. How was it?

(b) B: It was very nice and something hilarious happened while they said their vows.

(c) A: Weddings aren't supposed to be funny. What happened?

(d) B: A little girl ran up to Anna, then she hugged Anna's leg and (mustn't → **wouldn't**) let go.

| 해석 |
(a) A: 애나의 결혼식에 못 갔어. 어땠어?
(b) B: 매우 좋았어. 그리고 서약을 하는 동안 뭔가 재미있는 벌어졌어.
(c) A: 결혼식은 재미있는 게 아니잖아. 무슨 일인데?
(d) B: 작은 여자애가 애나한테 달려와선 애나의 다리를 잡고 놔주지 않으려 했어.

| 해설 |
조동사의 쓰임을 묻는 문제이다. must는 '~해야 한다' 는 의미와 '~임에 틀림없다' 가 있다. must not은 '~하지 말아야 한다' 는 의무의 부정형이고, 추측의 의미일 때 부정형은 cannot이 된다. 여기서는 의미상 must의 쓰임이 자연스럽지 않기 때문에 주어의 의지, 주장, 고집 등의 의미를 가진 would가 적절하다.

11.

(a) One of my favorite vacation destinations is Thailand. (b) Thailand has everything you could want, from tropical beaches to beautiful mountains and forests. (c) And of course there is the modern metropolis and capital city, Bangkok, a place to which I always (return to → **return**). (d) I love the city because it has a certain energy flowing through it that I've never felt anywhere else.

| 해석 |
(a) 내가 좋아하는 휴양지 중의 하나는 태국이다. (b) 태국은 열대 해변부터 아름다운 산과 숲까지 당신이 원하는 모든 것을 가지고 있다. (c) 물론 내가 항상 돌아가고 싶은 장소, 현대 도시이자 수도인 방콕도 있다. (d) 다른 곳에서는 느껴본 적 없는 어떤 에너지가 그곳에 흐르고 있기 때문에 그 도시를 사랑한다.

| 해설 |
동사 return이 자동사로 쓰일 때는 전치사와 함께 쓰인다. 그런데 여기서는 관계대명사 앞에 전치사 to가 있으므로(to which) 동사 뒤에 전치사 to를 없애야 한다.

12.

(a) Construction workers have been brought in to make the school look more sleek and modern. (b) However, their work has done nothing but cause a disturbance for the students and faculty. (c) Not only do they make loud, disruptive noises all day long, but also the dust from the construction gets everywhere making it hard to breathe. (d) Also, it covers all the desks and chairs so that each class period the students must (wipe their desks and chairs a layer of dust off → **wipe a layer of dust off their desks and chairs**).

| 해석 |
(a) 학교 외관을 더 멋지고 현대적으로 만들기 위해 건축업자들을 불렀습니다. (b) 그러나 아무것도 되지 않았고 학생들과 교직원에게 폐만 끼칠 뿐이었습니다. (c) 하루 종일 시끄럽고 소란스러운 소음을 냈을 뿐만 아니라 공사 먼지가 이곳저곳에 있어 숨을 쉬기 힘들게 했습니다. (d) 또한 먼지가 모든 책상과 의자를 덮어서 각 수업 시간마다 학생들은 먼지를 책상과 의자에서 닦아내야만 했습니다.

| 해설 |
문장의 구조를 묻는 질문이다. wipe은 4형식 동사가 아니기 때문에 목적어 두 개가 나란히 열거될 수 없다. wipe A off B는 'A을 B로부터 닦아내다' 라는 의미이다. 그러므로 여기서는 문장의 구조를 바로 잡아 wipe a layer of dust off their desks and chairs로 고쳐야 한다.

Day 9

Build Up

84p

1. (d)	2. (d)	3. (c)	4. (c)	5. (b)	6. (b)
7. (b)	8. (d)	9. (a)	10. (b)	11. (b)	12. (a)

1.

A: Hey, the bus is here! I have to go.

B: Okay. Remember! Dinner at six. _

____

(a) See there you!

(b) There you see

(c) You see there!

(d) **See you there!**

| 해석 |
A: 야, 버스 왔어. 나 가야 돼.
B: 알았어. 기억해! 저녁식사 여섯 시.

| 해설 |
See you there.은 '거기서 보자' 는 의미의 생활 영어 표현이다. 이 문장은 I will see you there.에서 앞에 I will이 생략된 표현이다.

2.

A: Benjamin placed first in the track tournament!

B: I'm not so surprised considering __________ training for it a year in advance.

(a) for him to begin
(b) of him to begin
(c) at him began
(d) that he began

| 해석 |

A: 벤자민이 육상 경기에서 일등을 했대.
B: 그가 일 년 전부터 그 경기를 위해 훈련을 시작한 것을 생각하면 전혀 놀랍지 않아.

| 해설 |

considering이 전치사로 쓰여서 바로 명사를 취하기도 하지만 여기서는 〈considering (that)＋주어＋동사〉의 어순으로 쓰였다. 그러므로 (d)가 가장 적절한 답이 된다. place first는 '일등하다' 라는 표현이다.

3.

A: Thank you so much for your help today.
B: No problem. Let me know if you have

_________________________.

(a) something of you to do
(b) something I want to do
(c) anything you want me to do
(d) anything do you want me to do

| 해석 |

A: 오늘 도와줘서 너무 고마워요.
B: 천만에요. 또 도울 일이 있으면 알려주세요.

| 해설 |

조건절에서는 something과 anything이 모두 쓰인다. 따라서 관계대명사 that이 생략되어 평서문의 절이 올바른 순서로 온 (c)가 정답이 된다.

4.

A: Were you in the middle of something when the fire alarm went off?
B: Yes, I was working on my essay, _________ my own business.

(a) mind
(b) to mind
(c) minding
(d) minded

| 해석 |

A: 화재 경보기가 울렸을 때 뭔가 하는 중이었니?
B: 응, 내 일만 신경 쓰면서 에세이를 쓰고 있었어.

| 해설 |

mind가 타동사이고 뒤에 목적어가 왔으므로 능동의 형태인 minding이 정답이 된다. minding my own business는 '내 일만 신경 쓰면서' 라는 관용적 표현이다.

5.

Because of the stock market crash, Mickey lost more than _________ and stocks.

(a) halving his earnings

(b) half of his earnings
(c) his half of earnings
(d) earnings in half

| 해석 |

주식 시장 폭락 때문에 미키는 그의 수입의 반 이상과 주식을 잃었다.

| 해설 |

〈half of＋명사〉는 '~의 절반' 이라는 의미이다. '수입의 절반' 이라는 의미가 되어야 하므로 (b)의 어순이 가장 적절하다.

6.

What gift should we get for John _________ his birthday?
(a) at
(b) on
(c) of
(d) upon

| 해석 |

존 생일에 무슨 선물을 사줄까?

| 해설 |

특정한 날 앞에는 전치사 on을 쓴다. 그러므로 (b)가 정답이 된다.

7.

James was in _________ to learn more about the student organization.
(a) hurry
(b) a hurry
(c) hurries
(d) the hurry

| 해석 |

제임스는 그 학생 기구에 대해 배우기 위해 서둘렀다.

| 해설 |

in a hurry는 '급히, 서둘러서' 라는 관용적인 표현이다. hurry 앞에 관용적으로 a가 쓰이므로 이 표현을 알아두도록 한다.

8.

The firefighters worked for seventeen hours to extinguish _________ spreading in different areas of the forest.
(a) blazes
(b) a blaze
(c) all blaze
(d) the blazes

| 해석 |

소방관들은 그 숲의 다른 지역으로 번지는 불길을 끄기 위해서 열일곱 시간을 일했다.

| 해설 |

blaze는 '불꽃, 화재' 라는 뜻으로 가산명사이다. 여러 개의 불꽃이 그 숲의 여러 지역에 번진 것이므로 (d)가 정답이 된다.

9.

(a) A: Are you okay? You seem (unfocusing → unfocused) and worried.
(b) B: I guess. I received a phone call from my mom about my cousin.
(c) A: Was it bad news?
(d) B: I'm not sure yet, but she told me that my cousin found a lump on her chest.

| 해석 |
(a) A: 괜찮니? 산만하고 걱정돼 보여.
(b) B: 응. 사촌에 대해서 엄마가 전화를 주셨어.
(c) A: 나쁜 소식이니?
(d) B: 아직 확실한 건 아닌데 사촌 가슴에서 혹이 발견됐대.

| 해설 |
seem 뒤에 보어로 분사가 왔다. '산만한'이라는 의미로 unfocused가 되어야 한다.

10.

(a) A: Why are you so happy?
(b) B: Our boss just promoted several people (included → including) me and others.
(c) A: That's fantastic! You definitely deserve it.
(d) B: Thank you! I worked hard for this promotion.

| 해석 |
(a) A: 너 왜 그리 기분이 좋아?
(b) B: 사장님이 나랑 다른 사람 여러 명을 승진시켰어.
(c) A: 잘됐다. 넌 충분히 받을 자격 있어.
(d) B: 고마워. 이번 승진을 위해 열심히 일했어.

| 해설 |
include는 타동사로서 included라는 수동의 의미를 가진 과거분사의 형태로 쓰이면 뒤의 명사구를 받을 수 없다. including은 '~을 포함해서'라는 의미로 뒤에 명사구를 받을 수 있다.

11.

(a) There are many reasons why the ecosystem is deteriorating. (b) One of the reasons (are → is) because of pollution. (c) Another reason is because people don't put in the effort to recycle or clean up the environment. (d) Also, humans destroy natural resources every year by demolishing and building over forests.

| 해석 |
(a) 생태계가 악화되는 데는 많은 이유가 있다. (b) 그 이유 중 하나는 오염 때문이다. (c) 또 다른 이유는 사람들이 재활용이나 환경을 정화하는 노력을 안 한다는 것이다. (d) 또한 사람들은 숲을 파괴하고 건설하면서 매년 천연 자원을 파괴한다.

| 해설 |
수의 일치에 관한 문제이다. 〈one of+복수 명사〉에서는 one이 주어가 되기 때문에 단수 동사가 와야 한다. 그러므로 are를 is로 고쳐야 한다.

| 어휘 |

deteriorate 나빠지다, 악화되다   demolish 파괴하다

12.

(a) Women should be careful at night-time and (for the good reason → for (a) good reason) too. (b) They are very vulnerable to sexual harassment and assault. (c) Women should carry around a whistle or other noise device for emergency situations. (d) They should also try not to walk alone because they are more susceptible to being attacked.

| 해석 |
(a) 여성들은 밤에 주의해야 하는데 그럴 만한 이유가 있다. (b) 여성들은 성희롱과 성폭행을 받기 쉽다. (c) 그들은 위급상황을 대비해서 호각이나 다른 소리 장치를 가지고 다녀야 한다. (d) 그들은 공격을 받기 쉽기 때문에 혼자 걸어 다녀서도 안된다.

| 해설 |
관사의 용법에 관한 문제이다. the가 오게 되면 특정한 이유가 되는데 여기서는 적절치 않다. for good reason 혹은 for a good reason은 '일반적인 그럴만한 이유로'라는 의미로 관용적인 표현으로 알아두도록 한다.

| 어휘 |
vulnerable 공격받기 쉬운, 상처받기 쉬운
sexual harassment 성희롱   assault 폭행
susceptible 가능한, 여지가 있는

Day 10

Build Up
92p

1. (d)	**2.** (b)	**3.** (c)	**4.** (d)	**5.** (c)	**6.** (c)
7. (b)	**8.** (c)	**9.** (a)	**10.** (d)	**11.** (c)	**12.** (c)

1.

A: Did you have fun playing tennis yesterday?
B: Yes! But I wish you __________ with me.
(a) played
(b) had play
(c) have played
(d) had played

| 해석 |
A: 어제 테니스 경기 재밌었니?
B: 응! 근데 너도 함께 했었으면 좋았을걸.

| 해설 |
wish를 이용한 가정법 문제이다. 〈wish+주어+과거 동사〉는 가정법 과거로 현재 사실의 반대를 가정하는 표현이다. 〈wish+주어+had p.p.〉는 가정법 과거완료로 과거 사실의 반대를 가정하는 표현이다. 여기서는 어제의 반대되는 상황을 가정하는 것이므로 가정법 과거완료로 표현하는

것이 적절하다.

2.

A: Do you know why there's going to be a parade next week?
B: It's because on August 12ᵗʰ the island __________ established for 200 years.
(a) was
(b) will have been
(c) must have been
(d) will be

| 해석 |
A: 다음주에 왜 퍼레이드가 있는지 알아?
B: 8월 12일이 이 섬이 세워진 지 200년이 된 날이야.

| 해설 |
시제를 묻는 문제이다. 미래완료는 미래의 한 시점을 기준으로 그 이전부터 그때까지의 동작이나 상태를 나타내며 will have p.p.로 표현한다. 여기서는 8월 12일이 미래의 기준 시점이 되므로 미래완료로 표현하는 것이 적절하다.

3.

A: Hi, Lloyd! __________ play on the school soccer team?
B: I'm not sure yet, they haven't announced the lineup.
(a) Would you
(b) Did you
(c) Were you chosen to
(d) Were you choosing to

| 해석 |
A: 안녕! 로이드! 학교 축구팀에 뽑혔니?
B: 아직 잘 모르겠어. 선수 명단을 아직 발표하지 않았거든.

| 해설 |
choose는 to부정사를 목적어로 취하는 동사이다. 여기서는 의미상 '선택되다'는 수동의 의미가 되어야 하므로 (c)가 가장 적절하다.

4.

A: I'm confused, __________? I thought it was further up the street.
B: No. It's always been right here, but many of these buildings have been renovated.
(a) where did we eat dinner last year
(b) where we ate dinner last year
(c) is this where did we eat last year
(d) is this where we ate dinner last year

| 해석 |
A: 헷갈리는데, 여기가 작년에 저녁을 먹었던 곳이니? 난 이 거리 훨씬 위쪽이라고 생각했는데.
B: 아니. 항상 여기 있었어. 그런데 여기 많은 빌딩이 개조되었어.

| 해설 |
문장의 어순을 묻는 문제이다. 먼저 빈칸 뒤에 이어지는 문장을 통해 빈칸이 의문사 의문문이 아님을 알 수 있으므로 의문사 의문문은 제외시킨다. 간접의문문의 순서는 〈의문사＋주어＋동사〉이다. 여기서 where 이하는 간접의문문이므로 (d)의 어순이 가장 적절하다. 관계부사 where 앞에는 장소의 선행사 the place가 생략되었다.

5.

We must teach young athletes __________ losing, but rather to learn from it.
(a) never hate
(b) no hate
(c) not to hate
(d) to hate not

| 해석 |
젊은 선수들에게 지는 것을 싫어하기보다는 그것으로부터 배우도록 가르쳐야 한다.

| 해설 |
〈teach＋목적어＋to부정사〉는 '~에게 …하라고 가르치다'라는 의미이다. to부정사의 부정은 to부정사 앞에 not이 들어간다. 그러므로 (c)가 정답이다.

6.

__________ of the thieve's guilt was found in his basement, where he stored the things he stole.
(a) Proofs
(b) A proof
(c) Proof
(d) The proofs

| 해석 |
훔친 것들을 저장해 둔 지하실에서 그 도둑의 죄의 증거가 발견되었다.

| 해설 |
이 문장에서 동사는 was이다. 그러므로 수의 일치 관점에서 (a)나 (d)는 답이 될 수 없다. a proof는 하나의 증거를 말하지만 그의 죄를 증명할 수 있는 것은 그의 지하실에 있는 모든 물건들이다. 따라서 '전체 증거'를 의미하는 proof가 적절하다.

7.

Young kids do not realize that cellphones were rare __________.
(a) too not in the distant past
(b) in the not too distant past
(c) past in the not too distant
(d) in not too the distant past

| 해석 |
어린아이들은 멀지 않은 과거에는 휴대폰이 드물었다는 것을 모른다.

| 해설 |
어순과 관련된 문제이다. in the past라는 기본적인 표현에 distant라는 형용사를 past(명사) 앞에 두고 부사 too를 형용사 distant 앞에 둔다. 또한 부정어 not은 부사 앞에 위치해야 하므로 (b)가 정답이 된다. 이렇

듯 어순과 관련된 문제는 무조건 외우려 하지 말고 기본적인 문법에 대입
하여 차근차근 고르도록 한다.

8.

___________ I am not fond of New York City, I
think the rest of the States is beautiful.
(a) Since
(b) But
(c) While
(d) When

| 해석 |
뉴욕은 맘에 들지 않지만 미국의 나머지 주들은 아름다운 것 같다.

| 해설 |
문장에 적절한 접속사를 고르는 문제이다. while은 기간을 나타내어 '~
하는 동안에' 라는 의미와 양보의 종속절을 이끌어 '~하는 반면에' 라는
의미가 있다. 여기서는 후자의 의미로 쓰였다.

9.

(a) A: The Smiths and the Walters are planning to
vacation (Florida → in Florida) this summer.
(b) B: Must we go to Florida again? We've been
there the last three summers.
(c) A: But wouldn't you rather go where our
friends are going?
(d) B: Not if it means seeing and doing the same
things we do every year.

| 해석 |
(a) A: 스미스 부부와 워터 부부는 이번 여름에 휴가를 플로리다에서 보
낼 계획이야.
(b) B: 플로리다에 또 가야만 해? 지난 세 번의 여름을 거기서 보냈잖아.
(c) A: 친구들이 가는 데로 가는 게 낫지 않을까?
(d) B: 매년 똑같은 것이라면 아니야.

| 해설 |
여기서 vacation은 자동사로 〈vacation＋전치사＋명사〉의 어순으로
'~에서 휴가를 보내다' 라는 의미가 있다. 그러므로 장소의 명사 Florida
앞에 전치사를 붙여야 한다.

10.

(a) A: What is the best way to gain advancement
in your career?
(b) B: I've always been told that making a five-
year plan is effective.
(c) A: That's right. And do you know why those
methods are effective?
(d) B: Because it helps keep your progress (on the
course → on course) for meeting your
goals.

| 해석 |
(a) A: 네 일에서 발전할 수 있는 가장 좋은 방법이 무엇이니?
(b) B: 5년 계획이 효과적이라고 항상 들어왔어.

(c) A: 맞아. 그런 방법들이 왜 효과가 있는지는 알아?
(d) B: 왜냐하면 목표를 이루기 위한 과정을 예정대로 계속 진행하는 데
도움을 주기 때문이지.

| 해설 |
여기서 course는 특정한 과정을 가리키는 것이 아니라 on course라는
관용적인 표현으로 '예정 방향으로 나아가' 라는 의미가 있다. 그러므로
the를 없애야 한다.

11.

(a) When learning to drive a car, the most
important lesson is to learn to be comfortable
while behind the wheel. (b) Too many drivers
focus too closely on the physical act of driving. (c)
A good driver is always aware of the road, the
cars, and the conditions, (at the same time → but
at the same time) perfectly comfortable and
relaxed. (d) Also, in order to be both aware and
comfortable, the driver should not be
concentrating on what could happen, but rather
on how to react to his or her surroundings.

| 해석 |
(a) 차를 운전하는 법을 배울 때 가장 중요한 교훈은 운전을 하는 동안
편안해지는 것을 배우는 것이다. (b) 너무 많은 운전자들이 운전의 육체
적인 행동에 지나치게 집중한다. (c) 좋은 운전자는 항상 도로와 차, 상
태를 경계하지만 동시에 완전히 편안한 마음으로 긴장을 푼다. (d) 또한
경계하면서 편안해하기 위해서 운전자는 무슨 일이 벌어질 수 있는지에
대해서 집중하지 말고 대신 그/그녀의 환경에 어떻게 대응할 수 있는지
에 대해 집중해야 한다.

| 해설 |
at the same time 뒤의 comfortable and relaxed를 연결할 접속사가
없다. 여기서는 의미상 대조되는 문장이 연결되므로 but이라는 대조의
등위접속사가 오는 것이 적절하다.

12.

(a) Native Americans were not always native in the
Western Hemisphere. (b) We call them native
because they were there long before the
Europeans ever realized those continents existed.
(c) (When did the Native Americans arrive →
When the Native Americans did arrive) they came
across the Bering Strait, which separates Russia
from Alaska. (d) During very cold winters the
Strait froze over, creating a safe, solid route from
Asia to the Americas.

| 해석 |
(a) 미국 원주민들이 항상 서반구에서 원주민이지는 않았다. (b) 유럽인
들이 그 대륙들이 존재한다고 알기 훨씬 전부터 그곳에 있었기 때문에 우
리는 그들을 원주민이라고 부른다. (c) 미국 원주민들이 도착했을 때 그
들은 알래스카와 러시아를 분리시키는 베링 해협을 건너서 왔다. (d) 매
우 추운 겨울 동안에 해협은 아시아에서 아메리카까지 안전하고 단단한
길을 만들면서 얼어붙었다.

| 해설 |

When did the Native Americans arrive는 의문사 의문문의 순서이다. 여기서는 시간 부사절이 되어야 하므로 did의 위치가 뒤로 와야 한다. 여기서 did는 강조의 용법으로 쓰였다.

Day 11
Build Up

1. (c)	2. (b)	3. (b)	4. (b)	5. (c)	6. (c)
7. (c)	8. (d)	9. (c)	10. (c)	11. (a)	12. (c)

1.

A: Do you want to rest before we go back?

B: Yes, I _________________ sleep for an hour since it's a long drive back.

(a) would like   (b) would have liked to

(c) would like to   (d) could like to

| 해석 |

A: 우리 돌아가기 전에 너 좀 쉬고 싶니?

B: 응, 오랫동안 운전해서 가야 하기 때문에 한 시간 정도 잠을 자두고 싶어.

| 해설 |

would like to는 '~하고 싶다' 는 뜻으로 의향을 나타내는 관용적인 표현이다. 그러므로 여기서는 (c)가 가장 적절하다.

2.

A: Congratulations! I'm so happy to hear that _________________ !

B: Wow, thanks! How did you find out about it so fast?

(a) you've engaged   (b) you're engaged

(c) engaged   (d) you're engaging

| 해석 |

A: 축하해. 네가 약혼했다는 소식을 듣게 되어 기뻐.

B: 고마워. 어떻게 그렇게 빨리 소식을 듣게 됐니?

| 해설 |

engage는 '약혼시키다' 는 의미의 타동사로 보통 수동태의 형태로 많이 쓰인다. 여기서도 약혼했다는 의미가 되야 하므로 수동의 형태인 (b)가 정답이 된다.

3.

A: Why was the mother so sad when the paramedics arrived?

B: Because they _____________ her child if they had arrived five minutes earlier.

(a) could save   (b) could have saved

(c) would save   (d) will save

| 해석 |

A: 그 엄마는 의료 보조팀이 도착했을 때 왜 그렇게 슬퍼했어?

B: 그들이 5분만 일찍 왔어도 그녀의 아이를 구할 수 있었기 때문이야.

| 해설 |

가정법 과거완료 용법과 관련된 문제이다. 과거 사실에 반대되는 가정을 할 때 가정법 과거완료 〈if+주어+had p.p.~, 주어+조동사 과거형 +have p.p.~〉를 사용한다. 그러므로 (b)가 정답이 된다.

4.

A: What type of bouquet would you like me to buy for your wife's dinner party?

B: You can choose something that is elegant, but definitely choose ___________ that has yellow roses in it.

(a) it   (b) one

(c) them   (d) those

| 해석 |

A: 사모님의 저녁 파티에 어떤 종류의 꽃다발을 원하십니까?

B: 뭔가 우아하고 노란색 장미가 들어간 것으로 해 주세요.

| 해설 |

one은 〈a/an+명사〉를 대신해서 쓰이며 동일한 종류의 것을 받는다. 지시대명사 it은 〈the/소유격+명사〉 대신 쓰이며 동일한 바로 '그것' 을 받는다. 그러므로 여기서는 one이 정답이 된다.

5.

I did not understand my professor's instructions, and _________________.

(a) my classmates neither did

(b) neither my classmates did

(c) neither did my classmates

(d) my classmates did neither

| 해석 |

나는 교수님의 설명을 이해하지 못했고 우리 반 친구들도 역시 이해하지 못했다.

| 해설 |

neither 뒤에 절이 오게 되면 도치가 이루어진다. 〈neither+(조)동사+주어〉의 어순이 되어 부정어구를 포함한 문 또는 절에서 '~도 역시 …아니다' 라는 의미로 쓰인다. 그러므로 (c)의 어순이 정답이 된다.

6.

_________________ his students were failing because of his unclear and complicated instructions.

(a) The professor little realized that

(b) The professor realized little that

(c) Little did the professor realize that

(d) Little did realize the professor that

| 해석 |

그의 불분명하고 복잡한 설명 때문에 학생들이 낙제했다는 것을 교수는
깨닫지 못했다.

| 해설 |

little은 '거의 ~않다'라는 의미의 부사로 문두에 위치하게 되면 문장이
도치가 된다. 그러므로 (c)가 정답이 된다.

7.

The airline reimbursed him and apologized

_________________________________.

(a) for him to the late arrival of the flight.
(b) him the late arrival of the flight
(c) to him for the late arrival of the flight
(d) the late arrival of the flight to him

| 해석 |

항공사는 그에게 변상했고 비행기 연착에 대해 사과했다.

| 해설 |

〈apologize to+사람+for~〉는 '…에게 ~에 대해 사과하다'라는 의미
가 있다. apologize는 자동사로 목적어를 취할 때 전치사를 필요로 한
다. 그러므로 (c)가 정답이 된다.

8.

It is not _______________ to inhale gasoline
fumes.

(a) safe you
(b) for you safe
(c) you are safe
(d) safe for you

| 해석 |

석유 가스를 흡입하는 것은 안전하지 않다.

| 해설 |

〈it is+형용사+for+명사+to V〉의 형식을 묻는 문제이다. 여기서 it은
가주어이며 〈for+명사〉가 의미상의 주어이고, to부정사가 의미상의 동
사가 된다. 그러므로 (d)가 정답이 된다.

9.

(a) A: What did you get this present from Chanel
for?
(b) B: It's because today is your birthday! Open it.
(c) A: You took the time and bought a present (to
→ for) me?
(d) B: Of course I did. I hope you have a happy
birthday.

| 해석 |

(a) A: 샤넬에서 이 선물은 왜 샀어?
(b) B: 오늘 네 생일이잖아. 열어 봐.
(c) A: 나를 위해 시간을 내서 선물을 샀다고?
(d) B: 물론이지. 행복한 생일 되길 바래.

| 해설 |

to가 대상의 용법으로 쓰일 때는 '~에게'이고, for가 대상의 용법으로

쓰일 때는 '~를 위해'라는 의미이다. 그러므로 여기서는 for가 적절하
다.

10.

(a) A: I am so exhausted from midterms!
(b) B: Yeah, you must be, since you had exams
every day!
(c) A: I'm looking forward to this weekend and (to
catch → catching) up on some sleep.
(d) B: Good! You definitely deserve it.

| 해석 |

(a) A: 중간고사 때문에 너무 지쳤어.
(b) B: 맞아. 매일 시험을 봤으니 당연하지.
(c) A: 이번 주말에는 그동안 못 잔 잠이나 잘 거야.
(d) B: 그래. 넌 충분히 그럴 자격이 있어.

| 해설 |

look forward to~는 '~을 기대하다, 고대하다'라는 의미로 to가 전치
사이므로 동사원형이 아닌 동명사 catching이 되어야 한다.

11.

(a) Many youth programs are being created to
suggest (to engage → engaging) in different
guidance programs. (b) Most programs that
encourage abstinence and safe sex are more
popular than ever. (c) Organizations that
discourage drug abuse are increasing as well. (d)
These programs are beneficial, especially in
urban cities where sexual promiscuity and drug
use are rampant.

| 해석 |

(a) 많은 청소년 프로그램이 다른 보호 프로그램들과 연계되도록 만들어
지고 있다. (b) 절제와 안전한 섹스를 장려하는 프로그램들이 예전보다
더 보편화되고 있다. (c) 약물 남용을 예방하는 기관들도 늘어나고 있다.
(d) 이러한 프로그램들은 유익하며 특히 문란한 성행위와 약물 복용이
만연한 도시 지역에 도움이 된다.

| 해설 |

suggest는 that절을 취하기도 하지만 동명사를 취하기도 한다. 그러나
to부정사는 취하지 않으므로 동명사의 형태로 바꾸어야 한다.

| 어휘 |

abstinence 절제   promiscuity 난잡함   rampant 만연하는

12.

(a) Arden always aspired to be a successful
actress in Hollywood. (b) She participated in
many talent and fashion shows and even posed
for magazine covers. (c) She recently landed a
role on a popular television show by, (which →
what) is known as *Heroes*. (d) There is no doubt
that she will make it big one day by landing a star
role in a successful movie!

(a) 아덴은 항상 할리우드에서 성공한 여배우가 되길 바랐다. (b) 그녀는 많은 연예쇼와 패션쇼에 참여했고 잡지 커버에도 실렸다. (c) 그녀는 최근 '히어로즈' 라고 알려진 유명한 TV쇼에서 역할을 맡게 되었다. (d) 성공적인 영화에서 주역을 맡음으로써 언젠가 그녀가 성공할 것이라는 데는 의심의 여지가 없다.

| 해설 |

which는 앞에 선행사를 필요로 하는 관계대명사다. 그러나 전치사 뒤에 명사절을 이끄는 관계대명사가 필요하므로 which를 what으로 바꾸어야 한다. 관계대명사 what은 자체에 선행사를 포함하여 명사절을 이끈다. by를 없앤다면 which도 가능하다.

| 어휘 |

aspire 열망하다, 큰 포부를 갖다   **land** 획득하다, 얻다

Day 12

Build Up
108p

1. (a)	2. (c)	3. (c)	4. (d)	5. (c)	6. (d)
7. (a)	8. (b)	9. (c)	10. (d)	11. (c)	12. (d)

1.

A: I hate winter, _____________________.
B: I agree. I get scared doing it, too.
(a) driving in the snow is too difficult
(b) the snow driving is too difficult
(c) it is too difficult for my drive in the snow
(d) it is too difficult that I drive in the snow

| 해석 |
A: 나는 겨울이 싫어. 눈길에 운전하는 건 너무 어렵거든.
B: 맞아. 나도 눈길에 운전하는 게 무서워.

| 해설 |
driving in the snow는 동명사구로서 단수 취급한다. 그러므로 의미상 어순이 가장 적절한 것은 (a)가 된다.

2.

A: Did you get a chance to see the Georgia O'Keeffe exhibition at the Art Museum?
B: I did, but I _________ it because I thought it lasted another month.
(a) am nearly missing
(b) nearly didn't miss
(c) nearly missed
(d) was nearly missing

| 해석 |

A: 미술관에서 조지아 오키프 전시회 봤니?
B: 응, 하지만 거의 놓칠 뻔 했어. 난 그 전시회가 한 달 더 하는 줄 알았거든.

| 해설 |
but이라는 대조를 나타내는 접속사가 나왔으므로 의미상 부정문인 (b)는 적절치 않다. 과거 시점의 이야기를 하는 것이므로 과거시제로 나타낸 (c)가 정답이 된다.

3.

A: Excuse me, do you know _________ I can give my completed paperwork to?
B: I can take that from you, sir. You can just wait in the waiting room till we're ready for you.
(a) when
(b) what
(c) whom
(d) whomever

| 해석 |
A: 실례합니다만 제가 누구에게 이 완성된 문서를 줘야 되는지 아십니까?
B: 제가 가져다 드리지요. 준비될 때까지 대기실에서 기다리십시오.

| 해설 |
빈칸에는 동사 give의 간접목적어가 필요하므로 목적격 관계대명사가 필요하다. 의미상 사람이 필요하므로 (c)가 정답이 된다.

4.

A: When can I see your band play live?
B: We _________ every weekend at a local jazz club.
(a) would perform
(b) can perform
(c) did perform
(d) perform

| 해석 |
A: 너희 밴드가 라이브로 연주하는 것을 언제 볼 수 있니?
B: 지역 재즈 바에서 주말마다 연주해.

| 해설 |
every weekend라는 표현을 통해 반복해서 일어나는 일임을 알 수 있다. 그러므로 현재시제가 가장 적절하다.

5.

_________ that pianist tonight at the symphony has made me want to start playing piano again.
(a) When hearing
(b) Of hearing
(c) Hearing
(d) By hearing

| 해석 |
오늘밤 연주회에서 그 피아니스트의 연주를 들은 것은 내가 다시 피아노를 시작하고 싶게끔 만들었다.

| 해설 |

이 문장의 동사는 has made이다. 그러므로 빈칸에는 that절을 이끌면서 문장의 주어가 될 수 있는 (c)가 가장 적절하다. 동명사는 단수 취급한다.

6.

For some busy families fast food restaurants often provide many kinds of the meals, __________ can be harmful to any person's health.

(a) that

(b) when

(c) such

(d) which

| 해석 |

바쁜 가족들을 위해서 패스트푸드 음식점들은 흔히 많은 음식들을 제공하는데, 이 음식들은 어떤 사람에게는 건강을 해칠 수도 있다.

| 해설 |

빈칸에는 many kinds of the meals를 받는 주격 관계대명사이면서 계속적 용법으로 쓰일 수 있는 것이 와야 하므로 which가 정답이 된다. that은 계속적 용법으로 쓰일 수 없으므로 정답이 될 수 없다.

7.

If I __________ travel cross-country, I wouldn't pack half as much baggage as you have.

(a) were to

(b) was to

(c) have to

(d) might

| 해석 |

내가 전국을 횡단하는 여행을 한다면 네가 싼 짐의 반은 싸지 않을 거야.

| 해설 |

〈If+주어+were to~, 주어+조동사 과거+동사원형〉의 어순이 되어 일어날 가능성이 희박한 일을 가정할 때 쓰인다. 그러므로 (a)가 정답이 된다. 또한 if 가정법 과거에서 be동사는 주어의 수와 상관없이 were를 사용한다.

8.

The swimmers __________ from the two sharks were hysterical and made it difficult for others to get to safety.

(a) who escape

(b) escaping

(c) for escaping

(d) to escape

| 해석 |

두 마리의 상어에게서 도망친 수영자들은 병적으로 흥분했고 그것이 다른 사람들을 안전한 곳으로 대피시키는 일을 어렵게 만들었다.

| 해설 |

분사가 명사를 후치 수식할 경우 〈주격 관계대명사+be동사〉가 생략된 경우가 많다. 여기서도 the swimmers who were escaping이 원래의

문장으로 (b)가 정답이 된다.

9.

(a) A: There is never enough work to do around the office during Christmas.

(b) B: Why do you have to work so many hours then?

(c) A: Well, I don't have to, but I definitely (would → **could/can**) use the extra money.

(d) B: Then, I guess I don't understand what you are complaining about.

| 해석 |

(a) A: 크리스마스 동안엔 일이 많지 않아.

(b) B: 근데 넌 왜 그렇게 일을 많이 해야 하니?

(c) A: 뭐 꼭 그럴 필요는 없어. 하지만 여분의 돈을 쓸 수가 있거든.

(d) B: 난 네가 불평하는 것을 이해할 수 없어.

| 해설 |

의미상 적절한 조동사를 찾아내는 것이다. 여기서는 막연한 추측을 나타내는 would보다는 가능성을 나타내는 could나 can이 적절하다.

10.

(a) A: Hello, William! I really like your suit. Did you get a new job?

(b) B: Actually, yes. I got the job downtown that I was telling you about last week.

(c) A: But I thought you weren't able to get an interview at that company?

(d) B: I wasn't, but last Friday I just walked in and (convinced to → **convinced**) the boss to give me the job.

(a) A: 안녕, 윌리엄! 네 양복 정말 멋지다. 새 직장을 구했니?

(b) B: 응. 지난주에 말했던 시내에 있는 일자리를 구했어.

(c) A: 그런데 난 네가 그 회사에서 인터뷰 할 수 없을 거라고 생각했는데.

(d) B: 못했지. 하지만 지난 금요일에 그냥 회사에 가서 나에게 일자리를 주도록 사장을 설득했어.

| 해설 |

convince는 '확신시키다' 라는 의미의 타동사로 목적어를 바로 취한다. 그러므로 전치사 to를 제거해야 한다.

11.

(a) When I was walking home from my friend's house last night something very strange happened. (b) I didn't see any other people most of the way home, but I saw one person wearing a big wool jacket. (c) Passing my right side, (I was addressed by the man → **the man addressed me by name**). (d) Immediately I turned around to see who it was, but there was no one there!

| 해석 |

| 해석 |
(a) 어젯밤에 친구 집에서 돌아올 때 뭔가 매우 이상한 일이 벌어졌다. (b) 나는 집에 오는 길 내내 다른 사람은 보지 못했는데 큰 울 재킷을 입은 사람을 보게 되었다. (c) 내 오른쪽을 지나가면서 그 남자는 내 이름을 불렀다. (d) 나는 그가 누구인지 보기 위해 바로 돌아섰지만 거기엔 아무도 없었다!

| 해설 |
생략된 분사구문의 주어와 주절의 주어가 일치하지 않아 생긴 비논리적 구문이다. 여기서 생략된 분사구문의 주어가 I라면 내용이 맞지 않기 때문에 주절의 주어를 the man으로 해서 올바르게 바꿔줘야 한다.

12.

(a) A friend of mine went to apply for a passport last month. (b) Once she got there she found out that she missed one of the documents needed to get her passport. (c) She went home to search for the document, but unfortunately, she does not keep her house very organized. (d) She searched and searched, and after a week of looking the missing document (has located → **has been located**).

| 해석 |
(a) 내 친구는 지난달에 여권을 신청하러 갔다. (b) 그녀는 거기에 도착했을 때 여권에 필요한 서류 중 하나를 가져오지 않았다는 것을 알았다. (c) 서류를 찾기 위해 집으로 갔지만 불행히도 그녀는 집 정돈을 잘 하지 않는다. (d) 그녀는 찾고 또 찾았지만 없어진 서류를 찾아 헤맨 지 한 주가 지나서야 찾게 되었다.

| 해설 |
locate는 타동사로 '(장소를) 알아내다, 찾아내다' 라는 의미가 있다. 그러므로 여기서는 능동이 아닌 수동으로 나타내야 한다.

Day 13

Build Up
116p

1. (a)	2. (a)	3. (c)	4. (c)	5. (a)	6. (d)
7. (a)	8. (d)	9. (a)	10. (a)	11. (b)	12. (b)

1.

A: Amos is really __________ about getting married next week!
B: He should be, since Alice is a wonderful woman!
(a) excited
(b) to excite
(c) exciting
(d) for excite

| 해석 |
A: 아모스는 다음주에 결혼하는 것에 대해 매우 흥분되어 있어!
B: 앨리스는 매우 좋은 여자니까 그가 그러는 것도 당연하지!

| 해설 |
excite는 감정을 나타내는 타동사이다. 주어가 사람일 경우 과거분사(p.p.)의 형태가, 사물일 경우 현재분사(-ing)의 형태가 오게 된다. 여기서는 주어가 사람이므로 외부의 영향에 따라 흥분되는 수동의 관계가 성립하므로 과거분사 형태인 excited가 정답이 된다.

2.

A: I have to leave town for a couple of days.
B: Okay, but I really don't understand __________ you have to do this now.
(a) why
(b) what
(c) when
(d) how

| 해석 |
A: 며칠 동안 마을을 떠나야만 해.
B: 알겠어. 근데 네가 왜 지금 이렇게 해야 하는지 정말 이해가 안 돼.

| 해설 |
의미상 알맞은 의문사를 고르는 문제이다. 여기서는 이유를 나타내는 것이 가장 적절하므로 (a)가 정답이 된다.

3.

A: What are you looking for?
B: My cellphone! I forgot __________ it from the charger!
(a) unplug
(b) unpluging
(c) to unplug
(d) having unplugged

| 해석 |
A: 무엇을 찾고 있니?
B: 내 휴대폰! 충전기에서 빼는 것을 잊었어!

| 해설 |
forget은 to부정사와 동명사를 목적어로 다 취하는 동사이다. 그러나 이미 완료된 일을 잊는다는 의미일 때에는 '동명사' 를, 앞으로 할 일을 잊는다는 의미일 때에는 to부정사를 취한다. 여기서는 후자의 의미가 적절하므로 (c)가 정답이 된다.

4.

A: What kind of questions should I expect at the interview?
B: A popular one is "__________ to apply for this job?"
(a) What make you to decide
(b) What did make you to decide
(c) What made you decide
(d) What decision you make

| 해석 |
A: 어떤 질문을 인터뷰에서 기대해야 할까요?

B: 가장 많이 묻는 질문은 '당신은 왜 이 직업을 지원하기로 결정했습니
까?' 입니다.

| 해설 |

〈What made/makes you＋동사원형~〉은 '왜 당신은 ~합니까?' 라
는 이유를 묻는 의미의 관용적인 표현이므로 알아두도록 한다.

5.

How was I supposed to know __________ the
store closed down and relocated?

(a) that   (b) which
(c) where   (d) who

| 해석 |

내가 어떻게 그 가게가 문을 닫고 이전했는지 알았겠니?

| 해설 |

여기서 that은 know라는 동사의 목적절을 이끄는 접속사의 역할을 한
다. 관계대명사 that과 접속사 that의 차이점은 '완벽한 절' 의 유무에 있
다. 여기처럼 접속사로 쓰였을 경우 뒤에 '완벽한 절' 이 오게 된다.

6.

Amnesty International has created many human
rights programs __________ spread awareness
about human rights violations in many countries.

(a) to succeed to
(b) that succeeding to
(c) succeeded to
(d) that have succeeded to

| 해석 |

국제사면위원회는 많은 나라에서 인권침해에 대한 경각심을 알리는 데
성공시킨 인권 프로그램을 만들었다.

| 해설 |

create는 3형식 동사로 (a)처럼 목적어 뒤에 to부정사가 올 수 없다. 또
한 분사의 형태인 (c)는 수동의 의미이므로 의미상 맞지 않다. 그러므로
관계대명사 that으로 연결시킨 (d)가 가장 적절하다.

7.

Among last week's guest celebrities __________
Michael Jordan of the Chicago Bulls.

(a) was
(b) is
(c) were
(d) are

| 해석 |

지난주 게스트 연예인들 중에는 시카고 불스의 마이클 조던도 있었다.

| 해설 |

빈칸에 올 동사의 주어는 guest celebrities가 아니라 Michael Jordan
이다. 이 문장은 부사구(Among last week's guest celebrities)가 강
조되어 문두로 가면서 도치가 이루어진 문장이다. 그러므로 단수 동사이
면서 과거 시점을 나타내는 (a)가 정답이 된다.

8.

The Thanksgiving dinner is tentatively __________
at McKinley Foundation.

(a) to hold
(b) be held
(c) holding
(d) to be held

| 해석 |

추수 감사절 저녁식사가 임시로 맥킨리 재단에서 열리기도 되어 있습니다.

| 해설 |

be to~는 예정, 의무, 가능, 의도, 운명 등의 의미로 쓰이는데 여기서는
예정의 의미로 쓰였다. 또한 의미상 '개최되는' 의 수동의 의미이므로 to
be p.p.의 형태로 쓰인 (d)가 정답이 된다.

9.

(a) A: I love (snacks → the snacks) that they
　　　 provide after each service.
(b) B: Do they serve anything besides crackers?
(c) A: Yes, they serve all kinds of distinctive
　　　 cheeses!
(d) B: Wow, I should stop by the snack table more
　　　 often.

| 해석 |

(a) A: 나는 식사 때마다 제공되는 스낵이 정말 좋아.
(b) B: 크래커 말고 다른 것도 있니?
(c) A: 응. 여러 종류의 특이한 치즈들도 있어.
(d) B: 와! 스낵 테이블에 더 자주 들러야겠다.

| 해설 |

여기서 snacks는 that절의 수식을 받고 있으므로 the가 있어야 한다.
(c)에서 cheese는 기본적으로 불가산명사이긴 하나 여기서는 '치즈의
종류' 를 의미하므로 가산명사화되었다.

10.

(a) A: (Do → Did) you have a good trip?
(b) B: Yes, it was a wonderful experience.
(c) A: That's good to know! What happened?
(d) B: They bumped me up to first class!

| 해석 |

(a) A: 여행은 재미있었니?
(b) B: 응, 정말 좋은 경험이었어.
(c) A: 잘됐다. 무슨 일이 있었니?
(d) B: 그들이 일등석에 나를 태워줬어.

| 해설 |

시제에 관한 문제이다. (b)의 응답으로 보아 의미상 과거의 행위에 대한
내용이 되어야 하므로 과거시제를 사용해야 한다. 현재시제는 '사실이나
습관적으로 반복되는 일' 등에 쓰이므로 적절치 않다.

11.

(a) The University's English department has new
and interesting courses this year! (b) For example,

there is a new multicultural literature class that
(are → is) now being offered. (c) There is also a
new course regarding the proliferation of
postmodern literature in the western hemisphere.
(d) I hope I can enroll in one of these courses!

| 해석 |

(a) 이 대학의 영문과에서는 새롭고 흥미로운 과목들을 이번 연도에 준
비했다! (b) 예를 들어 새롭게 개설되는 다문화 문학 수업이 있다. (c)
또한 서반구의 포스트모던 문학의 확산에 관한 새 수업도 있다. (d) 나는
이 중 한 과목에 등록하고 싶다.

| 해설 |

관계대명사 that의 선행사가 a new multicultural literature class이므
로 단수 동사가 되어야 한다. 따라서 are를 is로 고쳐야 한다.

12.

(a) Although I was very tired, I'm grateful that I
went to the informational meeting last night. (b)
Initially, I didn't want to go, but my roommate,
Ellie, had insisted that I (went → go). (c) If I hadn't
gone, I would've never learned about the North
Korean refugees. (d) Now I'm thinking about
joining the board to raise more awareness about
the injustice in North Korea.

| 해석 |

(a) 나는 매우 피곤했지만 어젯밤 그 홍보 모임에 참석하게 되어 너무 기
쁘다. (b) 처음에는 가고 싶지 않았지만 나의 룸메이트 엘리가 가야 한다
고 했다. (c) 만약 가지 않았더라면 나는 탈북 난민들에 대해 배우지 못
했을 것이다. (d) 나는 지금 북한의 불의에 대해 더 자세히 알아보기 위
해 그 단체에 참여할까 생각 중이다.

| 해설 |

주장, 제안, 요구 동사(suggest, recommend, insist, demand) 등이
오게 되면 that절 이하가 아직 일어나지 않은 내용 즉, '~해야 한다, ~
하겠다'라는 제안의 의미가 있을 때 should가 생략됐다고 보고 동사원
형을 쓰게 된다. 그러므로 여기서도 과거동사 went가 아닌 go의 형태로
바꾸어야 한다.

Day 14

Build Up
124p

1. (a)	2. (d)	3. (d)	4. (c)	5. (b)	6. (d)
7. (a)	8. (c)	9. (c)	10. (d)	11. (d)	12. (b)

1.

A: Something about your apartment seems
different. Did you get new furniture?
B: No, all these things __________ here before.

(a) were

(b) was

(c) are

(d) will be

| 해석 |

A: 네 아파트가 뭔가 다른 것 같아. 가구를 새로 샀니?
B: 아니, 모두 전부터 여기 있던 것들이야.

| 해설 |

주어가 복수이고 before를 통해 과거시제가 적절함을 알 수 있으므로
(a)가 정답이 된다.

2.

A: Which perfume did you buy for Mom's birthday
present?
B: She wanted one __________ of vanilla, so I
bought her Armani Mania.

(a) smells   (b) to smell

(c) smelled   (d) smelling

| 해석 |

A: 어머니 생신에 어떤 향수를 선물로 사 드렸니?
B: 어머니는 바닐라 향기가 나는 것을 원하셨어. 그래서 아르마니 마니
아를 사 드렸어.

| 해설 |

one을 수식하는 알맞은 형식의 분사를 고르는 문제이다. smell은 자동
사이므로 의미상 능동인 현재분사 형식이 가장 적절하다. 그러므로 (d)
가 정답이 된다.

3.

A: What happened to your hat? It looked great on
you.
B: Thanks, but out of respect I __________ it when
I entered the building.

(a) will remove

(b) had removed

(c) remove

(d) removed

| 해석 |

A: 네 모자는 어떻게 했니? 너한테 잘 어울렸는데.
B: 고마워. 하지만 실례가 되지 않도록 건물에 들어올 때 모자를 벗었어.

| 해설 |

시제 관련 문제이다. 시간 부사절의 시제가 과거이므로 (a)와 (c)는 정답
이 될 수 없다. (b)는 의미상 종속절보다 먼저 일어난 일이기 때문에 답
이 될 수 없다.

| 어휘 |

out of respect 경의를 표하여

4.

A: You look as if you'd seen a ghost. Are you

alright?
B: I'm fine now, but I'd __________________.
(a) not rather be alone tonight
(b) rather tonight be not alone
(c) rather not be alone tonight
(d) not be rather alone tonight

| 해석 |
A: 넌 마치 귀신을 본 것 같아. 괜찮아?
B: 지금은 괜찮아. 그렇지만 오늘 밤은 혼자 있지 않는 게 좋겠어.

| 해설 |
would rather~는 '~하는 게 낫다' 라는 의미로 부정문은 rather 뒤에
부정어 not을 붙이면 된다. 그러므로 (c)가 올바른 어순의 답이 된다.

5.
At the beginning of the year, the boss
__________________ that the factory might have
to be shut down by the end of the year.
(a) had warned to his workers
(b) had warned his workers
(c) to his workers warned
(d) has warned his workers

| 해석 |
올해 초 사장은 직원들에게 이번 연도 말에 공장을 닫아야 할지도 모른다
고 말했다.

| 해설 |
at the beginning of the year라는 말이 과거의 시점을 나타내고 있으
므로 빈칸에는 과거 혹은 과거완료의 시제가 와야 한다. 또한 warn은
'경고하다' 라는 타동사로 바로 목적어를 취하기 때문에 (b)가 정답이
된다.

6.
__________ upon a more familiar subject, Jill
broke the uneasy silence with a question about
Adam's family.
(a) To fallen back
(b) Fallen back
(c) Fall back
(d) Falling back

| 해석 |
좀 더 친숙한 주제에 의지함으로써 질은 아담의 가족에 대한 질문 때문에
생긴 불편한 침묵을 깼다.

| 해설 |
fall back on/upon은 '~에 의지하다' 라는 의미로 fall은 자동사이다.
분사구문의 주어와 주절의 주어는 일치해야 하므로 생략된 분사구문의
주어는 Jill이 된다. 그러므로 능동의 분사구문인 (d)가 정답이 된다.

7.
Many people don't realize this, but one of the
most physically strenuous activities for the body

__________ swimming.
(a) is
(b) was
(c) are
(d) be

| 해석 |
많은 사람들이 깨닫지 못하지만 육체적으로 가장 활발한 운동 중 하나가
수영이다.

| 해설 |
〈one of+복수 명사〉는 '~중 하나' 라는 의미로 단수 취급한다. 또한 이
것은 '사실' 이기 때문에 현재시제로 표현하는 것이 적절하므로 (a)가 정
답이다.

8.
The organization's new headquarters will be built
and __________ with the help of donations from
its large number of benefactors.
(a) financing
(b) finance
(c) financed
(d) finances

| 해석 |
협회의 새 본부가 지어지고 많은 후원자들의 기부로 자금이 조달될 것이다.

| 해설 |
finance는 '자금을 조달하다' 라는 의미의 타동사이므로 의미상 수동의
형태인 (c)가 정답이 된다. financed 앞에는 will be가 생략 되었다.

9.
(a) A: Are there any more people coming? Or is
    this all of them?
(b) B: I don't know for sure. We will have to wait
    and see.
(c) A: We don't have any more time (waiting → to
    wait) right away. We need to start the
    presentation.
(d) B: Go ahead and start then, it shouldn't be a
    problem.

| 해석 |
(a) A: 올 사람이 더 있니? 아니면 이 사람들이 다야?
(b) B: 확실히 모르겠어. 기다려 봐야 될 것 같아.
(c) A: 더 기다릴 시간이 없어. 프레젠테이션을 시작해야 돼.
(d) B: 그렇다면 시작해. 문제될 것은 없어.

| 해설 |
time waiting은 '시간이 능동적으로 기다리고 있다' 는 의미가 되므로
적절치 않다. 그러므로 to부정사의 형태로 고쳐야 한다. 여기서 to wait
은 앞에 있는 명사를 꾸며주는 형용사적 용법으로 쓰였다.

10.
(a) A: Did you enjoy your summer vacation?

(b) B: I did. It was very rewarding.

(c) A: Why was it rewarding? What did you do?

(d) A: I spent two months down south (to helping → helping) rebuild damaged houses.

| 해석 |

(a) A: 여름 방학을 재미있게 보냈니?

(b) B: 응. 정말 보람 있었어.

(c) A: 왜 보람 있었니? 뭘 했는데?

(d) B: 파괴된 집들을 복구하는 것을 돕느라 남부에서 두 달을 보냈거든.

| 해설 |

〈spend+목적어+-ing〉는 '(시간)을 들이다, (때를) 보내다' 라는 의미이다. 그러므로 전치사 to를 없애고 동명사의 형태로 바꾸어야 한다.

11.

(a) Koalas are some of the longest sleepers in the animal kingdom. (b) Actually, most of their lives are spent sleeping. (c) On average, a koala sleeps for 22 hours a day, which helps their bodies to conserve energy. (d) In turn, koalas do not need to consume very (much vegetations → **much vegetation**) for food, because their bodies do not need much energy.

| 해석 |

(a) 코알라는 동물의 왕국에서 가장 잠을 오래 자는 동물 중 하나이다. (b) 사실 그들의 대부분의 삶은 잠을 자는 데 쓰인다. (c) 평균적으로 코알라는 하루에 22시간을 잔다. 이것은 그들의 몸이 에너지를 보존하도록 도와준다. (d) 또한 코알라는 음식을 위해 많은 식물을 소비할 필요가 없다. 왜냐하면 그들의 몸은 많은 에너지를 필요로 하지 않기 때문이다.

| 해설 |

vegetation은 불가산명사이므로 복수로 표시할 수 없다. 또한 much라는 한정어를 통해 불가산명사임을 알 수 있으므로 단수형으로 표시해줘야 한다.

12.

(a) Deep sea fishing has been a favorite pastime of seaside peoples for thousands of years. (b) Over time, navigational and fishing tools have increased in proficiency, (the activity less challenging → **making the activity less challenging**). (c) Besides this, other concerns have been raised in recent years. (d) The increase in seafood consumption and pollutants in the water has seriously threatened the future of many aquatic animals worldwide.

| 해석 |

(a) 깊은 바다 낚시는 수천 년 동안 바닷가 민족들이 가장 좋아하는 오락 활동이었다. (b) 시간이 지나면서 항해와 낚시 장비는 편리하게 개선되어 그런 활동을 덜 도전적인 것으로 만들었다. (c) 게다가 최근에는 또 다른 관심사가 생겨났다. (d) 해산물 소비와 수질 오염의 증가는 전 세계적으로 많은 해양 동물의 미래를 심각하게 위협하고 있다.

| 해설 |

문장의 구조를 묻는 문제이다. (b) 문장에서 콤마 뒤에 명사구(the activity less challenging)는 연결어구 없이 나열될 수 없다. 그러므로 분사구문의 형태로 만들어 주는 것이 의미상 가장 적절하다.

| 어휘 |

pastime 오락, 취미

Day 15

Build Up
132p

1. (c)	2. (a)	3. (c)	4. (b)	5. (b)	6. (d)
7. (c)	8. (b)	9. (c)	10. (d)	11. (b)	12. (c)

1.

A: I read in the tabloids that Reese Witherspoon and Ryan Philippe __________ after all.

B: Wow! That's so sad considering they were one of Hollywood's cutest couples.

(a) should be divorced

(b) had got divorced

(c) **did get divorced**

(d) has been divorcing

| 해석 |

A: 타블로이드판 신문에서 봤는데 리즈 위더스푼과 라이언 필립이 결국 이혼했대.

B: 와! 그들이 할리우드의 잉꼬 부부 중 하나였다는 걸 생각하면 그건 너무 안됐어.

| 해설 |

get divorced는 '이혼하다' 라는 의미이다. 여기서 did는 get divorced를 강조하기 위해 쓰였으며 이혼한 것이 과거이므로 강조 동사 do의 시제를 과거형으로 해야 한다.

2.

A: Do you know __________ for dinner?

B: I think Caroline said it's at 6:30 p.m., so we should probably leave at 6 p.m.

(a) **what time to leave**

(b) to leave what time

(c) what time leaving

(d) of leaving what time

| 해석 |

A: 저녁식사를 위해 몇 시에 떠나야 하는지 아니?

B: 캐롤라인이 6시 반이라고 한 것 같아. 그래서 아마도 6시에 떠나야 할 것 같은데.

| 해설 |

빈칸에는 know의 목적어가 와야 한다. 〈의문사+to부정사〉는 명사구로서 주어, 목적어, 보어 등으로 쓰인다. 그러므로 여기서는 (a)가 정답이 된다.

3.

A: Nathan told me __________ him, but I lost his number.

B: Oh, I think Emily has it!

(a) calling

(b) called

(c) to call

(d) to be called

| 해석 |

A: 나단은 전화해 달라고 말했지만 난 그의 번호를 잃어버렸어.

B: 오, 에밀리가 그의 전화번호를 가지고 있는 것 같아!

| 해설 |

〈tell+목적어+to부정사〉는 '~하라고 명하다, 분부하다' 라는 의미이다. 그러므로 빈칸에는 to부정사의 형태가 와야 한다. 또한 to부정사 뒤에는 목적어 him이 있으므로 능동의 형태인 (c)가 정답이 된다.

4.

A: Ben is a huge Chicago Bears fan, but not as __________ fanatic as Eddie.

B: Yeah, Eddie paints his face blue and orange for every game!

(a) a much

(b) much of a

(c) much of

(d) of a much

| 해석 |

A: 벤은 시카고 베어즈의 대단한 팬이야. 에디만큼 광팬은 아니지만.

B: 맞아. 에디는 매 시합마다 파란색과 오렌지색으로 얼굴을 칠하잖아.

| 해설 |

not much of a는 '대단한 ~는 아니다' 라는 의미이다. 예를 들어 He is not much of a singer.는 '그는 대단한 가수는 아니다' 라는 의미이다. 그러므로 (b)가 정답이 된다.

5.

I wouldn't have survived senior year __________ my friends' daily support.

(a) haven't it been for

(b) had it not been for

(c) weren't it for

(d) was it not for

| 해석 |

친구들의 매일 같은 도움이 없었더라면 4학년을 견뎌내지 못했을 것이다.

| 해설 |

가정법 if절에서 if가 생략될 때는 도치가 일어난다. 의미상 가정법 과거

완료가 되어야 하므로 (b)와 같은 어순이 된다.

6.

Josh takes working out consistently as seriously __________ Joel does.

(a) because

(b) since

(c) while

(d) as

| 해석 |

조쉬는 꾸준히 운동하는 것을 조엘만큼이나 진지하게 생각한다.

| 해설 |

as A as B는 'B만큼 A한' 이라는 동등 비교구문이다. 앞의 as는 부사이고 뒤의 as는 접속사로 뒤에 명사구(절)이 오게 된다. 그러므로 여기서는 (d)가 정답이 된다.

7.

The two children, __________ in the cave, were rescued and taken to safety.

(a) to be discovered

(b) discovering

(c) discovered

(d) having discovered

| 해석 |

동굴에서 발견된 두 아이는 구출되어 안전한 곳으로 옮겨졌다.

| 해설 |

discover는 '~을 발견하다' 라는 타동사로 여기서 앞에 있는 명사를 수식하기 위해서는 의미상 수동이 되어야 하므로 과거분사의 형태인 (c)가 정답이 된다.

8.

__________ that Jane would appreciate his gesture, Eddie bought her a dozen roses and had it delivered to her workplace.

(a) To think

(b) Thinking

(c) Thought

(d) Think

| 해석 |

에디는 제인이 그의 행동에 고마워 할 거라고 생각하고 장미 꽃다발을 사서 그녀의 직장에 배달시켰다.

| 해설 |

분사구문에 관한 문제이다. think는 타동사로 빈칸 뒤에 목적절인 that절이 오므로 능동의 형태가 되어야 한다. 그러므로 (b)가 정답이 된다.

9.

(a) A: What happened after the party this weekend?

(b) B: Not only is my house trashed from the

party, but I also crashed my parents' car!
(c) A: Oh, no! (Sound like → Sounds like) you're going to be in big trouble.
(d) B: That's for sure. They're coming back from vacation tomorrow!

(a) A: 이번 주말에 파티 후에 무슨 일이 있었니?
(b) B: 내 집이 파티 때문에 난장판이 되었을 뿐만 아니라 내가 부모님의 차도 박았어.
(c) A: 세상에! 너 큰일날 것 같은데.
(d) B: 당연하지. 내일 여행에서 부모님이 돌아오시거든!

| 해설 |

sound like~는 '~처럼 생각되다' 라는 의미로 여기서는 sound 앞에 주어 it이 생략된 것이므로 sounds가 되어야 한다.

10.

(a) A: Where did you get your two puppies from?
(b) B: I brought them from the shelter. They were rescued from an abandoned building.
(c) A: Wow, what luck! Who knows what would have happened to them?
(d) B: Yeah, they (won't → wouldn't) be alive if it weren't for the animal rescue team.

| 해석 |

(a) A: 강아지 두 마리는 어디서 온 거니?
(b) B: 보호소에서 데려왔어. 그들은 버려진 건물에서 구출됐거든.
(c) A: 와, 운이 좋다! 그들에게 무슨 일이 벌어졌는지 누가 알겠니?
(d) B: 맞아. 동물구조팀이 아니었더라면 그들은 살아 있지 못할 거야.

| 해설 |

(d)는 가정법 과거의 문장으로 주절의 시제는 미래형이 될 수 없다. 그러므로 wouldn't be로 고쳐야 한다. 가정법 과거 구문에서 if절의 be동사의 과거형은 주어와 상관없이 were를 쓴다.

11.

(a) With the increase of standards to enter a top University for high school students, it has become increasingly difficult to become an all-around high school student. (b) There are just too many students competing for the same University, (but → and) not enough spots to give away to each one. (c) So what should a perfect student do to get in to a top University? (d) It seems there's no choice, but to hope for the best.

| 해석 |

(a) 고등학생들이 최고의 대학을 들어가기 위한 기준들이 높아지면서 다재다능한 고등학생이 되는 것은 매우 어렵게 되었다. (b) 같은 대학에 들어가기 위해 경쟁하는 학생이 너무 많고 그들 각각에게 줄 수 있는 자리는 충분치 않다. (c) 그렇다면 완벽한 학생이 최고의 대학에 들어가기 위해서는 무엇을 해야 하는가? (d) 그저 최선을 바랄 뿐 다른 선택은 없는 듯 보인다.

| 해설 |

접속사 but의 앞 문장과 뒷 문장이 의미상 대조를 이루지 않으므로 나열의 의미인 and로 바꾸는 것이 적절하다. (d)에서 〈no choice but+to 부정사〉는 '~일 뿐이다, ~할 수 밖에 없다' 라는 의미이다.

| 어휘 |

all-around 해박한, 만능의

12.

(a) There has been a huge increase in HIV/AIDS victims in Africa in the past decade. (b) However, because of the lack of HIV/AIDS education, the statistics aren't decreasing. (c) African governments are trying to provide (an information → information) about HIV/AIDS and abstinence to prevent the spread of the disease. (d) They believe that this will help people make the right decisions to protect themselves from contracting the disease.

| 해석 |

(a) 지난 10년간 아프리카에서 에이즈의 희생자는 크게 증가했다. (b) 그러나 에이즈 교육의 부족으로 수치는 줄어들지 않고 있다. (c) 아프리카 정부들은 그 질병의 확산을 막기 위해서 에이즈와 금욕에 대한 정보를 제공하려고 노력 중이다. (d) 그들은 이것이 사람들로 하여금 에이즈에 걸리지 않도록 옳은 결정을 내리게 도와줄 것이라고 믿고 있다.

| 해설 |

information은 불가산명사로 부정관사 an을 취할 수 없다. 그러므로 부정관사 an을 없애야 한다. (b)에서 statistics는 '통계, 수치' 라는 의미로 쓰일 때에는 복수 취급하고 '통계학' 의 의미일 때에는 단수 취급한다. 여기서는 '수치, 통계' 라는 의미로 쓰였으므로 올바른 형태로 사용되었다.

| 어휘 |

abstinence 금욕

Day 16

Build Up   140p

| 1. (c) | 2. (a) | 3. (d) | 4. (c) | 5. (b) | 6. (d) |
| 7. (a) | 8. (c) | 9. (b) | 10. (c) | 11. (c) | 12. (a) |

1.

A: How many people _____________ for this seminar?
B: I expect at least 350 people will attend the lecture portion.
(a) will you think actually show up

(b) will actually show up you think

(c) do you think will actually show up

(d) do you actually show up will think

| 해석 |

A: 얼마나 많은 사람이 이번 세미나에 올 것 같니?

B: 적어도 350명은 강의 부분에는 참석할 것 같은데.

| 해설 |

의문사 의문문에 do you think라는 삽입어구가 들어가면 그 뒤의 문장은 〈주어＋동사〉의 어순이 된다. 그러므로 (c)가 올바른 어순이 된다.

2.

A: Hello, Ma'am. Are you finding everything satisfactory with your meal this evening?

B: Oh, yes. You said the salmon would be an excellent choice and __________.

(a) so it is

(b) so is it

(c) so doe it

(d) so it does

| 해석 |

A: 안녕하세요? 오늘 저녁식사가 다 만족스러우십니까?

B: 네. 당신이 연어 요리가 좋을 것이라고 했는데 정말 그렇네요.

| 해설 |

〈so＋주어＋동사〉에서 so는 yes의 의미가 되어 '정말 ～하다' 라는 의미이다. 〈so＋동사＋주어〉에서 so는 also의 의미가 되어 '～도 …하다' 라는 의미가 된다. 여기서는 전자의 의미로 쓰였기 때문에 도치될 필요가 없으므로 (a)가 정답이 된다.

3.

A: There's nothing better than a good massage, __________________?

B: Actually, I prefer to relax in a sauna when I can.

(a) wouldn't you think

(b) didn't you think

(c) can you think

(d) don't you think

| 해석 |

A: 좋은 마사지보다 더 좋은 것은 없어. 그렇지 않니?

B: 사실 난 내가 할 수 있을 때 사우나에서 쉬는 게 더 좋아.

| 해설 |

빈칸에는 앞 문장에 대한 의견을 묻는 질문이 나와야 한다. '좋은 마사지보다 좋은 것은 없다' 고 말하고 그 상황에서 상대방의 의견을 묻고 있으므로 현재시제로 물어봐야 한다. 그러므로 (d)가 정답이 된다.

4.

A: Are you glad that the coach chose you to be the team captain?

B: Not really, I don't know if I can handle __________.

(a) a position

(b) position

(c) that position

(d) those positions

| 해석 |

A: 코치가 너를 팀 주장으로 뽑은 것이 기쁘니?

B: 별로야. 내가 잘 할 수 있을지 모르겠어.

| 해설 |

여기서 position은 구체적으로 the team captain을 가리키고 있으므로 (c)가 정답이 된다. (a)의 a position은 불특정한 하나의 position을 의미하므로 적절치 않다.

5.

A local wildlife conservation group has decided that __________________ must be relocated to a northwestern national park.

(a) herd of purebred bison

(b) a herd of purebred bison

(c) herds of purebred bisons

(d) a herd of purebred of bisons

| 해석 |

지역 야생 동물 보존 단체는 순종 들소떼가 북서쪽 국립공원에 재배치되어야 한다고 결정했다.

| 해설 |

bison은 단수와 복수의 형태가 같은 명사이다. a herd of～는 '～의 떼' 라는 의미로 (b)의 형태가 가장 적절하다.

6.

I can't stand having to drive __________ snowy winter days.

(a) about

(b) in

(c) for

(d) on

| 해석 |

나는 눈 오는 겨울날에 운전해야 한다는 것을 참을 수가 없다.

| 해설 |

특정한 날(day)이나 요일 앞에는 전치사 on을 쓴다. 그러므로 (d)가 정답이 된다.

7.

I think it's funny that Jenny is so humble about her appearance, because she really is as beautiful __________.

(a) as they come

(b) as she comes

(c) as she is

(d) as they be

나는 제니가 자기 외모에 너무 겸손해 하는 게 웃기다고 생각해. 왜냐면 제니는 더할 나위 없이 아름답기 때문이지.

| 해설 |
as ~ as they come은 '매우, 더할 나위 없이'라는 뜻의 관용표현이다. 그러므로 (a)가 정답이다.

8.

My leg has felt one hundred percent better ___________ I had that surgery done.

(a) although
(b) whenever
(c) ever since
(d) why

| 해석 |
내 다리는 그 수술을 받은 후로 훨씬 좋아졌다.

| 해설 |
빈칸 뒤에 절이 있으므로 의미상 적절한 접속사를 골라야 한다. since는 '~이후로'라는 의미가 있다. 그러므로 (c)가 정답이 된다.

9.

(a) A: It will be quicker to get there if we take a taxi, won't it?
(b) B: I don't think it will be at this time of day. Didn't you see (all cars → all the cars) on the road?
(c) A: Oh yeah, I guess you're right.
(d) B: We should probably just take the subway, or else we'll be really late.

| 해석 |
(a) A: 택시를 타면 거기에 더 빨리 도착할 거야, 그렇지 않니?
(b) B: 오늘 같은 날은 안 그럴 거 같은데. 도로에 있는 차 안 봤니?
(c) A: 그래. 네 말이 맞는 것 같아.
(d) B: 지하철을 타야겠다. 아니면 우리 정말 늦을 것 같아.

| 해설 |
도로 위(on the road)의 특정한 모든 차를 의미하므로 the를 넣어야 한다.

10.

(a) A: Hi, I'm here to drop some children off for Children's Day.
(b) B: Okay, great. You just have to sign all their names and leave a contact number?
(c) A: Sure. (Will the children wait → Should the children wait) out here until I've finished?
(d) B: No, they can go in now. Just make sure they each get a name tag.

| 해석 |
(a) A: 안녕하세요? 어린이날을 위해 어린이들을 데리고 왔는데요.
(b) B: 네. 좋습니다. 아이들 이름을 다 적으시고 연락처를 남겨주세요.

(c) A: 네. 아이들은 내가 끝날 때까지 기다려야 하나요?
(d) B: 아니오, 아이들은 지금 들어가도 됩니다. 아이들이 이름표를 다 가지고 있는지만 확인해 주세요.

| 해설 |
질문에 대한 대답(No, they can go in now.)을 보면 '허락'을 하고 있으므로 미래의 조동사 will보다는 당위성의 의미를 지닌 should가 더욱 적절하다.

11.

(a) Blue prints are extremely important and useful tools for homeowners. (b) The architects, when designing the house, create a drawing from a bird's eye view to scale. (c) (Utilized → Utilizing) this map during construction, the electrical engineers add marks to the drawing showing, where and how they have installed the houses electrical wiring. (d) This communication by means of the blue prints proves to be a necessity when modifications are made years down the road.

| 해석 |
(a) 설계도는 집주인에게 매우 중요하고 유용한 도구이다. (b) 건축가들은 집을 설계할 때 일정한 비율로 조감도를 그린다. (c) 건축을 하는 동안 이 지도를 활용하면서 전기 엔지니어들은 어디에 그리고 어떻게 그들이 전선을 설치했는지 그림에 표시를 한다. (d) 설계도에 의한 이 의사소통은 몇 년 후 장래에 변경이 이루어질 때 꼭 필요한 것임이 증명된다.

| 해설 |
utilize는 '~을 활용하다'라는 의미의 타동사로 능동의 분사구문으로 쓰여야 한다. 수동의 분사구문으로 쓰이면 뒤에 목적어가 없어야 하는데 뒤에 목적어 this map이 있으므로 능동의 형태가 적절하다. (d)에서 years down the road는 many years later라는 의미이다.

12.

(a) Although my real name is Nicholas, I've always preferred (to call → to be called) Tim. (b) Most of the time people get confused when I tell them this; however, it goes all the way back to my early childhood, and it seems more normal to me. (c) My cousin would always call me Tim as a joke, and I always did so many things with him. (d) The name engrained itself in my impressionable head and I learned to like it.

| 해석 |
(a) 나의 진짜 이름은 니콜라스지만 나는 팀으로 불리는 것을 항상 좋아했다. (b) 사람들은 사실을 말해주면 대부분 혼란스러워 한다. 하지만 그 이름은 내 어린시절로 거슬러 올라가고 내게는 그게 더 정상적으로 보인다. (c) 내 사촌은 장난으로 항상 나를 팀으로 불렀고 나는 언제나 그와 함께 많은 것을 했다. (d) 그 이름은 인상적으로 내 머리에 남았고 난 그것을 좋아하게 된 것이었다.

| 해설 |
〈call+목적어+목적격 보어〉는 '~을 …라고 부르다'라는 뜻이다. 문맥

상 '팀이라는 이름으로 불리는 것을 더 좋아했다' 는 수동의 의미가 되어야 하므로 to부정사의 수동의 형태로 바꾸어야 한다.

Day 17
Build Up

148p

1. (a)	**2.** (d)	**3.** (d)	**4.** (a)	**5.** (a)	**6.** (d)
7. (c)	**8.** (d)	**9.** (d)	**10.** (a)	**11.** (b)	**12.** (c)

1.

A: Honey, should I wear the black dress __________ the red one?

B: I think the red one looks fabulous.

(a) or

(b) either

(c) as much as

(d) and

| 해석 |

A: 자기야, 검정 드레스랑 빨간색 중에 어떤 것을 입을까?

B: 빨간색이 멋진 것 같은데.

| 해설 |

알맞은 의미의 접속사를 고르는 문제이다. 의미상 선택의 뜻을 갖고 있는 or가 가장 적절하다.

2.

A: I am so excited about the wedding tomorrow.

B: So am I. I'm sure it __________ be a great event.

(a) should

(b) would

(c) might

(d) will

| 해석 |

A: 내일 결혼식이 너무 기대돼.

B: 나도 그래. 정말 멋진 결혼식이 될 거야.

| 해설 |

I'm sure라는 표현 뒤에 어울리는 조동사를 고르는 것이므로 의미상 확실성이 강한 미래 조동사 will이 적절하다.

3.

A: Should we drive home Saturday night or Sunday morning?

B: I think Saturday night is better, but

__________ is fine with me since you're driving.

(a) neither

(b) both

(c) every

(d) either

| 해석 |

A: 토요일 저녁에 집에 갈까, 일요일 아침에 갈까?

B: 토요일 저녁이 더 좋긴 한데 네가 운전을 하니까 난 언제라도 좋아.

| 해설 |

의미상 토요일 밤이나 일요일 아침 아무 때나 괜찮다는 뜻이 되어야 하므로 대명사 either(어느 한쪽, 어느 쪽이든)가 되어야 한다. neither는 '어느 ~도 아니다' 라는 부정의 의미이므로 여기서는 적절치 않다.

4.

A: Eddie's taco dip wasn't __________ delicious.

B: I disagree! It was the best taco dip I've ever tasted.

(a) that

(b) much

(c) far

(d) such

| 해석 |

A: 에디의 타코 딥은 그다지 맛이 없었어.

B: 아니야. 내가 먹어본 것 중에 최고의 타코 딥이었어.

| 해설 |

that은 정도의 부사로 '그만큼, 그 정도로' 의 의미가 있다. 그러므로 빈칸에는 부사인 that이 적절하다. much와 far는 형용사 비교급을 수식한다.

5.

Tracy's room is a lot more organized than her little brother __________.

(a) Jimmy's is

(b) Jimmy is

(c) Is Jimmy

(d) Jimmy

| 해석 |

트레이시의 방은 그녀의 남동생 지미의 방보다 훨씬 잘 정돈되어 있다.

| 해설 |

비교의 대상이 Tracy's room과 Jimmy's room이므로 (a)가 정답이 된다. 여기서 be동사가 생략되어 Jimmy's가 되어도 답이 될 수 있다.

6.

I have always wanted to know __________ to be a Hollywood movie star.

(a) what is it like

(b) what was it like

(c) what it was like
(d) what it is like

| 해석 |
헐리우드 영화배우가 된다는 게 어떤 것인지 난 항상 알고 싶었다.

| 해설 |
간접의문문의 순서는 〈의문사＋주어＋동사〉의 어순이다. what it is like~는 '~는 어때?' 라는 의미이다. 여기서 like는 전치사로서 '~같이, 처럼' 이라는 의미이다. 그러므로 (d)가 정답이 된다.

7.

I had no idea that Dad had so much __________ about Iranian history.
(a) insights
(b) an insight
(c) insight
(d) the insight

| 해석 |
나는 아빠가 이란 역사에 그렇게 식견이 높은지 몰랐다.

| 해설 |
insight는 '식견, 통찰력' 이라는 의미의 불가산명사이다. 또한 빈칸 앞에 양 표시어 much가 왔으므로 (c)가 정답이다.

8.

The more I study and prepare myself for the exam, __________ I will do well on it.
(a) likely
(b) likelier
(c) more likely
(d) the more likely

| 해석 |
시험을 위해 더 열심히 공부하고 준비할수록 시험을 더 잘 볼 것이다.

| 해설 |
〈the 비교급＋주어＋동사, the 비교급＋주어＋동사〉는 '~하면 할수록 더 ~한다' 라는 의미이다. 그러므로 (d)가 정답이 된다.

9.

(a) A: What's the most difficult part about having a husband who travels a lot?
(b) B: One thing that is hard is being alone with the kids.
(c) A: Is there anything else that makes it difficult?
(d) B: Yes, I just miss him and want to (speak him → speak with/to him).

| 해석 |
(a) A: 여행을 많이 다니는 남편을 둔 것에 대해 가장 힘든 부분이 무엇이니?
(b) B: 아이들과 홀로 있어야 한다는 것이 힘든 것 중 하나야.
(c) A: 또 다른 힘든 점이 있니?
(d) B: 응, 그저 그가 그립고 이야기를 하고 싶어.

| 해설 |
speak은 '~에게〔~와〕 이야기하다' 라는 의미로 전치사를 필요로 한다. 그러므로 전치사 to나 with가 함께 쓰여야 한다.

10.

(a) A: Mina, I just need a break! My boss (has been driven → has been driving) me crazy!
(b) B: Oh, no! Work's been that tough, huh?
(c) A: Yes! Not only do we have multiple deadlines, but my boss is so demanding!
(d) B: I'm sorry. Is there anything I can do to help you?

| 해석 |
(a) A: 미나, 난 휴식이 필요해! 사장이 날 미치게 하고 있어!
(b) B: 어머, 일이 그렇게 힘드니?
(c) A: 응! 끝마쳐야 하는 일이 여러 개일 뿐만 아니라 사장이 너무 지나친 요구를 해!
(d) B: 안됐다. 내가 도울 수 있는 게 있니?

| 해설 |
〈drive＋목적어＋보어〉의 어순으로 '~를 …한 상태에 빠뜨리다' 라는 의미가 된다. 뒤에 목적어를 취하므로 수동의 형태가 아닌 능동의 형태가 되어야 한다. 여기서는 현재완료진행의 시제로 사용되었다.

11.

(a) My parents are very overprotective and caring about everything I do. (b) They call me every other day because they (concerned → are concerned) about my health and wellbeing. (c) My mom sends me cookies and snacks at the beginning of each month. (d) Also, even though I work, my dad makes sure that I have enough money in my checking account at all times.

| 해석 |
(a) 내 부모님은 너무 과잉보호하셔서 내가 하는 모든 것에 참견하신다. (b) 그들은 나의 건강과 행복을 걱정해서 하루 걸러 한 번씩 내게 전화를 하신다. (c) 어머니는 매달 초에 쿠키와 스낵을 내게 보내 주신다. (d) 또한 내가 일을 하지만 아버지는 언제나 내 은행 계좌에 돈이 충분히 있는지 확인하신다.

| 해설 |
concern은 타동사로 '관계가 있다' 라는 의미가 있다. '걱정〔염려〕하다' 라는 의미로 쓰일 때는 수동의 형태가 되어 전치사와 함께 쓰인다. be concerned about은 '~에 대해 걱정하다' 라는 의미이다. 그러므로 능동의 형태를 수동의 형태로 고쳐야 한다. every other day는 '하루 걸러서' 라는 의미이고 at all times는 '항상, 늘' 이라는 의미이다.

12.

(a) HIV/AIDS is a deadly disease that has been on the rise in the past decade. (b) The problem with HIV/AIDS, however, is that drastic symptoms appear much later in the sickness. (c) Therefore, many people live without knowing that they have the deadly disease and can consequently spread it to (the others → others). (d) That is why it is important for people to receive proper HIV/AIDS education.

| 해석 |
(a) 에이즈는 지난 십 년간 증가 추세를 보여온 치명적인 질병이다. (b) 에이즈의 문제는 심각한 증상들이 발병 후 훨씬 뒤에 나타난다는 것이다. (c) 그래서 많은 사람들이 그 치명적인 질병을 가지고 있는지 모른 채 살다가 다른 사람들에게 전염시킬 수 있다. (d) 그것이 바로 사람들이 정확한 에이즈 교육을 받는 것이 중요한 이유이다.

| 해설 |
여기서는 의미상 그 병을 불특정 다수인 '다른 사람들'에게 전염시킬 수 있다는 의미가 되어야 하기 때문에 the를 없애야 한다. the others는 '(한정된 영역에서) 나머지 그 사람들'이란 의미이다.

Day 18
Build Up
156p

| 1. (b) | 2. (a) | 3. (d) | 4. (d) | 5. (b) | 6. (b) |
| 7. (a) | 8. (c) | 9. (c) | 10. (d) | 11. (b) | 12. (a) |

1.
A: What kind of restaurant do you want to take your parents to tonight?
B: __________ they feel like eating, I'll be happy with their decision.
(a) Whichever
(b) Whatever
(c) When
(d) What

| 해석 |
A: 오늘밤 어떤 종류의 레스토랑에 부모님을 모시고 싶으세요?
B: 드시고 싶으신 게 무엇이든 그분들의 결정에 따를 거예요.

| 해설 |
복합 관계대명사 관련 문제이다. 복합 관계대명사는 〈관계대명사+ever〉의 형태로 여기서는 양보의 부사절을 이끌어 no matter what의 의미가 있는 (b)가 정답이 된다.

2.
A: I don't think we can make it to the movie, the hour has become late.
B: That's okay. We can see it __________.
(a) another time
(b) the other time
(c) other time
(d) for the time

| 해석 |
A: 오늘 영화 못 볼 것 같은데. 시간이 너무 늦었어.
B: 괜찮아. 다음에 봐도 돼.

| 해설 |
의미상 '(정해지지 않은) 나중에'란 의미가 되어야 하므로 (a)가 정답이 된다. 비슷한 의미로 some other time, next time 등이 있다.

3.
A: I think we might get stuck in heavy traffic.
B: I __________. We can't be late today.
(a) hope not it
(b) hope no
(c) don't hope
(d) hope not

| 해석 |
A: 내 생각에는 차가 막힐 것 같은데.
B: 그러지 않길 바래. 오늘은 늦을 수 없어.

| 해설 |
부정하는 동사나 절 등의 생략 대용어로 not이 사용된다. hope 이외에도 expect, think, believe, suppose, be afraid 뒤에 이러한 구문을 취할 수 있다.

4.
The success of the golf outing depends ________ the weather next weekend.
(a) about
(b) for
(c) of
(d) on

| 해석 |
골프 여행의 성공 여부는 다음 주말 날씨에 달려 있다.

| 해설 |
depend on은 '~에 달려 있다'라는 의미이다. 여기서 전치사 on은 '~에 근거하여, ~한 이유로(조건으로)' 등의 의미가 있다.

5.
My grandfather likes to tell me that he only had to pay a nickel for a coke when he __________ a kid.
(a) had been
(b) was
(c) is
(d) could be

| 해석 |
할아버지는 그가 어렸을 적에 콜라 값이 5센트밖에 하지 않았다고 나에게 말씀하시는 것을 좋아하신다.

| 해설 |
적절한 시제를 찾는 문제이다. that절의 주절이 과거형이고 그것의 종속

절(when절) 시제를 찾는 문제이므로 (a)와 같은 대과거(had p.p.)는 맞지 않다. 그러므로 과거형인 (b)가 가장 적절한 시제가 된다.

6.

__________ since she was ten years old, Amber has high expectations about competing in the Olympics next year.

(a) Training
(b) Having trained
(c) To train
(d) To have trained

| 해석 |

앰버는 10살 때부터 훈련을 해 왔기 때문에 다음해 올림픽에 큰 기대를 하고 있다.

| 해설 |

having p.p. 분사구문은 주절의 시제보다 한 시제 앞설 때 사용한다. 기대를 하게 된 원인이 10살 때부터 훈련을 해 왔기 때문(As she has trained)이므로 (b)가 정답이 된다.

7.

Many health concerns __________ to cigarettes, for smokers and nonsmokers alike.

(a) are attributed
(b) have attributed
(c) attribute
(d) were attributing

| 해석 |

많은 건강 문제들은 흡연자와 비흡연자 공히 담배에 기인한다.

| 해설 |

attribute은 '~탓으로 돌리다' 라는 의미의 타동사로 수동태로는 be attributed to가 되어 '~에 기인하다' 라는 의미가 된다. 여기서는 의미상 수동이 되어야 하므로 (a)가 정답이 된다.

8.

David began __________ during class for no reason at all.

(a) to laughing
(b) of laughing
(c) laughing
(d) laughter

| 해석 |

데이비드는 수업 시간에 아무 이유 없이 웃기 시작했다.

| 해설 |

begin은 동명사를 취하는 동사이므로 (c)가 정답이 된다. begin이 to부정사를 취하기도 하지만 (a)는 전치사 too이므로 정답이 될 수 없다.

9.

(a) A: I hiked that mountain last year. It's a great hike.
(b) B: That one too? Are there any mountains you haven't hiked?
(c) A: Well, I have yet to climb (tall → the tallest) mountain in the state.
(d) B: Maybe I'll come with you when you finally do.

| 해석 |

(a) A: 작년에 그 산을 올랐어. 너무 좋았어.
(b) B: 그 산을 또? 아직 오르지 않은 산이 있니?
(c) A: 주에서 가장 큰 산은 아직 오르지 않았어.
(d) B: 네가 오르게 될 때 같이 가야겠다.

| 해설 |

have yet to do는 '아직 ~해야 한다, 아직 ~하고 있지 않다' 는 의미이다. mountain은 가산명사이므로 단수 혹은 복수 표시를 해야 하고, 의미상 주의 불특정한 (하나의) 큰 산을 오르지 않았다는 것보다는 최상급의 표현인 the tallest mountain(가장 높은 산)이 적절하다.

10.

(a) A: Where have you been for the past three weeks?
(b) B: I was vacationing on an island in the South Pacific.
(c) A: That sounds like fun. Who did you go with?
(d) B: I went by myself. I just wanted to relax for (few → a few) weeks.

| 해석 |

(a) A: 지난 3주간 어디 다녀왔니?
(b) B: 남태평양의 섬에 다녀왔어.
(c) A: 재미있었겠다. 누구랑 갔어?
(d) B: 혼자 갔어. 그냥 몇 주 쉬고 싶었거든.

| 해설 |

a few는 가산명사 앞에서 '약간' 의 의미이고 few는 가산명사 앞에서 '거의 ~않다' 는 의미가 있다. 여기서는 전자의 의미가 적절하므로 a few weeks로 고쳐야 한다.

11.

(a) Recently there have been complaints that food and beverages are being brought into the library. (b) I would like to remind all students that absolutely (anyone is not allowed → **no one is allowed**) to bring either food or beverages inside the building. (c) The remnants of snacks have been attracting insects and rodents, both of which are great hazards to a library. (d) Not only can these pests disturb students and faculty, but they can also cause irreparable damage to our books.

| 해석 |

(a) 최근 음식과 음료가 도서관에 반입되는 것에 대한 불만들이 있었다.

(b) 나는 건물 내에 누구도 음식이나 음료를 가져올 수 없다는 것을 모든 학생에게 상기시키고 싶다. (c) 남은 음식물 찌꺼기들은 벌레와 쥐를 끌어들여 도서관에 큰 위험을 준다. (d) 이런 해충들은 학생과 교직원에게 해가 될 뿐만 아니라 책에 돌이킬 수 없는 피해를 준다.

| 해설 |

anyone은 '누군가'라는 의미의 부정대명사로 '누구도 ~하지 않다'라는 의미가 되기 위해선 no one이란 대명사를 사용해야 한다. any를 포함한 대명사는 부정어 not 앞에 올 수 없다.

| 어휘 |

remnant 나머지 faculty 교직원 rodent (쥐나 다람쥐 등의) 설치동물 irreparable 돌이킬 수 없는

12.

(a) Thomas Jefferson is widely known as the third President of the United States of America, (he was → **but he was**) also successful in many other areas of study. (b) Many people don't know that Jefferson had a great knowledge and talent in the study of architecture. (c) He helped to make the Neo-Palladian style of architecture popular in America, and he designed his own home in Virginia, the now-famous Monticello. (d) On top of that, he invented multiple modern amenities, such as the swivel chair, for his home.

| 해석 |

(a) 토마스 제퍼슨은 미국의 3대 대통령으로 잘 알려져 있지만 학문의 다른 많은 분야에서도 성공을 거두었다. (b) 많은 사람들은 제퍼슨이 건축 분야에 많은 지식과 재능을 가졌다는 사실을 알지 못한다. (c) 그는 미국에서 네오 팔라디오 풍의 건축이 유행하게 했고 지금은 몬테첼로로 유명한 버지니아에 있는 자신의 저택을 직접 설계했다. (d) 그밖에 그는 회전의자와 같은 여러 가지 현대 시설을 그의 저택을 위해 발명했다.

| 해설 |

(a)는 연결어 없이 두 개의 문장이 있으므로 알맞은 접속사가 필요하다. 의미상 두 개의 문장이 대조를 이루므로 접속사 but이 와야 한다.

| 어휘 |

amenity 시설 swivel 회전 on top of that 그밖에

Day 19

Build Up

164p

| 1. (b) | 2. (b) | 3. (d) | 4. (b) | 5. (a) | 6. (a) |
| 7. (c) | 8. (c) | 9. (a) | 10. (c) | 11. (d) | 12. (a) |

1.

A: Where is the new sushi restaurant located?

B: It's _______________ the street from the pizzeria.

(a) under   (b) across
(c) through   (d) beyond

| 해석 |

A: 새 초밥 식당이 어디 있니?

B: 피자 가게 건너편에 있어.

| 해설 |

across는 '~을 가로질러, ~의 맞은편에'라는 의미의 전치사다. 이 문장에서는 의미상 across가 가장 적절하다.

2.

A: Does John know that the concert has been rescheduled?

B: I will tell him that the concert has been delayed when he _________.

(a) will come

(b) comes

(c) was coming

(d) came

| 해석 |

A: 존은 그 콘서트 일정이 변경된 것을 아니?

B: 그가 오면 콘서트가 연기됐다고 말할 거야.

| 해설 |

시간 · 조건 부사절에서는 현재나 현재완료가 미래의 표현을 대신한다. 그가 오는 상황은 미래의 일이지만 여기서는 시간의 부사절로 쓰였으므로 현재형으로 써서 미래의 의미를 갖게 된다. 그러므로 (b)가 정답이다.

3.

A: _________ to get an A⁺ on the paper when she is busy with two jobs?

B: She is very studious and manages her time well.

(a) How do you think did Janice manage

(b) How do you think did manage Janice

(c) How do you think Janice manage

(d) How do you think Janice managed

| 해석 |

A: 제니스는 두 가지 일을 하면서 어떻게 그 논문에서 용케도 A⁺를 받은 것 같니?

B: 그녀는 매우 열심히 하고 시간도 잘 관리하잖아.

| 해설 |

의문사 의문문에 do you think가 삽입되면 그 뒤의 문장은 〈주어+동사〉의 어순이 된다. 또한 의미상 과거시제가 와야 하므로 (d)가 정답이 된다.

4.

A: Nathan _________ run six miles every morning until he tore his Achilles' heel.

B: Oh, so that's why he doesn't run anymore.
(a) ought to
(b) used to
(c) will
(d) did

| 해석 |
A: 나단은 아킬레스건을 다치기 전까지는 매일 아침 6마일씩 달렸어.
B: 그래서 그가 더이상 뛰지 않는구나.

| 해설 |
used to~는 '~하곤 했다'는 과거의 습관적인 행위나 상태를 나타내는 표현이다. B의 응답을 통해 그가 더이상 달리기를 하지 않는다는 것을 알 수 있으므로 (b)가 정답이 된다.

5.
_______________ continue to fight and delay every group project.
(a) It is the two employees who
(b) The two employees who
(c) When the two employees who
(d) Which are the two employees who

| 해석 |
계속해서 모든 그룹 프로젝트를 지연시키고 싸운 사람은 그 두 직원이었다.

| 해설 |
it ~ that 강조 구문이다. it은 가주어로 it과 that 사이에 강조하고 싶은 어구가 위치하게 되는데 여기서는 강조어구가 사람이므로 that 대신 관계대명사 who가 쓰였다.

6.
Not all of the students were doing well, _____________, since some of them were failing the tests.
(a) it seems
(b) it seeming
(c) seemed
(d) seeming

| 해석 |
모든 학생이 다 잘 한 것 같지는 않았다. 왜냐하면 그들 중에 몇몇은 시험에 떨어졌기 때문이다.

| 해설 |
빈칸에는 의견을 나타내는 표현인 it seems(~인 듯 보인다)절이 삽입 어구로 들어가는 것이 가장 적절하다.

7.
The dinner included many types of foods, most of which ___________ my favorite to eat.
(a) is
(b) have
(c) are

(d) has

| 해석 |
저녁식사는 많은 종류의 음식이 있었는데 대부분이 내가 좋아하는 것들이었다.

| 해설 |
〈most of + 명사〉는 명사의 수에 수를 일치시킨다. 관계대명사 which는 many types of foods를 의미하기 때문에 복수 동사가 와야 한다. 그러므로 (c)가 정답이 된다.

8.
Michael, ___________ lovingly at his sleeping daughter, whispered "good night."
(a) smiles
(b) smiled
(c) smiling
(d) was smiling

| 해석 |
마이클은 잠든 딸에게 사랑스럽게 미소지으면서 '굿 나잇'이라고 속삭였다.

| 해설 |
빈칸에는 분사구문이 와야 한다. smile at은 '~에 미소 짓다'라는 의미의 자동사로 능동의 분사구문이 와야 한다. 그러므로 (c)가 정답이 된다.

9.
(a) A: Henry bought (Sony laptop → the Sony laptop) from Circuit City.
(b) B: He always wanted it. How much was it?
(c) A: It was on sale for $400.
(d) B: He got very lucky.

| 해석 |
(a) A: 헨리가 서킷 시티에서 소니 노트북을 샀어.
(b) B: 걔가 항상 사고 싶어 했잖아. 얼마였대?
(c) A: 할인해서 400달러였어.
(d) B: 운이 좋았다.

| 해설 |
laptop은 가산명사이므로 단수나 복수 표시를 해야 한다. 여기서는 '한 개'를 의미하고 B의 응답을 통해(He always wanted it.) 구체적인 제품을 이야기하고 있으므로 the가 와야 한다.

10.
(a) A: The troops need more medical assistance and resources as soon as possible!
(b) B: They'll receive some soon since the president sent medical teams over.
(c) A: Yes, but that (must have been done → should have been done) sooner before hundreds of soldiers died.
(d) B: It's better late than never.

| 해석 |
(a) A: 그 부대는 더 많은 의료 지원과 구호품이 가능한 빨리 필요해!

(b) B: 대통령이 의료팀을 보냈기 때문에 곧 일부를 받게 될 거야.

(c) A: 알아. 하지만 수백 명의 군인들이 죽기 전에 더 빨리 보내졌어야
했어.

(d) B: 안 하는 것보다 늦게라도 하는 게 낫지.

| 해설 |

의미상 '~했어야 했다'라는 과거 일에 대한 유감의 뜻을 나타내는 표현
이 와야 한다. must have p.p.는 '~였음에 틀림없다'라는 과거 일에
대한 강한 추측이므로 should have p.p.로 바꾸어야 한다.

11.

(a) The YMCA recently developed a new community outreach program for the impoverished youth in this area. (b) They provide practical lessons about life. (c) The lessons cover a broad range of topics like drugs, gangs, abuse, family, and even poverty. (d) The program not only gives general information about these topics, but they also teach children (how can they deal with such issues → **how they can deal with such issues**).

| 해석 |

(a) YMCA는 최근 이 지역의 가난한 청소년들을 위해 새 커뮤니티 복지
계획을 개발했다. (b) 그들은 삶에 대한 실용적인 수업을 제공한다. (c)
이 수업은 약물, 갱단, 학대, 가족 그리고 빈곤에 이르기까지 넓은 범위를
다룬다. (d) 이 프로그램은 이러한 주제들에 대한 일반적인 정보를 제공
할 뿐만 아니라 그들이 이러한 문제들을 어떻게 다룰 수 있는지 가르쳐
준다.

| 해설 |

간접의문문의 순서는 〈의문사＋주어＋동사〉의 어순이다. how can
they deal with such issues는 의문문의 어순이므로 주어와 (조)동사
의 위치를 바꾸어야 한다.

| 어휘 |

outreach 보다 넓은 지역 사회의 복지에 관한
impoverished 가난한, 힘없는

12.

(a) Sometimes, cancer can be completely eliminated if treatment (began → **begins**) in its early stages. (b) If cancer is detected in its early stages, doctors can remove cancerous cells before they spread to other parts of the body. (c) However, it is almost impossible to get rid of cancerous cells once they spread throughout the body, especially to vital organs. (d) That is why it is extremely important to get yearly health checkups.

| 해석 |

(a) 때때로 암은 초기 단계에 치료를 시작하면 완전히 제거될 수 있다.
(b) 암은 초기 단계에 발견되면 몸의 다른 부분에 퍼지기 전에 의사들이
암 세포를 제거할 수 있다. (c) 그러나 일단 암 세포가 몸을 거쳐, 특히
중요 기관에 퍼지기 시작하면 암 세포를 제거하는 것은 거의 불가능하다.

(d) 그러므로 해마다 정기 검진을 받는 것은 매우 중요하다.

| 해설 |

초기에 치료가 시작되면 암이 완전히 제거될 수 있다는 사실이므로 과거
형의 시제는 맞지 않다. 그러므로 현재형으로 시제를 바꾸어야 한다.

| 어휘 |

eliminate 제거하다 **detect** 발견하다 **cancerous** 암의, 불치의
vital 중대한

Day 20

Build Up

174p

1. (c)	**2.** (a)	**3.** (b)	**4.** (b)	**5.** (a)	**6.** (c)
7. (d)	**8.** (b)	**9.** (b)	**10.** (c)	**11.** (b)	**12.** (d)

1.

A: Did you know that Tom doesn't know how to ride a bicycle?

B: Really? ___________ learn how to ride when they are children.

(a) Most of the people

(b) The most people

(c) **Most people**

(d) People most

| 해석 |

A: 톰이 자전거를 못 탄다는 것을 알고 있었니?

B: 정말? 대부분의 사람들은 어렸을 때 자전거 타는 방법을 배우는데.

| 해설 |

여기서는 의미상 일반적인 사람을 의미하므로 most people이 정답이 된
다. most of the people은 '그 사람들 중 대부분'이라는 의미이고, the
most people은 '그 대부분의 사람들'이란 뜻으로 제한적인 의미이다.

2.

A: Have you been to New York?

B: Yes. I ___________ there by myself soon after I graduated from college.

(a) **went**

(b) have been

(c) had gone

(d) have gone

| 해석 |

A: 뉴욕에 가 본 적 있니?

B: 응. 대학 졸업하자마자 혼자 갔었어.

| 해설 |

시간의 부사절을 통해 과거의 시점을 이야기하고 있음을 알 수 있으므로

(a)가 정답이 된다. Have you~?로 물어본 질문에 Yes로 대답은 했지만 여기서는 Yes 뒤에 I have가 생략되었다.

3.

A: When do you want to go shopping?
B: In a little while. I'm __________ by the neighbor kids right now.
(a) having my washed car
(b) having my car washed
(c) having my car wash
(d) washing my car

| 해석 |
A: 언제 쇼핑가고 싶니?
B: 잠시 후에. 지금 이웃집 아이들이 내 차를 세차 중이거든.

| 해설 |
사역동사 have는 목적어 뒤에 동사원형이나 과거분사 형태가 올 수 있는데, 목적어와 목적 보어의 관계가 능동이면 동사원형을, 수동이면 과거분사 형태를 취한다. 여기서는 수동의 관계가 성립되므로 (b)가 정답이 된다.

4.

A: Did you have fun at the reunion?
B: It was a lot of fun, actually. There were

__________________.

(a) 100 people we thought more than
(b) 100 more people than we thought
(c) we thought more than 100 people
(d) more than 100 people we thought

| 해석 |
A: 동창회 재미있었니?
B: 많이 재미있었어. 생각보다 100명 더 많은 사람들이 왔어.

| 해설 |
문장의 어순에 관한 문제이다. 의미상 생각했던 것보다 100명이 더 왔다는 문장이 되어야 하므로 동사 were 뒤에 의미상의 주어인 명사구가 와야 한다. 그러므로 (b)가 가장 적절한 어순이 된다.

5.

His principal made his options very clear: either he starts doing his homework ________ he doesn't graduate.
(a) or
(b) nor
(c) but
(d) and

| 해석 |
교장 선생님은 그의 선택을 매우 확실하게 해주셨다. 숙제를 하든지 아니면 졸업을 못하든지 둘 중 하나라는 것이다.

| 해설 |
상관접속사 관련 문제이다. 상관접속사가 나오면 체크해야 할 사항이 몇 가지 있는데 먼저 연결어가 제대로 연결됐는지 확인한다. 그리고 문법적으로 동일한 요소가 병치 구조를 이루었는지 확인한다. 마지막으로 수의 일치 문제가 아닌지 확인하는 것이다. 여기서는 접속사 either가 사용되었으므로 이것의 연결어 or가 와야 한다.

6.

Jeff needed to have his birth certificate in order to obtain a passport, but he couldn't find ________.
(a) an original
(b) original
(c) the original
(d) one original

| 해석 |
제프는 여권을 신청하기 위해서 출생증명서가 필요했지만 원본을 찾을 수 없었다.

| 해설 |
특정한 원본을 가리키고 있으므로 the가 쓰여야 한다. 그러므로 (c)가 정답이 된다.

7.

After years of hard work and training, Alex is golfing ______ an equal level with the professionals.
(a) with
(b) in
(c) as
(d) on

| 해석 |
몇 년 간의 고된 노력과 훈련으로 알렉스는 전문가들과 동등한 수준으로 골프를 친다.

| 해설 |
전치사 관련 문제이다. on an equal level은 '동등한 수준으로' 라는 의미의 관용적인 표현이다. 그러므로 (d)가 정답이 된다.

8.

Even though Bill __________ his car at the moment, he still made time to play with his children before bed.
(a) had repaired
(b) was repairing
(c) has repaired
(d) had been repairing

| 해석 |
빌은 그때 차를 고치고 있었지만 자기 전에 그의 아이들과 놀 시간을 만들었다.

| 해설 |
at the moment라는 시간 부사를 통해 과거에 일시적으로 진행되는 상태임을 알 수 있다. 그러므로 과거진행의 시제가 적절하다.

9.

(a) A: Is it true that they will implement a new

testing system next year at school?

(b) B: Yes, it is, (and → **but**) it will not be for us, only for the new freshman.

(c) A: That's a relief. I was not looking forward to an unfamiliar testing system.

(d) B: Well, it wouldn't be fair for them to change our testing program.

| 해석 |

(a) A: 학교에서 내년에 새로운 시험제도를 실행한다는 것이 사실이니?

(b) B: 응, 사실이야. 그런데 우리는 아니고 신입생들에게만 적용되는 거야.

(c) A: 잘됐다. 난 낯선 시험제도는 원하지 않거든.

(d) B: 우리 시험 제도를 바꾸는 것은 공평하지 않을 거야.

| 해설 |

적절한 의미의 접속사를 고르는 문제이다. 접속사 뒤의 내용이 대조를 이루므로 나열의 접속사 and가 아닌 but이 적절하다. That's a relief.는 '안심이 된다' 라는 표현으로 알아두도록 한다.

10.

(a) A: I don't think we should eat Italian tonight, I don't really like spaghetti.

(b) B: You don't have to get spaghetti. How about lasagna?

(c) A: No, (I don't like neither spaghetti nor lasagna → **I don't like either spaghetti or lasagna / I like neither spaghetti nor lasagna**).

(d) B: But you like pizza, right? I will split a pizza with you.

| 해석 |

(a) A: 오늘밤엔 이탈리안 음식을 먹지 않는 것이 좋겠어. 난 스파게티가 정말 싫거든.

(b) B: 스파게티 먹지 않아도 돼. 라자냐 어때?

(c) A: 아니. 스파게티도 라자냐도 싫어.

(d) B: 그런데 피자는 좋아하잖아? 피자를 나눠 줄게.

| 해설 |

neither A nor B는 'A도 아니고 B도 아닌' 이란 의미로 이 자체가 부정의 의미를 담고 있기 때문에 부정문에는 쓰일 수 없다. 그러므로 I don't like either spaghetti or lasagna.로 쓰든지 I like neither spaghetti nor lasagna.의 형태로 써야 한다.

11.

(a) Recent studies show that the number of Americans suffering from vision loss or blindness is increasing at a rapid rate. (b) Eye diseases (most common → **most commonly**) affect middle-aged and elderly people. (c) As the children of the baby-boomer era grow up and technological advances allow people to live longer, the number of elderly people increases by great strides. (d)

Studies project that nearly six-million Americans could suffer from eye diseases by the year 2020, thus increasing the burden upon both local and national governments.

| 해석 |

(a) 최근 연구는 시력 감퇴나 실명으로 고통 받는 미국인들의 숫자가 급격히 증가하고 있다는 사실을 나타내고 있다. (b) 눈 관련 질병은 일반적으로 중년이나 노년층에 영향을 준다. (c) 베이비 붐 시대의 아이들이 자라고 기술 발전이 사람을 더 오래 살 수 있게 하면서 노년층의 수는 큰 폭으로 증가하고 있다. (d) 거의 육백만 명의 미국인들이 2020년까지 눈 관련 질병으로 고통 받을 수도 있다고 연구 결과는 추정하고 있기 때문에 지역과 국가 정부에 부담을 가중시킬 것으로 예상하고 있다.

| 해설 |

common은 형용사의 형태로 명사를 수식하거나 보어의 역할을 하는데 여기서는 적절치 않다. 그러므로 부사의 형태인 commonly로 바꾸어 동사 affect을 수식해야 한다.

| 어휘 |

project 예상하다, 계획하다

12.

(a) Recently, voices around the community have been calling for the conservation of our countryside. (b) The natural beauty of the town attracts developers who want to destroy the land by building both residentially and commercially lucrative structures. (c) However, these developments remain unwanted by local citizens. (d) A bill is in the works, which, if passed, will (be warded off → **ward off**) the developers by officially recognizing our surrounding lands as a state park.

| 해석 |

(a) 최근 지역 사회에 우리 시골을 보존해야 한다는 요구가 높아지고 있습니다. (b) 마을의 아름다운 자연 경관이 주거용 및 상업적인 용도의 돈이 되는 건축물을 짓느라고 땅을 파괴하길 원하는 개발업자들을 끌고 있습니다. (c) 그러나 이 개발은 지역 주민들은 원하지 않는 일입니다. (d) 법안이 진행 중인데 통과가 되면 공식적으로 우리 땅이 주립 공원으로 인정되면서 그들을 몰아내게 될 것입니다.

| 해설 |

ward off는 '~을 물리치다' 라는 의미가 있다. 여기서 의미상 이 법안이 개발업자를 물리치는 것이므로 수동이 아닌 능동의 형태가 되어야 된다. 그러므로 will ward off로 고쳐야 한다. in the works는 '일이 진행중인' 이라는 뜻의 관용적인 표현이다.

| 어휘 |

call for 요구하다   **lucrative** 돈이 벌리는

Final Check

178p

1. (b)	**2.** (a)	**3.** (d)	**4.** (c)	**5.** (b)
6. (b)	**7.** (b)	**8.** (c)	**9.** (b)	**10.** (a)
11. (c)	**12.** (b)	**13.** (b)	**14.** (d)	**15.** (b)
16. (c)	**17.** (d)	**18.** (b)	**19.** (d)	**20.** (c)
21. (b)	**22.** (d)	**23.** (a)	**24.** (c)	**25.** (c)
26. (a)	**27.** (d)	**28.** (c)	**29.** (c)	**30.** (c)
31. (b)	**32.** (d)	**33.** (c)	**34.** (c)	**35.** (b)
36. (a)	**37.** (b)	**38.** (d)	**39.** (c)	**40.** (a)
41. (a)	**42.** (c)	**43.** (b)	**44.** (b)	**45.** (b)
46. (c)	**47.** (b)	**48.** (d)	**49.** (d)	**50.** (a)

Part 1

1.

A: Before I hire you, ___________ me a list of references to do a background check.

B: That's not a problem. I have all of the information with me.

(a) I'd like to give

(b) I'd like you to give

(c) I'd like that you gave

(d) I'd like you give

| 해석 |

A: 채용하기 전에 배경 조사를 위해 신원 보증인 명단을 저에게 주셨으면 좋겠는데요.

B: 문제없습니다. 모든 정보를 가지고 있어요.

| 해설 |

I'd like to~는 '~하고 싶다' 라는 표현이고, 〈I'd like + 목적어 + to~〉는 '…가 ~하면 좋겠다' 라는 표현이다. 여기에서는 후자의 용법으로 쓰였으므로 (b)가 정답이 된다.

2.

A: Have you heard what is happening with Jerry and his business?

B: Yes, he's ___________ attack from a group of animal rights activists.

(a) under

(b) about

(c) in

(d) by

| 해석 |

A: 제리와 그의 사업에 무슨 일이 벌어지고 있는지 들었니?

B: 응, 동물 권리 보호자 단체로부터 공격을 받고 있대.

| 해설 |

가장 어울리는 전치사를 고르는 문제이다. 이 문장에서 attack과 가장 어울리는 전치사를 골라야 하는데 under attack은 '공격을 받는' 이란 의미이다.

3.

A: I thought the speaker gave a really nice speech today.

B: I didn't think so. In fact, a lot of the things he said ___________ offended me.

(a) all kinds of

(b) a kind of

(c) kinds of

(d) kind of

| 해석 |

A: 오늘 연설자가 너무 멋진 연설을 한 것 같아.

B: 그런 것 같진 않은데. 사실, 나는 그가 언급한 많은 부분이 불쾌했어.

| 해설 |

kind of는 '약간, 좀' 이라는 의미의 관용적 표현이다. all kinds of는 '온갖 종류의' 란 의미이고, a kind of는 '일종의' 라는 의미로 여기에서는 어울리지 않는다. 그러므로 (d)가 정답이다.

4.

A: I'm getting sick of having such long hair.

B: It's probably about time that you had ________.

(a) cut it

(b) the cut

(c) it cut

(d) cutting it

| 해석 |

A: 긴 머리 이제는 질려.

B: 머리를 깎아야 할 때가 됐나 보다.

| 해설 |

have가 사역동사로 쓰일 때에는 〈have + 목적어 + 동사원형〉 혹은 〈have + 목적어 + p.p.〉의 형태로 쓰인다. 목적어와 목적 보어의 관계가 능동이면 동사원형을, 수동이면 과거분사 형태를 취하므로 (c)가 정답이 된다. 여기에서 cut은 과거분사이다.

5.

A: Is there anyone here who wants to pick up Bill from the airport?

B: Here. I ___________ do it.

(a) had to

(b) will

(c) may

(d) would

| 해석 |

A: 빌을 공항에서 데려오고 싶은 사람 없니?

B: 내가 할게.

| 해설 |

의미상 적절한 조동사를 고르는 문제이다. 여기서는 의미상 주어의 의지

를 담고 있는 미래의 조동사 will이 가장 적절하다. may와 would는 모두 확실성이 will보다 덜하므로 적절치 않다.

6.

A: If I __________ facing the same situation as you, I would get a new job.
B: Thanks for your advice; I know I can always trust you.

(a) was
(b) were
(c) could be
(d) am

| 해석 |
A: 내가 너와 같은 상황에 놓였다면 난 새 직업을 얻었을 거야.
B: 충고 고마워. 널 항상 믿을 수 있다는 걸 알아.

| 해설 |
가정법 과거와 관련된 문제이다. 현재 상황에 반대되는 것을 가정할 때 가정법 과거의 형태를 취한다. 〈if＋주어＋과거 동사~, 주어＋조동사 과거형(would, could, etc.)＋동사원형〉. 이때 if절에서 동사가 be동사이면 과거형은 주어와 상관없이 were를 쓴다. 그러므로 (b)가 정답이 된다.

7.

A: Hello, my truck needs __________ by tomorrow. Can you help me?
B: I don't know, sir. I'll have to take a look at it first.

(a) to repair
(b) repairing
(c) repaired
(d) repair

| 해석 |
A: 안녕하세요, 제 트럭이 내일까지 수리되어야 해요. 도와줄 수 있나요?
B: 글쎄요. 먼저 한번 볼게요.

| 해설 |
need는 to부정사를 취하기도 하지만 동명사를 취할 경우 수동의 의미가 된다. 여기서는 의미상 트럭이 수리되는 수동의 의미가 되어야 하므로 (b)가 정답이 된다. to부정사로 쓰였을 경우 to be repaired가 되어야 한다.

8.

A: How did the football team play in their game last weekend?
B: __________ by the size of the other team's players, they didn't play very well.

(a) Intimidating
(b) To intimidate
(c) Intimidated
(d) Intimidation

| 해석 |
A: 지난 주말에 그 축구팀이 경기에서 어땠니?
B: 상대팀 선수들의 크기에 주눅이 들어서 경기를 잘하지 못했어.

| 해설 |
intimidate은 '~을 협박하다, 겁주다' 라는 타동사이다. 그들이 겁을 먹은 수동의 뜻이 되어야 하므로 과거분사의 분사구문이 되어야 한다. 그러므로 (c)가 정답이 된다.

9.

A: The boss wanted me to tell you not to organize things that way.
B: I know this job better than he does. I couldn't care __________ what he thinks.

(a) any
(b) less
(c) a little
(d) some

| 해석 |
A: 사장님이 일을 그렇게 정리하지 말라고 당신에게 전하라고 하시는데요.
B: 이 일은 내가 그보다 더 잘 압니다. 그가 무엇을 생각하는지는 전혀 관심 없습니다.

| 해설 |
I couldn't care less는 '조금도 개의치 않는다, 아무래도 상관없다' 라는 관용적인 표현이다. 그러므로 (b)가 정답이 된다.

10.

A: Did your son enjoy his first Christmas in a cold climate?
B: He loved it. I can't explain to you __________ to see snow for the first time.

(a) how excited he was
(b) how he was excited
(c) how excited was he
(d) how was excited he

| 해석 |
A: 네 아들은 추운 기후에서 맞은 첫 번째 크리스마스를 즐겁게 보냈니?
B: 너무 좋아했어. 처음으로 눈을 보고 얼마나 흥분했는지 몰라.

| 해설 |
간접의문문은 〈의문사＋주어＋동사〉의 어순이다. how가 방법이 아닌 정도를 나타낼 때에는 how 뒤에 형용사나 부사가 오게 된다. 여기서 how는 방법이 아닌 정도이므로 (a)가 정답이 된다.

11.

A: Will you be able to finish your project before the weekend?
B: I'm expecting __________, but I'll have to have complete concentration all week.

(a) that
(b) about

(d) to do

| 해석 |

A: 주말 전에 프로젝트를 마칠 수 있을 것 같니?
B: 그럴 거라고 생각하는데 주중에 완전히 집중을 해야 할 거야.

| 해설 |

대부정사 문제이다. 명사의 반복을 피하기 위해서 대명사가 있고, 동사의 반복을 피하기 위해서 대동사를 쓰듯이 같은 to부정사의 동사구의 반복을 피하기 위해서 동사구를 생략하고 to까지만 쓰는 것을 대부정사라고 한다. 그러므로 (c)가 정답이 된다.

12.

A: Were you able to join the writing group you wanted to join?
B: No, by the time I applied the committee had objected __________ any new members.

(a) acceptance

(b) to accepting

(c) to accept

(d) accepting

| 해석 |

A: 네가 하고 싶었던 글쓰기 모임에 가입할 수 있었니?
B: 아니, 내가 지원했을 때 협회는 더 이상 새 회원을 받아들이는 것을 반대했어.

| 해설 |

object to -ing는 '~을 반대하다' 라는 의미로 여기서 to는 전치사이므로 동명사의 형태가 와야 한다. 그러므로 (b)가 정답이 된다.

13.

A: Did Amy go with you to the symphony?
B: She __________ about going, but in the end decided not to.

(a) would think

(b) had thought

(c) has thought

(d) would have thought

| 해석 |

A: 에이미가 너와 그 연주회에 갔었니?
B: 갈려고 생각했었는데 결국에는 안 가기로 결정했어.

| 해설 |

과거완료는 과거의 어느 시점보다 먼저 일어난 행동이나 상태를 나타내는 표현이다. 여기서도 가지 않기로 결정한 것(decided not to)보다 가는 것을 고려한 것이 먼저 일어났으므로 (b)가 정답이 된다.

14.

A: How was the winter in Maine this year?
B: We had __________ weather. The snow was beautiful, but it wasn't too cold.

(a) such an amazing

(b) amazing such

(c) an amazing such

(d) such amazing

| 해석 |

A: 메인에서 이번 해 겨울은 어땠어?
B: 멋진 날씨였어. 눈은 아름다웠고 너무 춥지도 않았어.

| 해설 |

⟨such+an/a+형용사+명사⟩의 어순이지만 weather는 불가산명사이므로 부정관사가 올 수 없다. 그러므로 (d)가 정답이 된다.

15.

A: How __________ to get to Phoenix?
B: It's going to take at least thirteen hours. You might as well take a nap.

(a) do you think it is going to take

(b) long do you think it is going to take

(c) long do you think is it going to take

(d) do you think it is going to take long

| 해석 |

A: 피닉스에 가는 데 얼마나 걸릴 것 같니?
B: 적어도 13시간 걸릴 거야. 낮잠이나 자는 게 좋을 걸.

| 해설 |

의문문에서 do you think가 삽입되면 그 뒤에는 ⟨주어＋동사⟩의 어순이 된다. 그러므로 (b)의 어순이 정답이 된다.

16.

A: Has the museum decided to build the addition yet?
B: No. It was only yesterday __________ they had the meeting, and they haven't reached a decision yet.

(a) where

(b) of which

(c) when

(d) about

| 해석 |

A: 그 박물관이 증축물을 짓기로 결정했니?
B: 아니. 어제야 미팅을 가져서 아직 결정하지 못했어.

| 해설 |

빈칸 뒤에 완벽한 문장이 왔으므로 빈칸에는 관계부사가 와야 한다. 여기서는 선행사가 날짜를 의미하므로 when이 적절하다.

17.

A: Okay, kids, every __________ person will be on the defensive team.
B: Teacher, what happens if the teams are uneven?

(a) double

(b) two

(c) again

(d) second

| 해석 |
A: 알았어. 애들아. 두 번째 사람마다 수비팀이 될 거야.
B: 선생님, 팀들이 (실력이) 고르지 않으면 어떻게 되죠?

| 해설 |
〈every+기수+복수 명사〉, 〈every+서수+단수 명사〉가 된다. 기수인 two가 오면 뒤의 명사는 people(every two people)이 되어야 하므로 (d)가 정답이 된다.

18.

A: Will you try to get into the advanced math class next year?
B: No way. Math tests are __________ difficult for me to get a passing grade in that class.

(a) a lot
(b) far too
(c) so much
(d) some

| 해석 |
A: 내년에 고급 수학반을 들을 거니?
B: 아니. 그 반에서 수학 시험 통과 점수를 받기는 나에겐 너무 어려워.

| 해설 |
부사 far는 비교급이나 다른 부사를 수식한다. 그러므로 too는 형용사 difficult를 수식하고 부사 far는 부사 too를 수식하므로 (b)가 정답이 된다. much는 형용사의 최상급이나 비교급을 수식하므로 원급의 difficult를 수식할 수 없다.

19.

A: Jenny was thinking of bringing her dog along on the trip. Do you mind?
B: Honestly, I would rather she __________. I'm allergic to dog hair.

(a) couldn't
(b) can't
(c) hadn't
(d) didn't

| 해석 |
A: 제니는 여행에 그녀의 강아지를 데려올까 생각 중이래. 어떻게 생각해?
B: 솔직히 안 데려왔으면 좋겠어. 강아지 털에 알레르기가 있거든.

| 해설 |
〈would rather+주어+과거 동사〉는 '주어가 ~하는 게 좋겠다' 라는 의미로 현재나 미래의 일을 의미한다. 그러므로 여기서도 과거 동사 (d)가 정답이 된다.

20.

A: This is just a trial copy, right?
B: Correct. __________ you not approve of the software, there will be no charge to your account.

(a) Until
(b) When
(c) Should
(d) Unless

| 해석 |
A: 이거 시험판이죠?
B: 네, 승인하지 않으시면 돈을 지불하지 않으셔도 됩니다.

| 해설 |
이 문장은 가정법 미래에서 if가 생략되어 도치가 된 구문이다. 원래 if you should not approve of the software이다. 그러므로 (c)가 정답이 된다.

Part 2

21.

The hurricane hit the southern coast of Florida hard, __________ the destruction of many homes and businesses.

(a) resulted in
(b) resulting in
(c) as a result of
(d) having resulted

| 해석 |
허리케인은 플로리다 남부 해안을 강타해서 많은 집과 사업체를 파손시켰다.

| 해설 |
result in은 '끝나다, 결과를 초래하다' 라는 의미로 능동의 분사구문이 적절하다. as a result of~는 '~의 결과로서' 라는 의미로 원인과 결과를 볼 때 논리적으로 맞지 않으므로 (c)는 정답이 될 수 없다.

22.

The mountain pass rose __________ steeply that my old truck overheated on the way up.

(a) much
(b) very
(c) quite
(d) so

| 해석 |
산길이 너무 가팔라서 내 낡은 트럭은 올라가는 도중에 과열되었다.

| 해설 |
so ~ that ...은 '너무 ~해서 …하다' 라는 의미이다. 그러므로 빈칸에는 부사 so가 적절하다.

23.

The company will remain in its current location for the holidays, __________ we are searching for a better suited location for after the New Year.

(a) however,
(b) then
(c) unless

(d) because

회사는 휴일 동안은 현재의 위치에 있게 될 것이다. 그렇지만 신년 이후를 위해 더 나은 장소가 있는지 찾아보는 중이다.

| 해설 |
콤마 앞뒤의 문장이 대조를 이루므로 대조의 접속사를 골라야 한다. 그러므로 여기서는 대조의 의미(그러나, 그렇지만)가 있는 (a)가 정답이 된다.

24.

The judge demanded that all reporters and media correspondents __________ from the court room.
(a) were removed
(b) to be removed
(c) be removed
(d) are removed

| 해석 |
판사는 모든 기자와 언론 관계자들을 법정에서 나가도록 요구했다.

| 해설 |
주장, 요구, 제안 동사 뒤에 that절이 올 경우 that절 이하의 내용이 아직 일어나지 않은 일에 대해 '제안'의 의미를 가질 때 should가 생략됐다고 보고 동사원형을 쓴다. 그러므로 (c)가 정답이 된다.

25.

I've always thought seeing music performed __________ to be more satisfying than listening to a record at home.
(a) alive
(b) to live
(c) live
(d) lively

| 해석 |
나는 실황으로 연주되는 음악 공연을 보는 것이 집에서 레코드를 듣는 것보다 더 만족스럽다고 항상 생각해왔다.

| 해설 |
live는 '실황으로, 생방송으로'라는 의미의 부사로 동사 performed를 수식한다. 부사 lively는 '힘차게, 생생하게'라는 의미이다. 여기서는 직접 연주한다는 의미가 되어야 하므로 (c)가 정답이 된다.

26.

To earn the promotion to chief inspector, you must build a reputation for examining the products __________ than others.
(a) more thoroughly
(b) most thoroughly
(c) more thorough
(d) a lot thorough

| 해설 |
최고 검사관으로 승진하기 위해서는 제품들을 다른 사람들보다 더 철저

하게 조사한다는 명성을 쌓아야만 한다.

| 해설 |
빈칸 뒤에 비교급 접속사 than이 왔으므로 최상급이 아닌 비교급이 와야 하고 examining을 수식해야 하므로 부사의 형태인 thoroughly가 와야 한다. 그러므로 (a)가 정답이 된다.

27.

Before beginning the tour, there is __________ to store your coats and other belongings just inside the doors and to your left.
(a) the place
(b) a placement
(c) any place
(d) a place

| 해석 |
투어를 시작하기 전에 문 안쪽 여러분 왼쪽에 코트와 다른 소지품을 넣을 장소가 있습니다.

| 해설 |
placement는 '배치'라는 의미로 여기서는 적절치 않다. 또한 (a)의 the place는 상대방이 알고 있는 장소를 가리키므로 내용상 옳지 않다. 그러므로 '장소'라는 의미의 (d)가 정답이 된다.

28.

__________, this university has one of the most intensive application processes in the country.
(a) All the requirements given
(b) The given all requirements
(c) Given all the requirements
(d) Giving all the requirements

| 해석 |
모든 필요조건이 주어지면 이 대학은 이 나라에서 가장 집중적인 지원 과정 중 하나를 갖게 된다.

| 해설 |
given은 considering(~을 고려하면)과 마찬가지로 분사이지만 하나의 관용적인 어구로 접속사 역할을 하여 '~라고 가정하면, ~이 주어지면'이란 의미를 가진다. 그러므로 (c)가 정답이 된다.

29.

Anyone caught trespassing on the premises after operating hours __________ immediately reported to the authorities.
(a) was
(b) were
(c) will be
(d) has been

| 해석 |
운영 시간 이후에 그 구역에 침입하다가 적발되면 누구든지 즉시 당국에 보고될 것이다.

의미상 적절한 시제를 고르는 문제이다. 주어가 Anyone(누구든지)이므로 미래시제가 가장 적절하다.

| 어휘 |

trespass 침입하다

30.

A university study shows that a reevaluation of residential planning __________ many people, should another hurricane evacuation be required.
(a) can benefit
(b) can have benefited
(c) could benefit
(d) could have benefited

| 해석 |

대학 연구는 만약 또 다른 허리케인 대피가 필요하게 되면 주거 계획의 재평가가 많은 사람들에게 혜택을 줄 수 있을 것이라는 점을 보여 준다.

| 해설 |

〈If+주어+should+동사원형~, 주어+조동사(기본/과거형)+동사원형〉은 '(혹시라도) ~한다면 …할 것이다'라는 의미이다. 이때 if가 생략되면서 문장의 도치가 이루어진다. 의미상 '혜택을 줄 수 있다'는 가능성이 맞으므로 (c)가 정답이 된다.

31.

There were reports of wildlife mysteriously __________ in the area long before the disease was known to have reached this part of the world.
(a) dead
(b) dying
(c) has died
(d) died

| 해석 |

그 질병이 이 지역에 도달했다고 알려지기 훨씬 전에 이해할 수 없이 죽어가는 야생생물에 관한 보고가 있었다.

| 해설 |

빈칸에는 wildlife를 수식하는 분사 형태가 와야 한다. die는 자동사이므로 현재분사 형태가 적절하다.

32.

Music industry experts __________ that the industry is on the verge of some major changes.
(a) are believed
(b) were believed
(c) are to believe
(d) believe

| 해석 |

음악 산업 전문가들은 이 산업이 중대한 변화에 직면했다고 여긴다.

| 해설 |

의미상 전문가들이 that 이하라고 여기다라는 능동의 의미가 적절하므로 (d)가 정답이 된다. be to~는 예정, 의무, 의도 등의 의미가 되므로 (c)

는 적절치 않다.

| 어휘 |

on the verge of ~하기 직전에

33.

The defendant admitted __________ at the hotel on December 6th, but said he was having dinner at the time the crime was committed.
(a) to be stayed
(b) to stay
(c) to staying
(d) to being stayed

| 해석 |

피고인은 12월 6일에 그 호텔에 머문 사실을 인정했지만 사건이 일어날 때에는 저녁을 먹고 있었다고 말했다.

| 해설 |

〈admit+to+-ing〉는 '~에 대해 인정하다'라는 의미이며 to는 전치사이기 때문에 뒤에 동명사가 와야 한다.

34.

My brother is turning forty next week, but I can't imagine __________ because he still has the energy of a twenty years old.
(a) he is that old
(b) he was that old
(c) his being that old
(d) his having been that old

| 해석 |

내 형은 다음주에 40세가 된다. 그런데 그는 여전히 20대 같은 에너지를 갖고 있기 때문에 나는 그가 그렇게 늙었다는 것을 상상할 수 없다.

| 해설 |

imagine은 동명사를 취하는 동사이다(imagine+-ing). 동명사의 의미상의 주어는 소유격으로 나타낸다. 그러나 구어체에서는 목적격으로 나타낼 수도 있다. e.g. Would you mind my/me smoking?

35.

Alan became __________ musician that he was able to quit the office job he had always hated.
(a) such successful
(b) so successful a
(c) so a successful
(d) very successful

| 해석 |

앨런은 성공한 음악가가 돼서 그가 항상 싫어했던 사무직을 그만둘 수 있었다.

| 해설 |

〈so+형용사+a/an+명사〉의 어순이다. such는 〈such+a/an+형용사+명사〉의 어순이다. 그러므로 (b)가 정답이다.

36.

Ted and Mary O'Conner traveled the world for
years, __________ in New Zealand.

(a) finally settling down
(b) to settle finally down
(c) finally settled down
(d) and finally settling down

| 해석 |

테드와 메리 오코너는 몇 년간 세계를 여행한 끝에 결국 뉴질랜드에 정착
했다.

| 해설 |

콤마 전까지 완벽한 절이 왔으므로 빈칸 이하는 부사구가 되어야 한다.
그러므로 분사구문의 형태인 (a)가 가장 적절하다. settle down은 '정
착하다' 라는 의미의 자동사이므로 능동의 분사구문을 써야 한다.

37.

Ted moved away from home when he was
eighteen, but __________ that he would never
return to his hometown again.

(a) little he knew
(b) little did he know
(c) little had he known
(d) he little knew

| 해석 |

테드는 18살 때 집을 떠났지만 자신이 다시는 고향으로 돌아가지 않을
것이라는 사실을 알지 못했다.

| 해설 |

부정부사 little이 문두에 오면 도치가 이루어진다. 시제상 과거가 맞고 일
반동사일 경우 조동사 do가 주어 앞에 위치하게 되므로 (b)의 어순이 정
답이다.

38.

Marilyn no longer believes in love at first sight
since she __________ her husband.

(a) will divorce
(b) divorces
(c) has divorced
(d) divorced

| 해석 |

마릴린은 남편과 이혼한 후에는 더 이상 첫눈에 반하는 사랑을 믿지 않는
다.

| 해설 |

since가 '~이후 지금까지' 의 뜻을 지닐 때 since가 이끄는 종속절은 주
로 과거형을 쓴다. 그러므로 (d)가 정답이 된다.

39.

The company's new line of environmentally-
friendly cars __________ better than any of their
other models.

(a) are sold
(b) is sold
(c) are selling
(d) is selling

| 해석 |

이 회사의 환경친화적인 새로운 차종은 그들의 다른 어떤 모델들보다 훨
씬 더 잘 팔린다.

| 해설 |

sell은 타동사일 때는 '~을 팔다' 라는 의미이고 자동사일 때는 '팔리다'
라는 의미가 된다. 여기서는 후자의 경우에 속하므로 (c)가 정답이 된다.

40.

The concert is supposed to start in half an hour,
so it's about time we __________ for the theater.

(a) left
(b) will leave
(c) have left
(d) did leave

| 해석 |

콘서트는 30분 후에 시작하기로 되어 있다. 그러므로 지금 극장으로 가
야 한다.

| 해설 |

〈It is (about/high) time+주어+과거 동사〉는 가정법의 관용적인 어구
로 '~해야 할 시간이다' 라는 의미이다. 그러므로 과거 동사인 (a)가 정
답이 된다.

Part 3

41.

(a) A: Do you (find it appropriately → find it
         appropriate) to question the decisions of
         your president?
(b) B: Of course! We are supposed to challenge
         the decisions of our government.
(c) A: I guess you have a point. It just seems
         disrespectful to me.
(d) B: It's disrespectful not to ask questions.
         That's our duty as citizens of a democracy.

| 해석 |

(a) A: 대통령의 결정에 대해 질문하는 것이 적절하다고 생각하세요?
(b) B: 물론이지요! 우리는 정부의 결정에 대해 당연히 이의를 제기할
        수 있어요.
(c) A: 당신 말이 맞는 것 같아요. 난 다만 그게 조금 실례가 되는 것 같
        아서요.
(d) B: 질문을 안 하는 게 실례예요. 그것이 민주국가의 시민으로서의 의
        무잖아요.

| 해설 |

〈find+목적어+목적 보어〉를 취하는 동사이다. 보어의 자리에는 부사가
올 수 없으므로 형용사의 형태로 바꾸어야 한다. 〈find+it+형용사+to
부정사〉의 형태에서 it은 가목적어, to부정사가 진목적어가 된다.

42.

(a) A: Hello. Can I purchase those two sofas in the corner?

(b) B: Absolutely, sir. Do you want us to deliver them for you as well?

(c) A: Yes, please. I'd like (to deliver them → them to be delivered / to have them delivered) by Friday, if that's possible.

(d) B: I don't think that will be a problem.

| 해석 |

(a) A: 안녕하세요? 코너에 있는 저 두 개의 소파를 사고 싶은데요.

(b) B: 물론이죠. 배달해 드릴까요?

(c) A: 그래 주세요. 가능하면 금요일까지 배달이 되었으면 좋겠어요.

(d) B: 문제없을 것 같은데요.

| 해설 |

I'd like to deliver them은 '내가 배달하고 싶다'는 의미이므로 적절치 않다. 그러므로 〈I'd like+목적어+to 부정사〉의 형식으로 바꾸든지 사역동사를 이용해 '소파가 배달되었으면 좋겠다'는 수동의 의미로 바꾸어야 한다.

43.

(a) A: Is there anything I can help you with today?

(b) B: Yes, I need to buy (the truck → a truck).

(c) A: Do you know what kind of truck you're looking for?

(d) B: I don't know anything about trucks, that's why I need your help.

| 해석 |

(a) A: 무엇을 도와드릴까요?

(b) B: 네. 트럭을 사고 싶은데요.

(c) A: 특별한 종류의 트럭을 찾고 계신가요?

(d) B: 트럭에 대해서는 아는 게 없어요. 그래서 당신의 도움이 필요합니다.

| 해설 |

the는 특정한 것을 지칭할 때 쓰인다. 여기서는 특정한 트럭(the truck)을 찾고 있는 것이 아니라 불특정한 트럭을 찾고 있는 것이므로 a truck으로 고쳐야 한다.

44.

(a) A: How has your leg been feeling?

(b) B: It's been feeling a lot better (before → since) last week.

(c) A: Are you going to be able to play in the soccer game this weekend?

(d) B: Unfortunately, no. The doctor says I should stay off of it for three more weeks.

| 해석 |

(a) A: 다리는 어떠니?

(b) B: 지난주 이후로 훨씬 좋아지고 있어.

(c) A: 이번 주말에 축구 경기에서 뛸 수 있을 것 같니?

(d) B: 안타깝지만 안 돼. 의사 선생님이 3주는 더 축구를 하지 말아야

한다고 했거든.

| 해설 |

의미상 '지난주 전에'라는 말은 맞지 않으므로 전치사를 since(~이후로)로 바꾸어야 한다. stay off는 '~을 삼가다, ~을 멀리하다'라는 의미이다.

45.

(a) A: What would you like me to do with this coffee table?

(b) B: You can (move in it → move it in) next to the sofa in the living room.

(c) A: I don't think it will fit in there right now.

(d) B: Oh, you're right. Just leave it for now while I clean out the living room.

| 해석 |

(a) A: 이 커피 테이블은 어떻게 하길 원하니?

(b) B: 거실 소파 옆으로 옮겨 줘.

(c) A: 거기에는 지금 맞을 것 같지 않은데.

(d) B: 맞아. 거실을 치울 동안 잠시 놔둬야겠다.

| 해설 |

〈타동사+대명사+부사〉의 어순에 관한 문제이다. 명사일 경우 부사 뒤에 위치할 수 있지만 대명사일 경우는 타동사와 부사 사이에 위치해야 한다.

Part 4

46.

(a) Last night I introduced my two good friends, Dave and Mike, for the first time. (b) I knew they would get along fine, but I may have underestimated how much they have in common. (c) Once they (were begun → began) talking about music they never stopped. (d) Also, they are both very knowledgeable when it comes to music, so it made for an interesting conversation to listen to.

| 해석 |

(a) 지난밤에 나는 나의 가장 친한 친구 데이브와 마이크를 처음으로 소개해 주었다. (b) 나는 그들이 잘 어울릴지는 알았지만 얼마나 많은 공통점을 가지고 있었는지는 과소평가한 것 같다. (c) 그들은 일단 음악에 대해서 이야기를 시작하면 절대 멈추지 않았다. (d) 또한 음악에 관해서라면 둘 다 아는 게 많아서 듣기 재미있는 대화가 되었다.

| 해설 |

동사 begin 뒤에 목적어(talking about~)가 있으므로 수동의 형태는 맞지 않다. 그러므로 능동의 형태로 고쳐야 한다. when it comes to~는 '~에 관해서라면'이라는 뜻으로 to는 전치사이므로 뒤에 명사가 오는 것이 올바르다.

| 어휘 |

underestimate 과소평가하다   make for ~에 이바지하다

47.

(a) Frank Johnston created a convincing world

and strong characters in his classic novel *Powercrash*. (b) The future world that he created is (actual → **actually**) not only convincing, but prophetic, as his predictions for the future were correct. (c) Although he wrote the book twenty-five years ago, he was able to predict and successfully implement many of the technological advances that we now take for granted. (d) Ideas such as the internet, modern video games, video cell phones, and high-tech navigation equipment are each described perfectly in the story, which was written long before their time.

| 해석 |
(a) 프랭크 존스톤은 그의 고전 소설 '파워크래쉬' 에서 설득력 있는 세계와 강한 캐릭터를 만들어냈다. (b) 그가 만들어낸 미래는 설득력 있을 뿐만 아니라 예언적이다. 왜냐하면 그의 미래에 대한 예견은 맞았기 때문이다. (c) 그는 이 책을 25년 전에 썼지만 우리가 지금 당연하게 받아들이는 많은 기술적 발전을 성공적으로 구현하고 예측할 수 있었다. (d) 인터넷, 현대 비디오 게임, 비디오 휴대폰, 그리고 하이테크 네비게이션 장비 같은 생각들은 그 이야기에서 각각 완벽하게 묘사되었고 이것은 그것들의 시대 훨씬 전에 쓰여졌다.

| 해설 |
actual은 형용사로서 같은 형용사 convincing을 수식할 수 없다. 그러므로 actual을 부사의 형태(actually)로 바꾸어야 한다.

| 어휘 |
convincing 납득이 가는, 설득력 있는 **implement** 이행하다, 충족시키다 **prophetic** 예언적

48.

(a) Besides the application process, the most competitive universities often require an interview process as well. (b) The interviews are similar to job interviews, and they are conducted in order to find the best students for the school. (c) Selective schools like to have outgoing and social students among their student body. (d) The interviews are useful because (it gives → **they give**) the schools a glimpse at the personalities of the prospective students.

| 해석 |
(a) 지원 과정과 함께 종종 가장 경쟁적인 대학들은 인터뷰 과정도 요구한다. (b) 인터뷰는 취업 인터뷰와 비슷한데 학교에 가장 맞는 학생들을 찾기 위해서 실시된다. (c) 좀 까다로운 학교들은 학생들 중에 외향적이고 사교적인 학생들을 좋아한다. (d) 인터뷰는 학교가 예비 학생들의 인성을 들여다볼 수 있는 기회를 주기 때문에 유용하다.

| 해설 |
대명사의 수와 관련된 문제이다. 여기서 it은 앞의 the interviews를 가리키므로 단수 대명사 it이 아닌 복수인 they가 와야 한다. 이에 맞추어 동사의 수도 일치시켜야 한다.

| 어휘 |
selective 선택하는, 가리는 **glimpse** 일견, 일별

49.

(a) The Regional Performance Arts Competition will accept submissions until the end of August. (b) At that time, ten applicants will be chosen to perform their pieces live before a panel of judges. (c) One winner will be announced on September 30th, after which he or she will be flown to Chicago for the national finals. (d) The contestant is allowed to (bringing → **bring**) one friend or family member, and all flight and hotel expenses will be provided.

| 해석 |
(a) 지역 퍼포먼스 아트 대회에서는 8월 말까지 신청서를 받을 것이다. (b) 그때가 되면 10명의 신청자들이 심사 패널 앞에서 그들의 작품을 공연하도록 선택될 것이다. (c) 한 명의 우승자가 9월 30일에 발표될 것이고 그 후에 그 우승자는 국내 결승전을 위해 시카고로 가게 될 것이다. (d) 참가자는 한 명의 친구나 가족을 데리고 올 수 있으며 모든 항공요금과 숙박비가 제공될 것이다.

| 해설 |
allow는 〈allow+목적어+to+동사원형〉의 5형식 동사로 to는 전치사가 아니므로 to 뒤에는 동사원형이 와야 한다.

| 어휘 |
submission 복종, 신청서 **contestant** 참가자

50.

(a) In recent years, many middle-class families (have been adopted → **have adopted**) children from less fortunate foreign nations. (b) This has proven to be beneficial to both parties. (c) Families unable to bear children naturally get a healthy young son or daughter, and the children are given a chance to grow up in a prosperous and safe environment. (d) Also, in the coming decades this will create a new and interesting dynamic in the ethnic make-up of our society.

| 해석 |
(a) 최근 많은 중산층 가족들이 불운한 외국 국가들로부터 아이들을 입양하고 있다. (b) 이것은 양측에 이롭다는 것이 입증되었다. (c) 자연적으로 아이를 가질 수 없는 가족들은 건강한 아들이나 딸을 갖게 되고 아이들은 부유하고 안전한 환경에서 자랄 수 있는 기회를 갖게 된다. (d) 또한 다가오는 수십 년 안에 이것은 우리 사회의 소수 민족 구성에 새롭고 흥미로운 동력을 가져올 것이다.

| 해설 |
adopt는 '~를 입양하다' 라는 의미의 타동사이다. 뒤에 children이라는 목적어가 있으므로 수동의 형태가 아닌 능동의 형태로 바꾸어야 한다.

| 어휘 |
fortunate 운이 좋은 **prosperous** 부유한 **dynamic** 동력 **ethnic** 소수 민족의, 인종의

Test of English Proficiency
Seoul National University

수험번호

성 한글
명 한자

좌 석 번 호

Ⓐ Ⓑ Ⓒ Ⓓ Ⓔ
① ② ③ ④ ⑤ ⑥ ⑦

청 해 Listening Comprehension	문 법 Grammar	어 휘 Vocabulary	독 해 Reading Comprehension

고사실란 감독관 만족도

100 / 90 / 80 / 70 / 60 / 50 / 40 / 30 / 20 / 10

문제지번호

답안수정개수 감독관확인란

〈답안작성시 유의사항〉

1. 답안지 작성은 반드시 컴퓨터용 싸인펜만을 사용하셔야 합니다.

2. 답안을 정정할 경우 수정테이프(수정액불가)를 사용하셔야 합니다.

3. 본 답안지는 컴퓨터로 처리되므로 훼손하시면 안되며, 답안지 하단의 타이밍마크(Ⅲ)를 찢거나, 낙서 등을 하시면 본인에게 불이익이 발생할 수 있습니다.

4. 답안은 문항당 정답을 1개만 골라 ● 와 같이 정확히 기재하여야 하며, 필기구 오류나 본인의 부주의로 잘못 표기한 경우에는 당 관리위원회의 OMR판독기의 판독결과에 따르며, 그 결과는 본인이 책임집니다.

Good ● Bad ◐ ⊙ ◑ Ⓧ Ⓥ

5. 감독관의 확인이 없는 답안지는 무효처리됩니다.

〈부정행위 처리규정〉

1. 모든 부정행위 적발 및 이에 대한 조치는 TEPS 관리위원회의 처리규정에 따라 이루어집니다.

2. 부정행위 현장적발 뿐만 아니라 사후에도 적발될 수 있으며 모두 동일한 조치가 취해집니다.

3. 부정행위 적발 시 당해 성적은 무효화되며 사안에 따라 최대 5년까지 TEPS 관리위원회에서 주관하는 모든 시험의 응시자격이 제한됩니다.

4. 문제지 이외에 메모를 하는 행위와 시험문제의 일부 또는 전부를 유출하거나 공개하는 경우 부정행위로 처리됩니다.

5. 각 파트별 시간을 준수하지 않거나, 시험 종료 후 답안 작성을 계속할 경우 부정행위로 처리됩니다.

서 약 본인은 필기구 및 기재오류와 답안지 훼손으로 인한 책임을 지고, 부정행위 처리규정을 준수할 것을 서약합니다.

TEPS

뒷면

성	영문	
명	서명	

응시일자 : 20   년   월   일

수 험 번 호 / PASSWORD

주 민 등 록 번 호

성   명 (성·이름순으로 기재)

EX HONG GIL DONG

단 체 구 분

학생	일반
◯	◯

질 문 란

1. 귀하의 TEPS 응시목적은?
ⓐ 입사지원   ⓑ 인사정책
ⓒ 개인실력측정   ⓓ 입시
ⓔ 국가고시지원   ⓕ 기타

2. 귀하의 영어권 체류 경험은?
ⓐ 없다   ⓑ 6개월미만
ⓒ 6개월이상1년미만   ⓓ 1년이상3년미만
ⓔ 3년이상5년미만   ⓕ 5년이상

3. 귀하께서 응시하고 계신 고사장에
   대한 만족도는?
ⓐ 0점   ⓑ 1점
ⓒ 2점   ⓓ 3점
ⓔ 4점   ⓕ 5점

4. 최근 2년내 TEPS 응시횟수는?
ⓐ 없다   ⓑ 1회
ⓒ 2회   ⓓ 3회
ⓔ 4회   ⓕ 5회이상

학 력

학교	재학	졸업
초등학교	◯	◯
중 학 교	◯	◯
고등학교	◯	◯
전문대학	◯	◯
대 학 교	◯	◯
대 학 원	◯	◯

계 열

인 문 학	◯
사회과학 · 법학	◯
경제학 · 경영학	◯
자 연 과 학	◯
의학 · 약학 · 간호학	◯
공 학	◯
교 육 학	◯
음악 · 미술 · 체육	◯
기 타	◯

직 업

공 무 원	◯
고시준비	◯
교 사	◯
군 인	◯
의 료 인	◯
자 영 업	◯
학 생	◯
회 사 원	◯
무 직	◯
기 타	◯

직 종

고 위 임 직 원	◯	무 역	◯
전 문 직(과학,공학)	◯	외 환	◯
전 문 직(교육)	◯	자 금	◯
전문직(법률,회계,금융)	◯	공 무	◯
기 술 직	◯	업 무	◯
영 업	◯	품 질 관 리	◯
홍 보	◯	전 산	◯
총 무	◯	행 정 직	◯
인 사	◯	생 산 관 리	◯
경 리	◯	서 비 스	◯
기 획	◯	기 타	◯
구 매	◯		

직 책

임 원	◯
부 장	◯
차 장	◯
과 장	◯
대 리	◯
계 장	◯
사 원	◯
인 턴	◯
기 타	◯

목표 점수 앞당기는

GRAMMAR

Handy Book

사람in
saramin.com

〈TEPS 달인이 되는 법-Final-문법〉 Handy Book 활용법

TEPS의 문법 문제는 똑같은 유형의 문제가 계속적으로 반복되는 경우가 많다. 그러나 문법 문제를 풀 때 틀린 문제를 계속 틀리는 경우가 많으므로 이를 '오답노트'로 바로 잡아야 한다. 틀린 문제를 계속 틀리는 것은 그 문제의 유형을 제대로 파악하지 못하기 때문이다. 그러므로 오답노트를 스스로 정리하면서 그 문제의 유형을 파악하고 구조를 정리해야 한다. 오답노트를 정리함으로써 자신이 약한 부분이 무엇인지 파악하고 그 문제를 다시는 틀리지 않도록 유의한다.

1. 문제: 문제를 스스로 작성함으로써 정확하게 문제를 파악하고 오래 기억하게 한다.
2. 출처: 반드시 작성하고 나중에 찾아 보고 싶을 때 참고한다.
3. 어휘: 모르는 단어가 있으면 정리하되 문법 문제는 모르는 어휘가 많지 않으므로 없으면 정리하지 않아도 된다.
4. 해석: 문법에서는 해석이 많이 필요하지 않기 때문에 필요한 경우에만 간단한 해석을 해 본다.
5. 문법정리: 반드시 이해를 하고 정리한다. 그 문제의 문법 사항이 파악이 되지 않을 경우 해당 영역을 다시 공부하고 정리하도록 한다.
6. 복습횟수: 복습횟수에 체크하면서 여러 번의 복습을 통해서 틀린 문제를 다시 틀리지 않도록 한다.

Sample

출처	Day 1. Build Up 1
복습횟수	1☐ 2☐ 3☐ 4☐ 5☐ 6☐ 7☐ 8☐ 9☐ 10☐
문제	A: What did the witness say? B: The witness testified that she ______________ the convicted murderer in the alleyway behind the diner at 9:13p.m. (a) saw　　　　(b) see (c) have seen　　(d) had seen
해석 및 문법정리	A: 목격자가 뭐라고 말했어? B: 그 목격자는 9시 13분에 식당차 뒤 골목길에서 살인자를 보았다고 말했어. 알맞은 시제를 고르는 문제이다. 여기서는 과거를 나타내는 시점 부사 at 9:13 p.m.와 함께 과거의 한 시점의 일어났던 일을 말하고 있으므로 단순 과거인 (a)가 정답이 된다. 과거 완료 (d)는 과거의 한 시점을 기준으로 그 이전부터 그 과거 시점까지를 어우르는 기간의 개념이므로 여기서는 적절치 않다.
어휘	**Alleyway** 골목길　**diner** 식당차

출처	
복습횟수	1☐ 2☐ 3☐ 4☐ 5☐ 6☐ 7☐ 8☐ 9☐ 10☐
문제	
해석 및 문법정리	
어휘	

출처	
복습횟수	1☐ 2☐ 3☐ 4☐ 5☐ 6☐ 7☐ 8☐ 9☐ 10☐
문제	
해석 및 문법정리	
어휘	

출처	
복습횟수	1□ 2□ 3□ 4□ 5□ 6□ 7□ 8□ 9□ 10□
문제	
해석 및 문법정리	
어휘	

출처	
복습횟수	1☐ 2☐ 3☐ 4☐ 5☐ 6☐ 7☐ 8☐ 9☐ 10☐
문제	
해석 및 문법정리	
어휘	

출처	
복습횟수	1□ 2□ 3□ 4□ 5□ 6□ 7□ 8□ 9□ 10□
문제	
해석 및 문법정리	
어휘	

출처	
복습횟수	1☐ 2☐ 3☐ 4☐ 5☐ 6☐ 7☐ 8☐ 9☐ 10☐
문제	
해석 및 문법정리	
어휘	

출처	
복습횟수	1□ 2□ 3□ 4□ 5□ 6□ 7□ 8□ 9□ 10□
문제	
해석 및 문법정리	
어휘	

출처	
복습횟수	1☐ 2☐ 3☐ 4☐ 5☐ 6☐ 7☐ 8☐ 9☐ 10☐
문제	
해석 및 문법정리	
어휘	

출처	
복습횟수	1□ 2□ 3□ 4□ 5□ 6□ 7□ 8□ 9□ 10□
문제	
해석 및 문법정리	
어휘	

출처	
복습횟수	1☐ 2☐ 3☐ 4☐ 5☐ 6☐ 7☐ 8☐ 9☐ 10☐
문제	
해석 및 문법정리	
어휘	

출처	
복습횟수	1□ 2□ 3□ 4□ 5□ 6□ 7□ 8□ 9□ 10□
문제	
해석 및 문법정리	
어휘	

출처	
복습횟수	1☐ 2☐ 3☐ 4☐ 5☐ 6☐ 7☐ 8☐ 9☐ 10☐
문제	
해석 및 문법정리	
어휘	

출처	
복습횟수	1□ 2□ 3□ 4□ 5□ 6□ 7□ 8□ 9□ 10□
문제	
해석 및 문법정리	
어휘	

출처	
복습횟수	1□ 2□ 3□ 4□ 5□ 6□ 7□ 8□ 9□ 10□
문제	
해석 및 문법정리	
어휘	

출처	
복습횟수	1□ 2□ 3□ 4□ 5□ 6□ 7□ 8□ 9□ 10□
문제	
해석 및 문법정리	
어휘	

출처	
복습횟수	1☐ 2☐ 3☐ 4☐ 5☐ 6☐ 7☐ 8☐ 9☐ 10☐
문제	
해석 및 문법정리	
어휘	

출처	
복습횟수	1☐ 2☐ 3☐ 4☐ 5☐ 6☐ 7☐ 8☐ 9☐ 10☐
문제	
해석 및 문법정리	
어휘	

출처	
복습횟수	1□ 2□ 3□ 4□ 5□ 6□ 7□ 8□ 9□ 10□
문제	
해석 및 문법정리	
어휘	

<table>
<tr><td>출처</td><td></td></tr>
<tr><td>복습횟수</td><td>1☐ 2☐ 3☐ 4☐ 5☐ 6☐ 7☐ 8☐ 9☐ 10☐</td></tr>
<tr><td>문제</td><td></td></tr>
<tr><td>해석
및
문법정리</td><td></td></tr>
<tr><td>어휘</td><td></td></tr>
</table>

<table>
<tr><td>출처</td><td></td></tr>
<tr><td>복습횟수</td><td>1☐ 2☐ 3☐ 4☐ 5☐ 6☐ 7☐ 8☐ 9☐ 10☐</td></tr>
<tr><td>문제</td><td></td></tr>
<tr><td>해석
및
문법정리</td><td></td></tr>
<tr><td>어휘</td><td></td></tr>
</table>

Day 1 시제

영어의 시제는 매우 세분화되어 있다. 다행히 TEPS에서는 세밀한 시제 차이를 묻는 질문은 잘 나오지 않고 시제의 큰 그림을 묻는 편이다. 그러므로 시험에 빈출되는 시제 유형을 중심으로 시험에 대비하도록 한다.

1. 현재시제: 현재 상태나 습관, 일반적 사실, 자연 법칙처럼 확실성이 큰 상황에 사용한다. 또한 빈도부사와 함께 자주 사용된다.

I usually get up early. (반복적 동작)
나는 주로 일찍 일어난다.
Steve drives a bus. (사실) 스티브는 버스를 운전한다.
(운전기사라는 의미)
cf. **Steve is driving a bus.** (현재 진행: 현재의 일시적 시점을 나타냄) 스티브는 (지금) 버스를 운전한다.

2. 과거 표시 단어나 부사구가 있으면 반드시 과거시제를 사용한다.

last~, yesterday, at that time, ago, the other day 일전에 **just now** 방금

I saw her last week. 지난주에 그녀를 보았다.

3. 현재완료: 과거에서 현재까지 이어지는 기간의 개념이다.

I think I have met her once before.

(과거부터 지금까지)

그녀를 전에 한 번 봤던 것 같다.

4. 과거완료: 기준 시점이 과거이고 그보다 이전의 일에 대해 언급할 때 〈had+p.p.(대과거)〉를 사용한다. 주로 두 가지의 과거 일이 언급될 때 그 중 하나가 이전의 일임을 강조할 때 쓰인다.

They had already left when I arrived at the office.

내가 사무실에 도착했을 때 그들은 이미 떠나고 없었다.

5. 미래완료: 기준 시점이 미래이고 그 미래 시점 이전에 완결된 미래의 행동을 의미할 때 사용한다. 〈by+시간 부사구〉나 by the time과 함께 자주 쓰인다.

I will have studied for 3 hours by the time my mom comes home.

엄마가 집에 오실 때가 되면 나는 3시간을 공부한 것이 된다.

6. 시간 · 조건 접속사(if, when, as, after, before, until, as soon as, etc.)가 나오는 절에서는 현재나 현재완료가 미래를 대신한다. 그러나 이러한 부사절이 나온다고 해서 무조건 시제를 현재나 현재완료로 하는 것이 아니라 주절이 미래형이나 명령문일 때 이러한 문법이 형성됨을 잊지 말자.

When you arrive tonight, we will go out for dinner.

오늘 밤 당신이 돌아오면 우리는 외식하러 나갈 거예요.

Day 2 조동사

TEPS에서 조동사 관련 문제가 나오면 대부분 해석을 통해 풀어야 하는, 조동사의 본래 의미를 물어보는 문제이다. 또한 〈조동사 과거형 + have p.p.〉의 쓰임이 가장 많이 나온다.

1. would, could, might, should는 과거형 이외에 조동사 본연의 뜻을 가지고 있다.

That could be true. 그것이 진실일 수도 있다.
You might meet Eric after the concert.
너는 그 콘서트 후에 에릭을 만날 수도 있다.
He would be in time. 그는 제시간에 올 것이다.
He should study harder. 그는 더 열심히 공부해야 한다.

2. 주어의 강한 의지, 고집, 습성을 나타내는 will(~할 것이다, ~하려고 하다, ~하기 마련이다)

This window won't open.
이 창문은 열리지 않는다. (고집)

3. 과거의 습관을 나타내는 would와 used to (~하곤 했다)

I would take a nap after lunch.
점심을 먹고 낮잠을 자곤 했다.
그러나 과거의 상태를 말할 때는 used to를 써야 함을 기억하자.
He used to be a singer. 그는 가수였다.
He would be a singer. (X)

4. 조동사 과거형＋have p.p.

I shouldn't have done it. 그것을 하지 말았어야 했다.
I could have arrived earlier.

좀 더 일찍 도착할 수 있었다.

5. must (~임에 틀림없다) ↔ cannot (~일 리 없다)

must not (~해서는 안 된다)
must have p.p. (~였음에 틀림없다),
should have p.p. (~했어야 했다)

**You must have been very tired by the time
you finished the exams.**
시험을 끝냈을 때 매우 피곤했었겠다.

6. 관용적 표현

1) **may well V** V 하는 것은 당연하다

She may well be proud of her daughter.
그녀가 딸을 자랑스러워하는 것은 당연하다.

2) **would rather A than B** B하느니 A하는 것이 더 낫다

**I would rather stay at home than go with
him.** 그 남자와 함께 가느니 차라리 집에 있겠다.

3) **cannot ~ too+(형용사/부사)** 아무리 ~해도 지나치
지 않다

**You cannot be too careful when you drive a
car.** 차를 운전할 때는 아무리 조심해도 지나치지 않다.

Day 3 수동태

자동사가 수동태로 쓰이지 않았는지 Part III와 Part IV에서 확인해야 한다.

1. 전형적인 자동사는 수동태가 불가능하다.

happen, occur, arrive, become, remain, appear, disappear, fall, come

The house has been remained empty for a long time. (X)
The house has remained empty for a long time. (O) 그 집은 오랫동안 비어져 있다.

2. It ~ that 구문으로 수동태로 쓰이는 동사

believe, consider, find, report, think, say, expect, suppose, know

It is said that he was once famous.
그는 한때 유명했다고 한다.

3. 수동태 뒤에 명사(구)가 올 수 있는 4형식·5형식 동사

give, offer, consider, call, elect
They gave her the money.
그들은 그녀에게 돈을 주었다.
→ She was given the money (by them).
We elected her mayor. 우리는 그녀를 시장으로 선출했다.

→ She was elected mayor (by us).

4. 지각동사, 사역동사의 목적격 보어인 원형부정사는 수동태
에서는 to부정사로 바뀐다.

She saw him break the window.
그녀는 그가 창문을 깨는 것을 보았다.
→ **He was seen to break the window.**
그가 창문 깨는 것이 목격되었다.

5. 감정 동사(scare, frighten, interest, disappoint,
surprise, satisfy)가 수동태로만 쓰인다는 생각을 버려야
한다.

The result satisfied me.
그 결과는 나를 만족시켰다. (능동태)
I was satisfied with the result.
나는 그 결과에 만족했다. (수동태)

6. 자동사와 타동사 둘 다 가능한 동사

write 쓰다/ 써지다   **cut** 자르다/(날이) 들다
sell 팔다 /팔리다   **read** 읽다/~라고 쓰여 있다
clean 청소하다/깨끗해지다   **hurt** 다치게 하다/아프다
grow 기르다/자라다   **peel** 벗기다/벗겨지다

The house has been sold. 그 집은 팔렸다. (타동사)
The books sell well. 그 책들은 잘 팔린다. (자동사, 수동 불
가능)

Day 4 가정법

1. 가정법 과거: 현재와 반대되는 상황을 가정한다.

If+S+과거형 동사(be동사 → were),
S+would/could/should/might+동사원형:
~한다면 ~할 텐데 (현재로 해석함)

If I knew his number, I would invite him to the
party. 그의 전화번호를 안다면 그를 파티에 초대할 텐데.

2. 가정법 과거완료: 과거와 반대되는 상황을 가정한다.

If+S+had p.p., S+would/could/should/might+
have p.p. : ~했다면 ~했을 텐데 (과거로 해석함)

If I had known his number, I would have
invited him to the party.

그의 전화번호를 알았다면 그를 파티에 초대했을 텐데.

3. 도치: if절에서 if를 생략하면 도치가 이루어진다.

If it had not been for your help, I wouldn't
have finished this project in time.
= Had it not been for your help, I wouldn't
have finished this project in time.

당신의 도움이 아니었더라면 나는 이 프로젝트를 제시간에 끝낼 수 없
었을 것이다.

4. 제안, 요구, 주장, 소망 표현

행동의 중요성을 표현하는 명사, 형용사, 동사 뒤에 that절이 오는 경우 that절의 동사는 〈(should+) 동사원형〉을 쓴다.

동사: **suggest, recommend, insist, demand, propose, advise, decide, claim, require**

형용사: **essential, important, advisable, required, urgent, necessary, imperative**

명사: **suggestion, wish, advice, decision, request, command, requirement**

He suggested that the government (should) pay more attention to the handicapped.

그는 정부가 장애자들에게 더 많은 관심을 가져야 한다고 제안했다.

7. 가정법 특수 구문

1) **It is (high/about) time (that)+S+과거동사**:

~할 때이다

It is about time you studied harder.

이제 더 열심히 공부해야 할 때다.

2) **주어+wish+(that) 주어+과거 동사**: 현재 사실 반대 소망

had p.p.: 과거 사실 반대 소망

3) **as if/as though 주어+과거 동사**: 마치 ~인 것처럼

had p.p.: 마치 ~였던 것처럼

She talks as if she ran the company.

그녀는 마치 그녀가 그 회사를 운영하는 것처럼 말한다.

Day 5 to부정사

1. 의문사 + to V: 명사구로서 주어, 목적어, 보어로 쓰인다.

〈의문사 + to부정사〉를 목적어로 취하는 동사
know, wonder, discover, find out, show, see, explain, understand, tell, learn
I don't know what to say.
나는 무슨 말을 해야 할지 모르겠다.

2. to부정사가 목적격 보어가 되는 경우: V + O + to V (5형식 문장)

force, ask, enable, cause, want, allow, encourage, expect, persuade, require, urge, compel
He forced me to sign the paper. 그는 나에게 서류에 사인하도록 강요했다.

3. N + to V: 명사를 후치 수식하여 '~할', '~하기 위한'의 의미가 있다. (한정 용법)

the only, the first, ~thing + to V
She does not have friends to play with.
그녀는 함께 놀 친구가 없다.

4. 자동사 + to V

never fail to V 반드시 ~하다   **manage to V** 간신히[용케] ~해내다   **come to V** 서서히 ~하다

get to V ~하게 되다   **deserve to V** ~할 만하다
prove to V ~으로 판명되다   **afford to V** ~할 여유가 있
다 **seem/appear to V** ~처럼 생각나다(보이다)   **grow
to V** 서서히 ~하게 되다

5. to부정사를 목적어로 취하는 동사

**care, decide, determine, choose, expect, fail,
hope, manage, mean, plan, pretend,
promise, refuse, want, wish, hesitate, seek,
offer, afford**

6. to부정사의 관용표현: be + 형용사 + to부정사

be ready to V ~할 준비가 되어 있다
be able to V ~할 능력이 있다
be available to V ~할 수 있는 상황이다
be eager to V 열망하다
be hesitant to V ~하기를 주저하다
be sure/certain to V 반드시 ~하다
be reluctant to V ~하기를 꺼려하다
be likely to V ~할 가능성이 있다
be supposed to V ~하기로 예상되다
be apt to V ~하기 쉽다
feel free to V 마음껏 ~하다
be bound to V 틀림없이 ~하다
**be enough N to V / be 형용사
enough to V** 충분하다
be willing to V 기꺼이 ~하다

Day 6   동명사

1. 동명사의 의미상 주어는 소유격으로 표시한다.

I don't mind your smoking here.

여기서 담배 피우셔도 됩니다.

= I don't mind you smoking here. (구어체에서는 목적격도 가능)

2. need, want, require + -ing: 수동 의미

본래 to부정사 수동형을 취하나 그 의미가 수동일 때 동명사를 취할 수 있는 동사

My car needs washing. 내 차는 세차되어야 한다.
= My car needs to be washed.

3. 동명사를 목적어로 취하는 동사

finish, consider, enjoy, suggest, quit, abandon, avoid, mind, delay, permit, admit, resist, deny, prohibit, anticipate

He suggested going on a picnic.

그가 피크닉 가는 것을 제안했다.

4. 동명사를 취하는 관용어구

look forward to -ing ~을 기대하다
fall to -ing ~에 빠져들기 시작하다
be used to -ing ~하는 데 익숙하다
object/oppose to -ing ~을 반대하다

be devoted to -ing ~에 몰두하다
be committed to -ing 전념하다
be equal to -ing ~과 동등하다
be busy (in) -ing ~하느라 바쁘다
be worth -ing ~할 만한 가치가 있다
come close to -ing ~에 근접하다
there is no use/good -ing ~해도 소용없다
have difficulty/trouble/a hard time (in) -ing
~하는 데 어려움을 겪다
when it comes to -ing ~의 점에서는
What do you say to -ing? ~하는 것이 어떻습니까?

5. to부정사와 동명사를 취할 때 의미가 다른 경우

remember/forget + to V (앞으로 할 것)
      -ing (이미 완료된 것)
regret + to V 유감스럽다
   -ing 후회하다
try+ to V ~하려고 노력하다
  -ing 시험 삼아 ~해보다

Sam often forgets to lock the door.
샘은 종종 문 잠그는 것을 잊곤 한다.
I will never forget seeing the Alps for the first
time. 처음 알프스를 봤을 때를 잊지 못할 것이다.

Day 7　분사

1. 명사를 수식하는 분사가 현재분사인지 과거분사인지를 확인하는 절차

① 동사가 타동사인지 자동사인지 확인한다.
② 타동사일 땐 명사(의미상 주어)와 분사(의미상 동사)의 관계가 능동인지 수동인지를 파악하여 결정한다.
③ 자동사일 땐 명사(의미상 주어)와 분사(의미상 동사)의 관계가 진행인지 완료인지를 파악하여 결정한다.

2. 분사 + 명사

a sleeping baby 자는 아기 (sleep은 자동사 – 진행의 의미)
a returned solider 돌아온 군인 (return은 자동사 – 완료의 의미)
an exciting show 흥미진진한 쇼 (excite는 타동사 – 능동의 의미)
disappointed people 실망한 사람들 (disappoint는 타동사 – 수동의 의미)

3. 명사 + 분사: 〈주격 관계대명사＋be동사〉가 생략된 경우가 많다.

The man (who is) talking over the phone is the manager of the restaurant.
전화 통화중인 저 남자가 그 레스토랑 매니저다.

4. 감정 동사의 분사 용법

감정의 원인은 현재분사(능동)를 쓰고, 감정을 느끼는 주체(주로 사람)에게는 과거분사(수동)를 사용한다.

bore 지루하게 하다	**interest** 흥미를 일으키다
excite 흥분시키다	**surprise** 놀라게 하다
scare 겁나게 하다	**frighten** 놀라게 하다
satisfy 만족시키다	**please** 즐겁게 하다
amuse 즐겁게 하다	**disappoint** 실망시키다
confuse 당황하게 하다	**satisfy** 만족시키다
annoy 성가시게 굴다	**bewilder** 당황하게 하다
irritate 짜증나게 하다	**exhaust** 지치게 하다
astonish 놀라게 하다	**embarrass** 당황하게 하다

5. 분사구문 만드는 법: 종속절의 주어와 주절의 주어가 일치할 때 접속사와 종속절의 주어를 생략한다.

Since she was eliminated, she had to go back to the hotel immediately and pack her belongings.

여자는 탈락되었기 때문에 즉시 호텔로 돌아가 짐을 꾸려야 했다.

→ **Being eliminated, she had to go back to the hotel immediately and pack her belongings.** (분사구문에서 Being/Having been은 생략 가능하다.)

→ **Eliminated, she had to go back to the hotel immediately and pack her belongings.**

Day 8 명사와 관사

1. 가산명사인데 단수 표시 즉, 부정관사(a/an)를 붙이지 않거나 복수 표시(-s, -es)를 하지 않으면 틀린 문장이 된다. 이와 관련된 문제가 Part Ⅲ에서 자주 출제된다. 또한 가산명사 앞에 붙는 수 표시어(many, few, a few)와 불가산 명사에 붙는 양 표시어(much, little, a little)를 구별하여 알아두어야 한다.

2. 부정관사: (a/an) '하나, ~에, ~당, 어떤' 이라는 의미를 갖는다.

He didn't say a word about it.
그는 그것에 대해 한 마디도 하지 않았다
She visits her parents once a week.
그녀는 일주일에 한 번 부모님을 방문한다.

3. 부정관사의 쓰임: 같은 명사라 하더라도 그 의미에 따라 가산명사 혹은 불가산명사 취급을 받을 때가 있다. 대체적으로 그 단어가 일반적인 의미로 쓰일 때는 불가산명사로 보고, 구체적인 하나의 개별체로 볼 때는 가산명사로 본다. 이와 관련된 문제가 출제되니 그 의미 파악을 먼저 하도록 한다.

hair 머리 숱	**a hair** 머리카락
noise 소음	**a noise** 소리
room 공간	**a room** 방
paper 종이	**a paper** 신문; 논문

work일   **a work** 작품
light 빛   **a light** 조명

4. 정관사: 부정관사가 '막연한 것'을 가리키는 반면 정관사는 '특정한 것'을 지칭한다.

형용사구〔절〕나 전치사구에 의해 수식을 받을 때, last, only, next, same, 형용사의 최상급, 서수사 등이 명사를 수식하여 그 명사가 특정한 사람이나 사물을 가리키게 될 때, 〈by the+단위 명사〉 등의 경우에 정관사 the가 그 명사 앞에 붙는다.

All the candidates in B group are safe.
B그룹에 있는 모든 후보는 통과했다.
He is paid by the week. 그는 주급을 받는다.

5. 관사의 위치

1) **such, many, quite, what+ (a/an)+** 형용사+명사
   It's quite an easy question. 그건 꽤 쉬운 질문이다.
2) **so, how, too +** 형용사+**(a/an)+** 명사
   This is too good an opportunity.
   너무 좋은 기회이다.

Day 9 대명사

1. 대명사가 나오면 그것이 가리키는 명사와 수, 성, 격이 일치
하는지를 반드시 확인한다.

**They are taking preliminary steps to protect
themselves.**

그들 자신을 보호하기 위해 조기 조치를 취하고 있다.

2. **one**: 〈a ＋명사〉 대신 쓰이며 동일한 종류의 것을 받는다.

it: 〈the/소유격＋명사〉 대신으로 쓰이며 동일한 바로 '그
것' 을 받는다.

A: I bought this dress in Zara yesterday.

나 어제 이 드레스 자라에서 샀어.

B: ① **It's beautiful. I want to buy one.**

(동일한 종류의 드레스를 사고 싶다는 의미)

② **It's beautiful. I want to buy it.**

(A가 산 옷을 B가 사고 싶다는 의미)

3. 부정대명사

부정대명사란 정해지지 않은 막연한 사람이나 사물, 수량을 나타내는
대명사로 some, any, one, another, other, each, every 등이 있
다.

1) **any, no, some, the + other +단수 명사**
   There is no other way. 다른 방법이 없다.

2) **another + 숫자+ 복수 명사**: another 가 '더 많은' 이라
   는 의미를 지칭할 때

Could you wait for another ten minutes for me? 10분만 더 기다려 주시겠어요?

3) **every+ 숫자 + 복수 명사**
She works at the store every two weeks.
그녀는 이 주일에 한 번씩 그 가게에서 일한다.

4. 〈so+주어+동사〉의 어순: so는 yes의 뜻이 되어 '정말 그래'의 뜻.

〈so+동사+주어〉의 어순: so는 also의 뜻이 되어 '~도 역시 그래'의 뜻.

You said the concert would be awesome and so it was. 그 콘서트가 멋질 거라더니 정말 그렇더라.
His father was a singer and so is he.
그의 아버지는 가수셨는데 그도 가수이다.

5. 관용적 용법

1) **(A is) one thing, (B is) another** A와 B는 별개다
2) **one ~, the other ...** (둘 중에서) 하나는 ~, 다른 하나는 …
one ~, another ... the other/third (셋 중에서) 하나는 ~, 둘째는 …, 셋째는 –
3) **one ~, the others ...** (셋 이상 중에서) 하나는 ~, 나머지 전부는 …
4) **some ~, others ...** 어떤 것(사람)들은 ~, 다른 일부(사람)는 … (전체 수가 정해지지 않았을 때)
5) **each other**는 '(둘 사이에) 서로 서로,'
one another는 '(셋 이상의 사이에) 서로 서로'

Day 10 형용사

명사를 수식하며 보어로 쓰인다.

1. 서술적 용법으로만 쓰이는 형용사

afraid 두려운   **alike** 같은   **alive** 살아 있는
alone 혼자인   **ashamed** 부끄러운   **asleep** 잠든
awake 깨어 있는   **aware** 알고 있는

When you enter the building, you need to be aware that you shouldn't forget to bring your ID card.

그 건물에 들어갈 때 ID 카드를 가지고 가는 것을 잊으면 안 된다.

2. 복합 형용사

명사 앞에 하이픈(-)으로 연결된 어군이 명사를 수식하는 경우가 있는데 이를 하나의 복합 형용사로 본다. 이때 수식하는 명사는 반드시 단수형으로 쓴다.

It's a two-days trip. (X)
It's a two-day trip. (O)   이틀간의 여행이다.

3. 수량 형용사

1) many + 명사의 복수형

〈many a/an + 단수 명사〉는 단수로 취급한다.

Many a student likes the band.

많은 학생이 그 밴드를 좋아한다.

2) much + 명사의 단수형

I have too much homework to do.
해야 할 숙제가 너무 많다.

3) a few와 a little

a few + 가산명사의 복수형: 소수의

a little + 불가산명사의 단수형: 소량의

some은 수와 양을 모두 나타낼 수 있다.

4) few 와 little: '별로 없는, 거의 없는' 이라는 부정의 의미를 나타내
는 표현이 된다.

There is little hope. 희망이 별로 없다.

cf. **There is a little hope.** 약간의 희망이 있다.

5) 수의 단위인 hundred, thousand, million, billion, trillion 등은
그 앞에 복수의 수가 붙어도 복수형으로 쓰지 않는다.

two hundreds (X)   two hundred (O)

6) hundred, thousand, million이 복수형으로 뒤에 위치한 명사와
of로 연결되면 '수백, 수천, 수백만' 의 뜻을 갖는다.

**Hundreds of fans are waiting for him in front
of his house.**

수백 명의 팬들이 그의 집 앞에서 그를 기다리고 있다.

Day 11 부사

부사는 동사, 형용사 또는 다른 부사를 수식하거나 문장 전체를 수식할 때 쓰이고 보어가 될 수 없다.

What he did for me makes me specially. (X)

→ What he did for me makes me special. (O)

그가 나를 위해 한 것이 날 특별하게 만든다.

1. 주의해야 할 부사

1) very는 형용사나 부사의 원급, 현재분사, 형용사화된 과거분사를 수식한다.

I am much tired. (X) → I am very tired. (O)

2) much는 동사, 형용사나 부사의 비교급·최상급, 서술적 형용사를 수식한다.

You should be much more careful.

좀 더 조심해야 한다.

2. 형용사와 부사의 형태가 같은 것

1) **hard** → 형용사: 어려운

→ 부사: 열심히

2) **fast** → 형용사: 빠른

→ 부사: 빠르게

3) **long** → 형용사: 긴

  → 부사: 오래

4) **late** → 형용사: 늦은

  → 부사: 늦게

3. 뜻이 다른 두 가지 부사의 형태

free 무료로 — **freely** 자유롭게
hard 열심히 — **hardly** 거의 ~않는
wide 넓게/완전히 — **widely** 널리(범위)
late 늦게 — **lately** 최근에
near 가까이 — **nearly** 거의
right 정확히 — **rightly** 올바르게
direct 똑바로 — **directly** 곧바로
sharp 정각에 — **sharply** 심하게
deep 깊게 — **deeply** 매우, 철저히
high 높게 — **highly** 매우, 대단히

I got up very late today.
오늘 늦게 일어났다.
Have you seen Tom lately?
최근에 탐 본 적 있니?

Day 12 관계사

1. 관계대명사가 나오면 다음 세 단계를 확인해야 한다.

    ① 알맞은 선행사가 쓰였는지 확인하기

    ② 관계대명사의 격 확인하기

    ③ 선행사와 수의 일치 확인하기

    ④ 관계대명사는 주어 혹은 목적어 역할을 하므로 뒤에 '불완전한 절' 이 와야 한다.

This is the table which I ordered it last week. (x)

This is the table which I ordered last week. (O)

(which가 관계대명사 목적격이므로 it을 생략해야 선행사와의 중복을 피할 수 있다.)

2. what: 자체에 선행사를 포함하고 있으므로 what 앞에 선행사가 올 수 없다.

The thing what he purchased yesterday was too expensive. (X)

What he purchased yesterday was too expensive. (O)

(선행사가 있기 때문에 what을 which/that으로 바꾸든지, the thing을 생략하고 what이 이끄는 명사절로 바꿔야 한다.)

3. that의 쓰임: that 앞에 전치사를 쓸 수 없고, 계속적 용법으로 쓰이지 않는다. 선행사를 한정해주는 어구(the only/same, 최상급, some, any, no)가 있는 경우 that이

쓰인다.

관계대명사 that + 불완전한 절
접속사 that + 완전한 절

It was the most amazing moment that I have ever had. (관계대명사 that) 생애 가장 놀라운 순간이었다.
I believe that he is innocent. (접속사 that)
그가 결백하다는 것을 믿는다.
cf. 관계대명사 what도 명사절을 이끌어 '~하는 것'이라는 의미가 있지만 뒤에 불완전한 절이 온다.
Do you know what I'm saying?
내가 무슨 말 하는지 아니? (say의 목적어가 없다)

4. 복합 관계대명사: 〈관계대명사＋ever〉의 형태로 명사절이나 양보 부사절을 이끈다.

I will give you whichever you choose.
네가 무엇을 고르든지 그것을 주겠다.
Whatever happens, I will still love you.
무슨 일이 일어나더라도 나는 여전히 당신을 사랑할 것입니다.

5. 관계부사

관계부사는 〈접속사＋부사〉의 역할을 하며 〈전치사＋관계대명사〉로 바꿔 쓸 수 있다. 그 종류에는 선행사에 따라 where, when, how, why가 있다.
This is the house where he was born.
= This is the house in which he was born.
이곳이 그가 태어난 집입니다.

Day 13 접속사

1. 등위접속사(and, or, but)와 상관접속사 관련 문제 체크
사항 익혀두기

① 문법 단위가 동일한 품사끼리 병렬 구조가 되었는지 확인하기

② 상관접속사의 연결이기기 알맞게 연결됐는지 확인하기

③ 수의 일치 확인하기

**The history class was interesting and
education. (X)**

**The history class was interesting and
educational. (O)**

그 역사 수업은 흥미롭고 교육적이었다.

2. 상관접속사

both A and B A와 B 모두 (복수 취급)

either A or B A 또는 B (B에 동사 일치)

neither A nor B A도 B 도 아닌

not only A but also B A 뿐만 아니라 B 도(B에 동사 일치)

Neither the boys nor Tom eats onions.

그 남자아이들도 톰도 양파를 먹지 않는다.

3. 종속접속사

시간 · 조건 부사절에서는 주절의 시제가 미래를 나타내거나 명령문일
때 현재시제로 미래를 대신한다.

1) 시간 접속사

    after, as, before, while, when, as soon as,

till, until

I will call you as soon as he comes back.

그가 돌아오자마자 너에게 전화할게.

2) 조건 접속사

if, in case, as long as, provided (that), supposing (that), as far as, unless

Why don't you get insurance in case you have an accident?

사고를 대비해서 보험을 드는 게 어때?

3) 양보 접속사

even if, even though, although, though

Although the weather was not good, they didn't cancel the game.

= Despite/In spite of the bad weather, they didn't cancel the game.

날씨가 좋지 않았지만 그들은 경기를 취소하지 않았다.

(despite, in spite of는 양보를 나타내는 전치사이므로 그 뒤에 명사(구)가 온다.)

4) 이유의 접속사

because, since, as, for, inasmuch as, seeing that, now that

Since he didn't pass the bar exam, he decided to go back to his hometown.

변호사 시험을 통과하지 못해서 그는 고향으로 돌아가기로 결정했다.

Day 14 전치사

전치사 뒤에는 명사(구)가 오게 된다.

1. 때/시간을 나타내는 전치사

at: 시간, 시점

on: 날짜, 요일

in: 월, 계절, 세기, 하루의 아침/오후/저녁(**주의** 밤: at night, 정오:
at noon, 새벽: at dawn)

at noon 정오에	**at night** 밤에
at dawn 새벽에	**at midnight** 한밤중에
at 10: 30 10시 30분에	**at sunset** 해질 무렵에
at present 현재는	**at that time** 그때에는
at this time of the year 일 년중 이맘때에는	
in spring 봄에	**in 2002** 2002년에
in the past 과거에	**in the future** 앞으로, 장차
in the 21st century 21세기에	
in the eighties 80년대에	
in one's life 자신 생애에	**in those days** 그 당시에는
in one's absence 부재 중에	
in one's early/mid/late twenties 20대 초/중/후반	
on May 4 5월 4일에	**on Saturday** 토요일에
on Valentine's Day 발렌타인 데이에	
on Christmas Day 크리스마스 날에	

2. ～때까지: by, till, until

by: (늦어도) ～까지 (완료) → 동작, 상태가 완료를 나타냄 (1회성으

로 끝나는 동작/상태)

until, till: ~까지 계속 (유지) → 동작, 상태의 계속을 나타냄.
**You should hand in the report by 9 o'clock
this Friday.** 금요일 9시까지 레포트를 내야 한다.
The shop opens until 10 p.m. every day.
그 가게는 매일 밤 10시까지 연다.

3. ~동안: for, during

for: ~동안 (일정한 기간) – How long~?에 대한 대답
during: ~동안 (특정 기간) – When~?에 대한 대답

4. 관용적인 전치사구 표현

out of sorts 기분이 언짢은   **out of work** 실직한
out of sight 보이지 않는
out of stock 품절된 (*cf.* in stock 재고가 있는)
at hand 가까이에   **at random** 닥치는 대로
at one's own risk 자기가 책임지고
at stake 위태로운   **at times** 때때로
at the moment 바로 지금 **at a stretch** 단숨에
in token of ~의 표시로
in terms of ~의 견지에서   **on strike** 파업 중
on leave 휴가 중
on sale 할인판매 중 (*cf.* for sale 판매중인)
in demand 수요가 있는 (*cf.* on demand 청구하는 대로)
to a great extent 크게   **for the time being** 당분간
at the expense of ~의 대가를 치르고
as a whole 대체로   **as a result of** ~의 결과로

Day 15 시험에 잘 나오는 문장 어순

목적격 보어로 to부정사를 취하는 타동사가 시험에 잘 나온다. 목적격 보어를 to부정사로 취하는 동사류를 암기하도록 한다.

1. 보어를 필요로 하는 불완전자동사

보어 자리에 부사는 올 수 없다.

keep, remain, stay, become, get, go, grow, look, feel, smell, sound, taste, seem, appear

It sounds strangely. (X)
It sounds strange. (O) 이상하게 들린다.

2. 목적격 보어를 취하는 타동사: V+O+OC

목적격 보어 자리에도 부사는 올 수 없다.

1) find, make, think, believe+ it(가목적어)+형용사 +to V

I found it difficult to solve the problem.

나는 그 문제를 푸는 것이 어렵다는 것을 알았다.

The noise made it impossible to hear her talking.

그 소음 때문에 그녀가 이야기하는 것을 듣는 것은 불가능했다.

2) 목적격 보어로 to부정사를 취하는 타동사: V+ O + to V
allow, urge, encourage, enable, cause, force, help, get, forbid

It is obvious that the new test system encourages students to study hard.
새 시험 제도가 학생들을 열심히 공부할 수 있게 한다는 것은 명백하다.

Day 16 어순

사역동사의 어순은 시험에 잘 나오므로 알아두도록 한다. 사역동사의 목적격 보어로는 현재분사는 올 수 없고 동사원형이나 과거분사만 올 수 있다.

1. 사역동사

목적격 보어로 동사원형이나 과거분사를 취한다.

1) 사역동사 + 목적어 + 동사원형 (목적어와 목적격 보어가 능동의 의미)

2) 사역동사 + 목적어 + 과거분사 (목적어와 목적격 보어가 수동의 의미)

I had him repair my radio.

그에게 내 라디오를 고치게 했다.

I had my radio repaired by him.

2. 준사역동사 get의 용법

1) get + 목적어 + to부정사 → 능동

I got him to mend my watch.

나는 그에게 시계를 수선하게 했다. (능동의 의미)

2) get + 목적어 + 과거분사 → 수동

I got my watch mended.

나는 시계를 수선시켰다. (수동의 의미)

3. 의문문의 순서

1) 직접의문문: 의문사 + 동사+ 주어
   What did you buy for Jane?
   제인을 위해 무엇을 샀니?

2) 간접의문문: 의문사 + 주어 + 동사
   Do you know where the post office is?
   우체국이 어디 있는지 아세요?

3) 의문사와 함께 think, suppose, believe, imagine, say가 동사로
   쓰일 때 의문사가 문두에 오게 된다.
   Who do you think his new girlfriend is?
   누가 그의 새 여자친구인 것 같니?
   Which do you think is better on me?
   어떤 것이 나에게 더 어울리는 것 같니?

Day 17 일치

대명사의 수 일치, 주어와 동사의 수 일치, 선행사의 수 일치 등은
시험에 자주 나온다. 특히 Part III나 Part IV에서 수 일치 문제가
자주 등장하니 주의하도록 한다.

1. 수 일치에서 확인해야 할 것

① 대명사의 수를 확인해야 한다.
② 동사와 멀리 떨어져 있는 주어의 수가 일치하는지 확인해야 한다.
③ 선행사의 수와 일치하는지 확인한다.

2. 시험에 잘 나오는 수의 일치

1) 기간, 거리, 가격, 무게를 나타내는 복수 명사가 '하나의 단위'를 나
타내는 경우 단수 취급을 한다.
Twenty pounds is all I've got.
20파운드가 내가 가진 전부이다.

2) 복수 취급하는 표현
both A and B: A와 B 둘 다
the + 형용사 = 복수 보통 명사

3) 동사 가까이에 있는 명사에 수를 일치시키는 표현들
Either A or B A 또는 B
Neither A nor B A도 B도 아닌
Not only A but also B A뿐만 아니라 B 역시
일부를 나타내는 표현 most of~, the majority of ~, the rest

of ~, half of ~, 분수 of ~

Neither the students nor the driver was responsible for the accident.

학생들이나 운전자는 그 사고에 책임이 없다.

4) **the number of** ~의 숫자(단수취급)

a number of 많은(복수취급)

The number of people attending the fashion show decreases every year.

그 패션쇼에 참석하는 사람의 숫자는 매년 줄어든다.

3. 주어와 동사의 수 일치

The students in this room are watching the movie *Hero*.

이 교실에 있는 학생들은 영화 '히어로' 를 보고 있다.

〈선행사 + 주격 관계대명사 + 동사〉의 수 일치

Julie isn't the only girl that/who has a laptop.

쥴리가 노트북을 가지고 있는 유일한 소녀는 아니다.

4. 명사와 대명사의 수 일치

I met Jane and Tom and had some fun with them. 나는 제인과 탐을 만나서 재미있게 놀았다.

Day 18 도치 구문을 잡아라

동사와 주어의 위치가 바뀌는 도치 구문을 주의해야 한다. TEPS에는 부정 부사 관련 도치와 so와 such의 어순이 잘 나온다.

1. 강조의 도치

부정부사가 문두에 오는 경우 → 일반 동사일 경우 조동사가 주어 앞으로 도치되고, be동사일 경우는 be동사 자체가 주어 앞으로 도치된다.
부정부사 **hardly, scarcely, rarely, barely, little, no sooner, not only, only** 부사구

Not only is she pretty, but she is also smart.
그녀는 예쁠 뿐 아니라 똑똑하기도 하다.
Little did they know that he would become such a great singer.
그들은 그가 이렇게 위대한 가수가 될 줄 전혀 몰랐다.
Only on weekends is Mary able to visit her parents.
메리는 주말에만 그녀의 부모님을 방문할 수 있다.

only는 외형적으로는 부정형이 아니지만 의미상으로는 부정적인 요소를 가지고 있다. only가 문두에 오면 도치가 일어날 수 있지만 꼭 그런 것은 아니다. 하지만 시험에 나올 경우 대부분은 도치로 쓰이므로 도치의 형식으로 알아두도록 한다.

2. so와 such의 어순

1) such, many, quite, what＋ a/an＋형용사＋명사
   The meeting lasted for half an hour.
   그것은 30분 동안 계속되었다.
   It's quite a horrible story.
   그것은 아주 무서운 이야기이다.

2) so , too＋형용사＋ a/an＋ 명사
   He is so clever a boy. 그는 너무 영리한 소년이다.
   I'm not as good a storyteller as you are.
   나는 당신처럼 이야기를 잘 하지 못한다.
   It's too small a T-shirt for me.
   그것은 내게는 너무 작은 티셔츠다.

3) 〈so＋주어＋동사〉의 어순:
   so는 yes의 뜻이 되어 '정말 그래' 의 뜻.
   〈so＋동사＋주어〉의 어순:
   so는 also의 뜻이 되어 '~도 역시 그래' 의 뜻.
   Julie has a laptop and so do I.
   줄리는 노트북이 있고 나도 그렇다.

Day 19 Part III를 바로 잡자

Part III는 대화문이다. 관용적인 표현은 LC 스크립트를 많이 따라 읽음으로써 자연스럽게 표현을 익히도록 한다. 동사 위주로 찾아보고, 시험에 자주 출제 되었던 부분들을 점검하도록 한다.

1. 관사의 missing을 찾아라.

관용적인 부정관사가 빠지지 않았는지 확인한다.

Have good time. (X) → Have a good time. (O)

(time 앞에는 보통 관사가 붙지 않지만 형용사가 오게 되면 부정관사가 붙는다.)

2. 수의 일치

대명사의 수 일치, 주어와 동사의 수 일치, 선행사와 동사의 수 일치를 확인한다.

3. 대부정사 문제가 아닌지 확인한다.

대부정사는 to부정사를 취하는 동사에서 동사구의 반복을 피하기 위해 to만 쓰는 것을 의미한다.

4. 관사의 쓰임이 제대로 되었는지 확인한다.

부정관사(불특정한 단수 명사를 수식함)와 정관사(특정한 단수/복수의 명사를 수식함)의 차이를 알아두자.

5. 조동사의 의미가 제대로 쓰였는지 확인한다.

조동사 관련 문제는 보통 해석을 통해 오류를 찾아야 하므로 문맥을 해석하여 오류를 찾아본다.

6. 어순

도치: 부정부사(hardly, scarcely, rarely, barely, little, no sooner, not only, only 부사구)가 문두에 오면 도치가 이루어진다.
간접의문문(의문사＋주어＋동사)
동사＋대명사＋부사

Check out it. (X) → Check it out. (O)

(동사와 부사 사이에 대명사는 가운데 위치한다.)

7. 전치사 to와 to부정사를 구별한다.

〈자동사＋전치사 to〉의 표현을 알아둔다.

8. 보어로 부사가 올 수 없다.

It makes the culture uniquely. (X)
It makes the culture unique. (O)

그것이 그 문화를 독특하게 만든다.

Day 20 Part IV가 고득점 관문이다

동사 위주로 오류를 먼저 찾아본다. 한 문장을 따로 떼어 놓았을 때의 오류뿐 아니라 전체 문맥 내의 시제 불일치 문제도 있으니 전체 단락을 파악한다.

1. 시제가 일치하는지 확인한다.

전체적인 내용이 일반적인 사실을 나타내고 있어서 현재시제로 나타내고 있는데 한 문장만 과거시제를 썼다면 의심해야 한다.

2. 수동태를 주목하라.

수동태의 동사 뒤에 목적어가 있으면 4형식 수여동사가 아닌 이상 오류이다. 또한 자동사(arrive, become, remain, appear, disappear, fall, come, occur)가 수동태가 되어 있지 않은지 확인하라.

3. 접속사

의미상 적절한 접속사가 쓰였는지 확인하고, 접속사 없이 두 개의 문장이 있으면 접속사를 넣어야 한다.

He loves Mary so much, but he popped the question to her. (X)
He loves Mary so much, so he popped the question to her. (O)
그는 메리를 사랑해서 청혼을 했다.

4. 분사와 분사구문을 주목하라.

분사구문의 주어와 주절의 주어가 논리적으로 연결되는지 확인한다.

Looking at the evidence, a decision was made. (X)

Looking at the evidence, they made a decision. (O)

증거를 보고 그들은 결정했다.

5. 관계대명사를 확인하라.

관계대명사 뒤에 완벽한 문장이 있다면 이것이 범인이다. 단, 접속사 that 뒤에는 완벽한 문장이 올 수 있다.

There is a famous spot which hundreds of tourists come every year in the city. (X)

There is a famous spot in which/where hundreds of tourists come every year in the city. (O)

그 도시에는 매년 수백 명의 관광객이 오는 유명한 장소가 있다.

6. 수의 일치

주어와 동사, 선행사와 동사의 수 일치, 대명사의 수일치, 수식어와 피수식어의 일치 등을 확인한다.